◎ 普通高校专业英语教程系列

新时代教育学专业英语

马　飞　刘志鹏　司爱侠　编著

清华大学出版社
北京

内 容 简 介

本书旨在切实提高读者的专业英语能力和教育教学理论水平。全书共12个单元，第1至第7单元主要介绍教育学领域的经典及常用理论，如行为主义理论、认知主义理论、建构主义理论等；第8至第12单元主要介绍现代信息技术对教学的影响，如互联网、大数据、虚拟仿真、创客、云计算、人工智能等在教学中的运用。本书还配有丰富的教学资源（含电子课件和习题答案），方便读者进行教学和自主学习。

本书既可作为本科和专科院校教育学相关专业的专业英语教材，也可供从业人员自学。作为教学培训教材，亦颇得当。

图书在版编目（CIP）数据

新时代教育学专业英语 / 马飞，刘志鹏，司爱侠编著 . —北京：清华大学出版社，2022.8
普通高校专业英语教程系列
ISBN 978-7-302-60958-2

Ⅰ . ①新… Ⅱ . ①马… ②刘… ③司… Ⅲ . ①教育学—英语—高等学校—教材 Ⅳ . ① G40

中国版本图书馆 CIP 数据核字（2022）第 089011 号

责任编辑：徐博文
封面设计：子 一
责任校对：王凤芝
责任印制：丛怀宇

出版发行：清华大学出版社
　　　网　　　址：http://www.tup.com.cn, http://www.wqbook.com
　　　地　　　址：北京清华大学学研大厦 A 座　　　　邮　　编：100084
　　　社 总 机：010-83470000　　　　　　　　　　　邮　　购：010-62786544
　　　投稿与读者服务：010-62776969, c-service@tup.tsinghua.edu.cn
　　　质量反馈：010-62772015, zhiliang@tup.tsinghua.edu.cn
印 装 者：北京同文印刷有限责任公司
经　　销：全国新华书店
开　　本：185mm×260mm　　　印　　张：14　　　字　　数：340 千字
版　　次：2022 年 8 月第 1 版　　　　　　　印　　次：2022 年 8 月第 1 次印刷
定　　价：69.00 元

产品编号：080080-01

前　言

教育兴则国家兴，教育强则国家强。"发展具有中国特色、世界水平的现代教育"既要继承中国传统优秀教育思想，又要开门办学，吸收有益的国外教育理念。要培养具有国际视野的学生，首先要培养具有国际视野的教师。随着全球化的持续推进和信息化的迅速普及，人们获取知识的渠道更加快捷、媒介更加多元，在世界范围内获取知识愈发变得可能和必要。世界上最新的学术成果大多以英文呈现，世界顶级学术刊物的语言载体也大多是英语。教师应了解国际教育界的最新动态，熟知教育学的最新理论，具备用英语获取本领域知识的能力。英语语言能力和世界经典教育理论对于提升教师的专业素质至关重要

本书主要介绍了教育学的经典概念和理论，如行为主义理论、认知主义理论，以及建构主义理论等，同时还介绍了信息技术对教育的影响，如大数据与教育、人工智能与教育、虚拟仿真与教育等。全书共 12 个单元。每个单元分 Text A、Text B 和 Supplementary Reading 三部分。Text A 为精读，Text B 为泛读，Supplementary Reading 可用于自学。每个单元的结构如下：课文——选材广泛、风格多样、切合实际，既有基本理论，又有最新案例；单词——课文中出现的核心词汇，读者由此可以积累教育专业的基本词汇；词组——课文中出现的常用词组，这些词组都是教育学专业英语中常用和必须掌握的；缩略语——课文中出现的、业内人士应该熟知的缩略语；习题——基于课文精心设计的练习可以巩固学习的知识、检验学习效果，提升思考能力；补充阅读——进一步培养读者的阅读能力，拓展读者的视野；参考译文——Text A 的参考译文，供读者对照阅读学习。

本书内容突出实用性和经典性，选材新颖，包括大量的实用内容和经典理论，让读者可以学习到目前最常用的、最新的知识，以便学以致用。本书按照教学规律做了精心设计，结构上符合认知逻辑，内容上循序渐进，适合组织教学。本书还配有丰富的教学资源（含电子课件和习题参考答案），读者可以从清华大学出版社网站（www.tup.com.cn）上下载，也可给我们发送邮件索取（邮箱地址：zqh3882355@163.com）。

由于时间仓促，编者水平有限，书中难免有疏漏和不足之处，恳请广大读者和同行提出宝贵意见，以便再版时进行修正。

编者

2022 年 3 月

Contents

Unit 4

Unit 5

Unit 6

Unit 7

Unit 8

Unit 9

Unit 10

Unit 11

Unit 12

Unit

1

Text A

Behavioral Learning Theory

1. Introduction

Learning is the process leading to permanent or potential behavioral change. In other words, as we learn, we alter the way we perceive our environment, the way we interpret the incoming stimuli, and therefore the way we interact, or behave. John B. Watson[1] (1878–1958) was the first to study how the process of learning affects our behavior, and formed the school of thought known as Behaviorism. The central idea behind Behaviorism is that only observable behaviors are worthy of research since other abstractions such as a person's mood or thoughts are too subjective. This belief was dominant in psychological research for over 50 years.

Perhaps the most well-known behaviorist is B. F. Skinner[2] (1904–1990). Skinner followed much of Watson's research and findings, but believed that internal states could influence behavior just as external stimuli. He is considered a radical behaviorist because of this belief, although nowadays it is believed that both internal and external stimuli influence our behaviors.

Behavioral psychology is basically interested in how our behavior results from the stimuli both in the environment and within ourselves. They study, often in minute detail, the behaviors we exhibit while controlling for as many other variables as possible. It's often a grueling process, but the results have helped us learn a great deal about our behaviors, the effect our environment has on us, how we learn new behaviors, and what motivates us to change or remain the same.

2. Classical and Operant Conditioning

One important type of learning, classical conditioning, was actually discovered accidentally by

---

1   John B. Watson：约翰·B. 华生，美国心理学家，行为主义心理学的创始人。

2   B. F. Skinner：B. F. 斯金纳，美国心理学家，新行为主义的代表人物。

Ivan Pavlov[1] (1849-1936). Pavlov was a Russian physiologist who discovered this phenomenon while doing research on digestion. His original research aimed at better understanding the digestive patterns in dogs. During his experiments, he put meat in the mouths of dogs to measure body responses. What he discovered was that the dogs began to salivate before the meat was presented to them. After that, the dogs began to salivate as soon as the person feeding them would enter the room. He soon began to gain interest in this phenomenon and abandoned his digestion research in favor of his now famous classical conditioning study.

Basically, the findings support the idea that we develop responses to certain stimuli that are not naturally occurring. When we touch a hot stove, our reflex pulls our hand back. It does this instinctually, no learning involved. It is merely a survival instinct. However, why now do some people, after getting burned, pull their hands back even when the stove is not turned on? Pavlov discovered that we make associations which cause us to generalize our response to one stimuli onto a neutral stimuli it is paired with. In other words, hot burner = ouch, stove = burner, therefore, stove = ouch.

To further explore this, Pavlov began pairing a bell sound with the meat and found that even when the meat was not presented, the dog would eventually begin to salivate after hearing the bell. Since the meat naturally results in salivation, these two variables are called the Unconditioned Stimulus (UCS) and the Unconditioned Response (UCR) respectively. The bell sound and salivation are not naturally occurring; the dog was conditioned to respond to the bell sound. Therefore, the bell sound is considered the Conditioned Stimulus (CS), and the salivation to the bell sound, the Conditioned Response (CR).

Many of our behaviors today are shaped by the pairing of stimuli. Have you ever noticed that certain stimuli, such as the smell of a cologne or perfume, a certain song, a specific day of the year, result in fairly intense emotions? It's not the smell or the song that are the cause of the emotion, but rather what the smell or song has been paired with—perhaps an ex-boyfriend or ex-girlfriend, the death of a loved one, or maybe the day you met your current husband or wife. We make these associations all the time and often don't realize the power that these connections or pairings have on us. However, in fact, we have been classically conditioned.

Another type of learning, very similar to the one discussed above, is called operant conditioning. The term "operant" refers to how an organism operates on the environment. It can be thought as learning due to the natural consequences of our actions. It is a method of learning that occurs through rewards and punishments for behavior. Behavior followed by pleasant consequences is likely to be repeated, and behavior followed by unpleasant consequences is less likely to be repeated.

The classic study of operant conditioning involves a cat who is placed in a box with only one way out; a specific area of the box had to be pressed in order for the door to open. The cat initially tries to get out of the box because freedom is reinforcing. In its attempt to escape, the area of the box is triggered and the door opens. The cat is now free. Once placed in the box again,

---

1　Ivan Pavlov：伊万·帕夫洛夫，苏联著名生理学家、心理学家。

the cat will naturally try to remember what it did to escape the previous time and will once again find the area to press. The more the cat is placed back in the box, the quicker it will press that area for its freedom. It has learned, through natural consequences, how to gain the reinforcing freedom.

We learn this way every day in our lives. Imagine the last time you made a mistake, you most likely remember that mistake and do things differently when the situation comes up again. In that sense, you've learned to act differently based on the natural consequences of your previous actions. The same holds true for positive actions. If something you did results in a positive outcome, you are likely to do that same activity again.

3. Reinforcement

The term "reinforcement" means to strengthen, and is used in psychology to refer to anything stimulus which strengthens or increases the probability of a specific response. For example, if you want your dog to sit on command, you may give him a treat every time he sits for you. The dog will eventually come to understand that sitting when told to will result in a treat. This treat is reinforcing because he likes it and will result in him sitting when instructed to do so.

This is a simple description of a reinforcer, the treat, which increases the response, sitting. We all apply reinforcers every day, most of the time without even realizing we are doing it. You may tell your child "good job" after he or she cleans his or her room; perhaps you tell your partner how good he or she looks when he or she dresses up; or maybe you got a raise at work after doing a great job on a project. All of these things increase the probability that the same response will be repeated.

There are four types of reinforcement: positive, negative, punishment, and extinction. The examples above describe what is referred to as positive reinforcement. Think of it as adding something in order to increase a response. For example, adding a treat will increase the response of sitting; adding praise will increase the chances of your child cleaning his or her room. The most common types of positive reinforcement are praise and rewards, and most of us have experienced this as both the giver and receiver.

Negative reinforcement can be thought as taking something negative away in order to increase a response. Imagine a teenager who is nagged by his mother because he does not take out the garbage week after week. After complaining to his friends about the nagging and suggested by them, he finally one day performs the task and to his amazement, his mother's nagging stops. The elimination of this negative stimulus is reinforcing and will likely increase the chances that he will take out the garbage next week.

Punishment refers to adding something aversive in order to decrease a behavior. The most common example of this is disciplining (e.g. spanking) a child for misbehaving. The reason we do this is that the child begins to associate being punished with the negative behavior. The punishment is not liked and therefore to avoid it, he or she will stop behaving in that manner.

When you remove something in order to decrease a behavior, this is called extinction. You are taking something away so that a response is decreased. For example, after Pavlov's dog was conditioned to salivate at the sound of the bell, it eventually stopped salivating to the sound after the bell had been sounded repeatedly but no meat came.

Research has found positive reinforcement is the most powerful of any of these. Adding a positive to increase a response not only works better, but allows both parties to focus on the positive aspects of the situation. Punishment, when applied immediately following the negative behavior can be effective, but results in extinction when it is not applied consistently. Punishment can also invoke other negative responses such as anger and resentment.

New Words

perceive [pə'si:v] v. 理解，感知

interpret [ɪn'tɜ:prɪt] v. 解释，说明

stimuli ['stɪmjʊlaɪ] n. 刺激，刺激物（stimulus 的复数）

behaviorism [bɪ'heɪvjərɪzəm] n. 行为主义

abstraction [æb'strækʃən] n. 抽象，抽象概念

psychological [ˌsaɪkə'lɒdʒɪkəl] adj. 心理的，心理学的

radical ['rædɪkəl] adj. 激进的

variable ['veərɪəbl] n. 变量，可变因素

digestion [daɪ'dʒestʃən] n. 消化

salivate ['sælɪveɪt] v. 分泌唾液，流口水

reflex ['ri:fleks] n. 反射动作，下意识反应

instinct ['ɪnstɪŋkt] n. 本能，直觉

association [əˌsəʊʃɪ'eɪʃən] n. 关联，联想

eventually [ɪ'ventʃʊəli] adv. 最终，最后

shape [ʃeɪp] v. 塑造，形成

pairing ['peərɪŋ] n. 配对

cologne [kə'ləʊn] n. 古龙香水

initially [ɪ'nɪʃəli] adv. 最初；开始

reinforcement [ˌri:ɪn'fɔ:smənt] n. 强化，加强

treat [tri:t] n. 款待，招待

reinforcer [ri:ɪn'fɔ:sə] n. 强化刺激（物）；增强剂

extinction [ɪk'stɪŋkʃən] n.（心理学）消退

nag [næg] v. 唠叨

aversive [ə'vɜ:sɪv] adj. 厌恶的，反感的

discipline ['dɪsəplɪn] v. 管教，训导

spanking ['spæŋkɪŋ] n. 打屁股

misbehave [ˌmɪsbɪ'heɪv] v. 举止失礼，行为不端

invoke [ɪn'vəʊk] v. 引起，唤起

resentment [rɪ'zentmənt] n. 愤恨，怨恨

Phrases

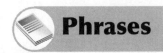

Behavioral Learning Theory 行为主义学习理论

Behavioral Psychology 行为主义心理学

in minute detail 详尽无遗

classical conditioning 经典条件反射　　come up 发生，出现
aim at 针对，目的在于　　positive reinforcement 正强化
in favor of 支持，有利于　　negative reinforcement 负强化
be paired with 与……配对　　in that manner 以那种方式
operant conditioning 操作性条件反射

 Abbreviations

Unconditioned Stimulus (UCS) 无条件刺激，非制约刺激
Unconditioned Response (UCR) 无条件反应，非制约反应
Conditioned Stimulus (CS) 条件刺激
Conditioned Response (UR) 条件反射

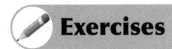 **Exercises**

Ex. 1 Give the English equivalents of the following Chinese expressions.

(1) 行为主义心理学　_____

(2) 经典条件反射　_____

(3) 操作性条件反射　_____

(4) 正强化　_____

(5) 无条件刺激　_____

(6) 详尽无遗　_____

(7) 针对；目的在于　_____

(8) 支持，有利于　_____

(9) 与……配对　_____

(10) 以那种方式　_____

Ex. 2 Explain the following terminologies in English.

(1) classical conditioning　_____

(2) operant conditioning　_____

(3) reinforcement　_____

(4) positive reinforcement　_____

(5) negative reinforcement _____

(6) extinction _____

Ex. 3 **Answer the following questions according to Text A.**

(1) What is learning in the perspective of behaviorists?

(2) How do internal state and external stimuli function upon us according to B. F. Skinner?

(3) How was classical conditioning discovered?

(4) Could you explain UCS, UCR, CS and CR with Pavlov's experiment as an example?

(5) Could you explain operant conditioning with examples from your life experiences?

(6) What are the four types of reinforcement? Which one is the most powerful type?

(7) Could you explain positive reinforcement with one example from real life?

(8) Could you explain negative reinforcement with one example from real life?

Ex. 4 **Fill in the blanks with the words given below.**

environmental	operant	differentiating	classical	natural
rewarding	observable	modified	molded	learned

Behaviorism is a learning theory that focuses on (1)_____ behaviors. It is broken into two areas of conditioning—(2)_____ and (3)_____. Most are familiar with operant conditioning, where one learns through (4)_____ the desired behavior. B. F. Skinner spent lots of time exploring operant conditioning through research with animals, which proved that behavior is a(n) (5)_____ response. Classical conditioning is a(n) (6)_____ reflex or response to stimuli. When a child feels apprehension at the thought of taking a test, he or she is exhibiting classical conditioning.

Skinner's research determined that the brain was not a part of conditioning, and learning was through (7)_____ factors, (8)_____ his ideas from others such as John Watson, and coining his theories as radical Behaviorism. All actions required a reaction, positive or negative, which (9)_____ behavior. With basic behaviorism theories, it is thought that the individual is passive and behavior is (10)_____ through positive and negative reinforcement. This means that a child's behavior can be changed and modified through reinforcement.

Text B

Behaviorism in Classroom

1. The Implications of Behaviorism

We already know behaviorists see learning as a change in behavior due to an external stimulus. This, in fact, means that learning is nothing more than the acquisition of new information. We are born as blank slates and have no predispositions. The external stimuli we receive mold us into who we are.

Behaviorists are concerned primarily with the observable and measurable aspects of human behavior, and discount mental activities. That is, behaviorists assume that the only things that are real are the things we can see and observe. We cannot see the mind, the ID, or the unconscious, but we can see how people act, react and behave. The object of the behaviorist's study interest is what people do, but not what they think or feel. Likewise, behaviorists do not look to the mind or the brain to understand the causes of a particular behavior. They assume that the behavior represents certain learned habits, and they attempt to determine how the habits are learned. The behavioral researchers are interested in understanding the mechanisms underlying the behavior of learners.

Although there are many theories encompassed in behavioral belief, all share several common assumptions: the importance of focusing on observable behavior, the blank-slate nature of organisms, classical and operant conditioning, the use of drill and practice for teaching basic skills, and an attention to the consequences of student behaviors. In behaviorists' view, human behavior can be learned and unlearned. Therefore, when behaviors become unacceptable, they can be unlearned. The acceptable behaviors should be reinforced.

Behaviorism assumes a learner is essentially passive, and will be shaped through positive or negative reinforcement. Learning is, therefore, defined as a change in behavior. It is believed that behavior is a function of its consequences, i.e., learners will repeat the desired behavior if positive reinforcement is given. The behavior should not be repeated if negative feedback is given. Giving immediate feedback, whether positive or negative, should enable the learners to behave in a certain way.

Behaviorism learning theory stresses the importance of repetition. The more frequent a stimulus and response occur in association with each other, the stronger the habit will become. This focus on repetition is seen in the drill and practice tutorials often associated with students learning basic skills. B. F. Skinner is one of the best known psychologists in the behaviorist tradition. His theory of operant conditioning proposes that "a response followed by a reinforcing stimulus is strengthened and therefore more likely to occur again". Skinner urges educators to focus on reinforcing student success rather than on punishing student failure. Behaviorism as an educational learning theory led to the development of several aspects of instruction and learning production, some of which we still use in classrooms today, including direct instruction, lecture, behavioral objective as classroom management, behavioral reward system, positive reinforcement, and individualized instruction, among other notions.

Behaviorism teaching style in education is more common than we would like to believe. In fact, it is used in every aspect of education. This style of teaching believes that information passed from a teacher to a student is basically the correct response to specific stimulus. Therefore, the purpose of education is to ensure that a student has appropriate collection of responses to specific stimuli and these responses are then reinforced. An effective reinforcement schedule requires consistent repetition of the material, small, progressive sequences of tasks, and continuous positive reinforcement. Without positive reinforcement, learned responses will quickly become extinct. This is because learners will continue to modify their behavior until they receive some positive reinforcement.

When applied to a classroom setting, Behaviorism focuses on conditioning student behavior with various types of behavior reinforcement and consequences called operant conditioning. There are four types of reinforcement: positive reinforcement, negative reinforcement, punishment and extinction, and each can be applied effectively to get the students to behave in the classroom. Positive reinforcement and punishment are easy to understand. Negative reinforcement occurs when the rate of a behavior increases because an aversive event or stimulus is removed or prevented from happening. For example, a child cleans his or her room, and this behavior is followed by the parent stopping "nagging" or asking the child repeatedly to do so. Here, the nagging serves to negatively reinforce the behavior of cleaning because the child wants to remove that aversive stimulus of nagging. Extinction is similar to punishment in that its purpose is to reduce unwanted behavior. It implies absence of reinforcement. In other words, extinction implies lowering the probability of undesired behavior by removing reward for that kind of behavior. Extinction can be seen when a child stops throwing tantrums when the parent wises up and stops giving into their demands (the reinforcer). If the child stops getting their demands, the tantrums will stop, or at the very least, decrease.

2. The Roles of Students and Teachers

Behaviorists hold the following assumptions about students:

● Everything a student does from thinking to feeling to acting should be regarded solely a behavior; the mind plays no role.

● Behaviors can be controlled simply by reinforced teaching of proper behaviors via the Stimulus, Response, and Reinforcement (S-R-R) process.

Behaviorism places students in a secondary role in the learning process. Behaviorists portray students as responders rather than actors. The students respond to stimuli. If their response is not the desired response, it is the role of the teacher to provide feedback that will discourage such response in the future or reprogram the students with a different response to the stimuli. Perhaps, one could argue it is the students' job to practice skills and behaviors, but taking behaviorism at its purest form it is the teacher who ultimately decides whether students will do the practice or work necessarily to learn a new skill or behavior.

According to behaviorists, the main objective of a teacher is to provide the correct stimuli to shape or condition the students into the desired end product. In layman terms the teacher provides the necessary inputs to get the desired output. Teachers are possessors of knowledge and it is their responsibility to impart facts and desired behaviors to students. Teachers control student behavior and learning with stimulus control via evaluation, repetition, and reinforcement techniques.

Behaviorists propose the following teaching process. First, a teacher must set a clear quantitative learning goal. In order to reach that goal, the teacher must evaluate the students to determine a starting point for instruction. This might take the form of a test to determine what students have already known. Once a goal has been set, the process must be broken down into small steps or stages. Each step or stage should be accompanied by repetition in the form of drill and practice, evaluation and reinforcement. Drill and practice with continuous reinforcement is necessary as per the law of exercise, which states the more a stimulus-response bond is practiced and feedback is provided, the stronger it becomes. What's inherent in this law then is the necessity for the teacher's constant feedback to student behavior and demonstration of acquired knowledge. Reinforcement should serve as a motivational tool. Once a skill is mastered, reinforcement should be reduced to a variable schedule. For example, once a math skill is mastered, instead of being covered on every test, it should be thrown into the mix intermittently. The reinforcement in this case is the grade the student receives on the test.

Manifestations of reinforcement take several forms. If the student studies the new skill and practices, they will hopefully receive a good grade, which reinforces their study habits. The opposite type of reinforcement is punishment. Punishment entails penalizing a student for their behavior by taking away some privilege like recess. Punishment creates a negative association for the student with that behavior thereby reducing the likelihood of its recurrence. Another type of reinforcement is extinction or non-reinforcement, which holds that responses that are not reinforced are not likely to be repeated. In other words, if a student interrupts without raising a hand, the teacher should ignore the student's comments or questions until the student follows the correct class rules.

It is worthwhile explaining the reinforcement in detail. The simplest way to apply positive reinforcement is to praise a student when he or she behaves well or successfully completes a task. We could employ a system of giving gold stars that result in a small prize when enough has been earned. We are encouraged to take advantage of the effectiveness of simple statements of praise. When offering praise, however, opt for a specific statement such as, "you really showed mature insight right there" as opposed to a vague statement such as "nice work". The fact is that students can sense when praise is generic or disingenuous. Reserve such comments when we really mean them, so our students won't take them as empty words. Meanwhile, saying nice things to our students will work fine for a while, but they might stop believing us unless we can show them exactly why their behavior warrants praise in the first place. Whenever possible, show them the proof, point out the specific act and explain why it is so important.

It is sometimes useful to utilize negative reinforcement. Negative reinforcement isn't punishment. Rather, it is a rewarding good behavior by taking away something your students see as negative. For example, our class clown always makes inappropriate comments during health lessons and disrupts the class. He also really doesn't like writing book reports because the writing is boring. We could offer to let him do his book report another way, perhaps as a diorama, on the condition that he behaves appropriately during health lessons. By removing something he sees as negative, we reinforce a separate, positive behavior.

Sometimes punishment is necessary to discourage undesirable behavior, but we must be careful not to go too far and embarrass our students. Just as there are positive and negative reinforcement for good behavior, two methods are appropriate for applying punishment. Presentation punishment is the type we are most familiar with: a student misbehaves and we act by adding a punishment like a detention or time-out. Removal punishment is similar to negative reinforcement: we remove something students see as good because they have behaved badly. For example, if they refuse to stop encouraging the class clown's inappropriate comments, we could threaten to cancel an upcoming field trip, or an upcoming class party.

New Words

implication [ˌɪmplɪ'keɪʃən] *n.* 意义，启示，影响

slate [sleɪt] *n.* 石板

predisposition [ˌpriːdɪspə'zɪʃən] *n.* 倾向，癖好；预设

discount [dɪs'kaʊnt] *v.* 低估，忽视

assume [ə'sjuːm] *v.* 假设；认为

unconscious [ʌn'kɒnʃəs] *adj.* 无意识的，潜意识的

likewise ['laɪkwaɪz] *adv.* 同样地；也

underlie [ˌʌndə'laɪ] *v.* 是……的原因；是……的基础

encompass [ɪn'kʌmpəs] *v.* 包含；环绕

assumption [ə'sʌmpʃən] *n.* 假定；设想

organism ['ɔːgənɪzəm] *n.* 生物体；有机体

essentially [ɪ'senʃəli] *adv.* 本质上

define [dɪ'faɪn] *v.* 给……下定义；解释

consequence ['kɒnsɪkwəns] *n.* 后果，结果

propose [prə'pəʊz] *v.* 提出（某观点、方法等）

notion ['nəʊʃən] *n.* 概念；见解

consistent [kən'sɪstənt] *adj.* 一致的，持续不变的

progressive [prə'gresɪv] *adj.* 进阶性的，逐步的

tantrum ['tæntrəm] *n.* 发怒，发脾气

solely ['səʊlli] *adv.* 仅仅；单独地

portray [pɔː'treɪ] *v.* 描绘，描写

ultimately ['ʌltɪmətli] *adv.* 最终，最后

objective [əb'dʒektɪv] *n.* 目的，目标

layman ['leɪmən] *n.* 外行，门外汉

impart [ɪm'pɑːt] *v.* 传授；给予

quantitative ['kwɒntɪtətɪv] *adj.* 量化的，定量的

evaluate [ɪ'væljʊeɪt] *v.* 评估，评价

accompany [ə'kʌmpəni] *v.* 伴随，陪伴

inherent [ɪn'hɪərənt] *adj.* 固有的，内在的

motivational [ˌməʊtɪ'veɪʃənl] *adj.* 动机的；激发性的

variable ['veərɪəbl] *adj.* 可变的，多变的

intermittently [ˌɪntə'mɪtəntli] *adv.* 间歇地，断断续续地

manifestation [ˌmænɪfe'steɪʃən] *n.* 体现；表现

entail [ɪn'teɪl] *v.* 使必要；牵连

penalize ['piːnəlaɪz] *v.* 处罚，惩罚

privilege ['prɪvəlɪdʒ] *n.* 特权；优待；好处

recess [rɪ'ses] *n.* 休息；休假

recurrence [rɪ'kʌrəns] *n.* 再发生；重现

insight ['ɪnsaɪt] *n.* 深刻见解；洞察力

disingenuous [ˌdɪsɪn'dʒenjʊəs] *adj.* 不真诚的，无诚意的

warrant ['wɒrənt] *v.* 使……显得必要；使……显得适当

utilize ['juːtəlaɪz] *v.* 使用，利用

inappropriate [ˌɪnə'prəʊprɪət] *adj.* 不适当的，不恰当的

diorama [ˌdaɪə'rɑːmə] *n.* 立体模型

embarrass [ɪm'bærəs] *v.* 使窘迫，使尴尬

detention [dɪ'tenʃən] *n.*（放学后）留校惩罚，留堂

time-out ['taɪm-aʊt] *n.* 隔离处分，闭门思过

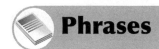

Phrases

blank slate 空白状态；一张白纸

in association with 与……相联系；与……联合

teaching style 教学方法，教学风格

apply to 应用到

throw a tantrum 发脾气，耍性子

portray... as 把……描绘成

end product 最终产品；最后结果

impart... to 传授；给予

break down into 分解成

as per 按照，依据

take advantage of 利用

opt for 选择

as opposed to 与……截然相反；而不是

in the first place 首先；原本

on the condition that 在……的条件下

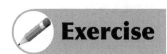

Exercise

Decide whether the following statements are true (T) or false (F) according to Text B. Give your reasons for the false ones.

(　　) (1) According to behaviorists, we human beings are born as a blank sheet. The stimuli we receive shape us into who we are.

(　　) (2) The behaviorists are interested in understanding the mechanisms underlying the mind of learners.

(　　) (3) In behaviorists' view, human behavior can be learned, but cannot be unlearned.

(　　) (4) Behaviorism learning theory stresses the importance of repetition.

(　　) (5) Without positive reinforcement, the knowledge learned will quickly become extinct.

( ) (6) In the view of behaviorists, everything a student does from thinking to feeling to acting should be regarded solely a behavior; the mind plays no role.

( ) (7) Behaviorism places students in a primary role in the learning process.

( ) (8) According to behaviorism, the major objective of a teacher is to provide the correct stimuli to shape the students into the desired end product.

( ) (9) Negative reinforcement is similar to punishment.

( ) (10) Punishment is the best way to stop a student's undesirable behavior.

 # Supplementary Reading

Text	Notes
The Audio-lingual Method[1]	[1] Audio-lingual Method 听说教学法
1. The Origin and Claims[2] of the Method	[2] claim *n.* 主张；要求
Until the Second World War, "Grammar Translation Method" and "Direct Method" could serve well to the United States in terms of foreign language teaching. However, during the war, the U.S. government felt the necessity of the personnel who were fluent in some European and other languages. Therefore, it was necessary to create a new training program for the army. Some universities in the country were entrusted to develop language programs for military staff. This is the so-called "Army Method".	
After the war, as America became an international power in the world, there was a growing demand for teaching English to new immigrants. For example, the students that came to America to attend universities had to learn English at first so that they could begin their studies. Many reasons like this caused an emergence of an approach to second language learning. The University of Michigan and some other universities borrowed the Army Method and developed an approach of foreign language teaching, which advocated aural training first, then pronunciation training, speaking, reading and writing. This approach came to be known as Audio-lingualism.	
The Audio-lingual Method, as a style of foreign language teaching, is based on behaviorist theory, which postulates[3] certain traits of living things, and in this case, humans could	[3] postulate *v.* 假定，认为

be trained through a system of reinforcement. The correct use of a trait would receive positive feedback while incorrect use of that trait would receive negative feedback. This approach to language learning was similar to the earlier Direct Method. Like the Direct Method, the Audio-lingual Method advises that students should be taught a language directly, without using the students' native language to explain new words or grammar in the target language. However, unlike the Direct Method, the Audio-lingual Method does not focus on teaching vocabulary. Rather, the teacher drills students in the use of grammar.

Audio-lingual Method claims that language occurs naturally. The native language and the target language have different linguistic[4] systems so they must be kept separate in order that the native language isn't used in the classroom environment. One of the teacher's major mission is to be a good model to students. Language learning is seen as a habit formation and repetition is said to make the habit stronger. Because errors may cause the formation of bad habits, they should be prevented. To help students develop correct habits, positive reinforcement can be used.

The objective of the Audio-lingual Method is accurate[5] pronunciation and grammar, the ability to respond quickly and accurately in speech situations, and knowledge of sufficient vocabulary to use with grammar patterns. Particular emphasis was laid on mastering the building blocks[6] of language and learning the rules for combining them. It was believed that learning structure, or grammar was the starting point for the student. The assumptions of the method include.

- Language learning is habit-formation;
- Mistakes are bad and should be avoided, as they are considered bad habits;
- Language skills are learned more effectively if they are presented orally[7] first, then in written form;
- Analogy[8] is a better foundation for language learning than analysis;
- The meanings of words can be learned only in a linguistic and cultural context.

The main teaching activities may include reading dialogues

[4] linguistic *adj.* 语言的，语言学的

[5] accurate *adj.* 准确的

[6] building block 构建模块；积木

[7] orally *adv.* 口头地

[8] analogy *n.* 类比，类推

aloud, repeating model sentences, and drilling. Key structures from the dialogue serve as the basis for pattern drills of different kinds. Lessons in the classroom focus on the correct imitation[9] of the teacher by the students. Not only are the students expected to produce the correct output, but attention is also paid to correct pronunciation. Although correct grammar is expected in usage, no explicit[10] grammatical instruction is given. It is taught inductively[11]. Furthermore, the target language is the only language to be used in the classroom.

[9] imitation *n.* 模仿

[10] explicit *adj.* 明确的，清楚的
[11] inductively *adv.* 诱导地；归纳地

2. The Classroom Teaching and Learning

Because it's a teacher-centered method, the teacher is active. We may associate the teacher with an orchestra[12] leader: directing and controlling students' behaviors and progress, the direction and speed of learning. The teacher models the language, observes and corrects the learners' performance when necessary. In this method, learning the language effectively can be achieved through active interactions between the teacher and the learners. In face of a failure, before blaming the method, we should question wether the teacher provides sufficient practice or not. As said before, as the method is teacher-centered, success or failure depends mostly on the teacher's efficiency[13].

[12] orchestra *n.* 管弦乐队

[13] efficiency *n.* 效率，效能

The teacher's role in Audio-lingual Method may be summarized as follows:

● Introduce, sustain[14] and harmonize[15] the learning of the four skills in this order: listening, speaking, reading and writing;

[14] sustain *v.* 维持，保持
[15] harmonize *v.* 协调，使和谐

● Use the target language in the classroom;

● Model various types of language behavior that the students are to learn;

● Teach spoken language in dialogue form;

● Direct choral response[16] by all or parts of the class;

[16] choral response 集体回答

● Teach the use of structure through pattern practice;

● Guide the student in choosing and learning vocabulary;

● Show how words relate to meaning in the target language;

● Get each individual student to talk;

● Reward trials[17] by students in such a way that learning is reinforced;

[17] trial *n.* 试验；演练

- Teach in a story and other literary forms;
- Establish and maintain a cultural island;
- Formalize[18] the rules on the first day according to which the language class is to be conducted and enforce[19] them.

[18] formalize *v.* 形成；使正规化

[19] enforce *v.* 实施，执行

Learners are expected to produce correct responses directed by the teacher. They are imitators of their model (the teacher or the supplied model speaker). Because they are not much active, they have little control over the speed or the style of their learning. They don't really understand the meaning of the dialogues at the first lesson, but as time goes, by listening to their teacher, imitating him/her correctly, they get better.

The following techniques are often used in the audio-lingual classroom.

- Dialogue memorization: It's generally used in the beginning of the lesson. Students memorize the dialogue and then practice the patterns that are included in it.

- Expansion drill: It's used when students have trouble with the long lines. It is also used to make students pay attention to new information.

- Repetition drill: It is used to teach the lines of the dialogue.

- Single-slot and multiple-slot substitution drills[20]: The students repeat the line the teacher says according to the cues he/she has given.

[20] single-slot and multiple-slot substitution drill 单一成分或多成分替换练习

3. The Decline[21] of the Method

[21] decline *n.* 消亡，衰退

The method lived its golden age in the 1960s. It was applied to teaching of foreign or second languages around the world. However, after some time, two major criticisms emerged. The first one was that the theoretical foundations of the method was said to be unsound[22]. It is a teacher-dominated method and the learner is in a passive role. It is also a mechanical method since it puts too much focus on pattern practice, drilling, and memorization. The second was that practical results fell short of[23] expectations. Learners couldn't transfer what they learn in the classroom to real life and most of them said that they found the method's procedures very boring.

[22] unsound *adj.* 没有根据的；不可靠的

[23] fall short of 达不到，低于

The theoretical criticism mostly emerged from Noam

Chomsky's[24] studies. Chomsky rejected behaviorist theory by claiming that language is not a habit structure. Linguistic behavior involves innovation[25], formation of new sentences and patterns in accordance with rules of great abstractness[26] and intricacy. Chomsky also argued that learning a language is similar to any other kind of learning because many of human language use is not imitated behavior but is created with the underlying rules. Chomsky's studies made linguists and psychologists begin to focus on the mental properties[27] people bring to language learning.	[24] Noam Chomsky 诺姆·乔姆斯基（麻省理工学院的语言学和哲学教授） [25] innovation *n.* 创新 [26] abstractness *n.* 抽象，抽象性 [27] property *n.* 属性，特性

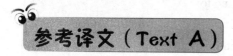

参考译文（Text A）

行为主义学习理论

1. 引言

学习是产生永久或潜在行为变化的过程。换句话说，当我们学习的时候，我们改变了感知环境和理解外来刺激的方式，进而改变我们的互动及行为方式。约翰·B. 华生（1878—1958）是第一个研究学习过程如何影响行为的人，并形成了被称为行为主义的思想学派。行为主义背后的核心思想是，只有观察到的行为才值得研究，因为其他如情绪或思想等抽象概念过于主观。在 50 多年的时间里，这种理念在心理学研究中一直占主导地位。

最著名的行为主义者或许是 B. F. 斯金纳（1904—1990）。斯金纳继承了华生的大部分研究和发现，但他认为，内部状态和外部刺激一样，都会影响行为。由于这个观点，他被认为是激进的行为主义者，尽管现在人们已经相信，内部和外部刺激都会影响我们的行为。

行为主义心理学主要感兴趣的是外部环境和自身刺激是如何影响我们的行为的。他们通常仔细研究我们所展现出的行为，同时控制尽可能多的其他变量。这通常是一个艰辛的过程，但其研究结果大大帮助我们了解了行为、环境对我们的影响，我们习得新行为的方式，以及促使我们改变或维持现状的原因。

2. 经典条件反射和操作性条件反射

作为一个重要的学习类型，经典条件反射，实际上是由伊万·帕夫洛夫（1849—1936）偶然发现的。洛夫是俄罗斯生理学家，他在研究消化的时候发现了这种现象。他最初的研究目的是更好地理解狗的消化方式。在实验中，他把肉放在狗的嘴里，以测量其身体反应。他发现，在把肉给狗之前，它们就开始分泌唾液。后来，当喂狗的人进入房间时，狗就开始分泌唾液。他很快就对这种现象产生了兴趣，并放弃了他的消化研究，转而研究现在变得著名的经典条件反射理论。

这些发现基本表明，我们会对某些非自然发生的刺激做出反应。当我们的手碰到热火炉时，我们的反射会让我们缩回手。这是一个本能反应，没有涉及学习，只是一种生存本能。然而，为什么有些人在被烫过之后，即使炉子并未打开，也会把手缩回来呢？帕夫洛夫发现，我们会进行关联，这会让我们把对刺激的反应推广到一个与其配对的中性刺激物。换句话说，热的燃烧器＝哎哟，炉子＝燃烧器，因此，炉子＝哎哟。

为了进一步探索这一问题，帕夫洛夫将铃声与肉配对并发现，即使没有提供肉，狗也会在听到铃声后分泌唾液。由于肉会自然导致唾液分泌，所以这两个变量分别被称为无条件刺激（UCS）和无条件反应（UCR）。铃声和唾液分泌不是自然发生的，这只狗只是习惯了对铃声做出反应。因此，铃声被认为是条件刺激（CS），听到铃声时分泌唾液是条件反应（CR）。

我们的许多行为都是由刺激的配对形成的。你是否注意到，某些刺激，比如古龙香水或香水的味道、某首歌、某一年的某一天，会让你产生相当强烈的情感？气味或歌曲并不是情感产生的原因，而是与气味或歌曲相配对的人或事——或许是前男友或前女友，亲人的离世，或是你遇见你现在的丈夫或妻子的那一天。我们一直在做这样的联想，而且往往不会意识到这些联想或配对对我们的影响。然而，事实上，我们已经受到了经典条件反射的影响。

另外一种学习方式，和上面讨论的非常类似，叫作操作性条件反射。"操作性"一词指的是生物体如何对环境做出反应。可以认为这是一种因为我们行为的自然后果而产生的学习。这是一种通过对行为的奖励或惩罚而产生的学习。如果某行为的后果是令人愉悦的，我们就很可能会重复这个行为；如果某行为的后果是令人厌恶的，我们就不大可能会重复这个行为。

操作性条件反射的经典研究与一只猫有关，它被放置在一个只有一个出口的箱子里。必须按下箱子中的一个特定区域，箱门才会打开。出于对自由的渴望，这只猫试图逃出这个箱子。在它尝试逃脱的过程中，箱子的那个区域被触发，门打开了，猫获得了自由。一旦再次被关进这个箱子，这只猫会自然地去回忆上次是如何逃出的，并且会再次发现那个需要按下的区域。这只猫被放回箱子的次数越多，它就会越快按下那个开关，以获得自由。猫通过自然后果学会了如何获得自由。

在生活中我们每天都以这种方式学习。设想你上次犯了一个错误，你很可能会记得那个错误，当情况再次出现时，你会做出不同的反应。从这个意义上说，你已经学会了根据自己之前行为的自然后果采取不同的行动。这个道理也适用于积极的行为。如果你所做的某件事取得了积极的结果，你很可能会重复那个行为。

3. 强化

"强化"一词的意思是加强，在心理学中，指任何能增强或提高某一特定反应的概率的刺激。比如说，你想让你的狗听从"坐下"的命令，可以在每次它听从你的命令坐下的时候给它一个奖励。狗最终会明白，听到"坐下"的命令时就坐下会得到奖励。这个奖励会强化它的行为，因为狗喜欢这个奖励，所以会在接到命令时坐下。

这是对"奖励"这一强化刺激的简单描述，它增强了"坐下"这个反应。我们每天都在使用增强剂，大部分时间甚至没有意识到我们在使用。当你的孩子打扫房间后，你会说"好棒"；当你的伴侣盛装打扮时，你会说"真漂亮／真帅"；在成功完成一个项目后，你会得到加薪。所有这些都增加了同样的反应会被重复的概率。

强化有四种类型：正强化、负强化、惩罚和消退。上面的例子描述的是正强化，可以把它看作是给予一些东西以增强反应。例如，给予奖励会增强狗"坐下"的反应；给予表扬会增加孩子打扫房间的概率。最常见的正强化是表扬和奖励，作为给予者或接受者，我们大多数人都经历过正强化。

负强化可以理解为，为了增加反应而去除一些负面的东西。设想有一个少年因为一直不扔垃圾而被母亲唠叨。在向他的朋友抱怨此事并接受了朋友的建议后，终于有一天他扔掉了垃圾，令他惊讶的是，他母亲的唠叨也停止了。这个负面刺激会强化，并很可能会增加他下周扔垃圾的概率。

惩罚是指为了抑制某个行为而采取一些令其厌恶的措施。最常见的例子就是管教行为不端的孩子（比如打屁股）。我们这样做是因为孩子会将被惩罚和不良行为联系起来。没有人喜欢被惩罚，因此为了避免惩罚，他们会停止不良行为。

当你移除某物以减少某个行为时，这就是"消退"，即你去除某物以减少某个反应。例如，帕夫洛夫的狗习惯了在听到铃声时分泌唾液，但当铃声反复响起，却没有给它喂肉的时候，狗最终会停止对铃声分泌唾液。

研究发现，正强化是最强有力的强化方式。通过正强化来增强反应不仅能更好地发挥作用，而且还能让双方专注于情况的积极方面。在不良行为后立即实施惩罚是有效的，但是如果不持续使用的话，就会产生消退现象。惩罚也可能会引发其他的负面反应，比如愤怒和怨恨。

Unit

2

Cognitive Theories of Learning

Learning theories describe how knowledge is absorbed, processed, and retained during learning. Cognitive, emotional, and environmental influences, as well as prior experience, all play a part in how understanding is acquired, a worldview is changed, and knowledge is retained. Behaviorists look at learning as an aspect of conditioning and advocate a stimulus-response system in learning. Cognitivists believe people are not "programmed animals" that merely respond to environmental stimuli. People are rational beings who are capable of active participation in order to learn, and whose actions are a consequence of thinking. Educators who embrace cognitive theory believe that the definition of learning as a change in behavior is too narrow and prefer to study the learners rather than their environment, and in particular the complexities of human mind.

Cognitive learning theorists believe learning occurs through internal processing of information. The cognitive approach to learning theory pays more attention to what goes on inside the learner's head and focuses on mental process rather than observable behaviors. Changes in behaviors are observed, and used as indicators as to what is happening inside the learner's mind. That is, cognitivism focuses on the inner mental activities—opening the "black box" of the human mind is valuable and necessary for understanding how people learn. Mental process such as thinking, memory, knowing, and problem-solving are the foci of exploration. Cognitivists see knowledge as schema, and learning may be defined as change in a learner's schemata. Cognitivists also use the metaphor of the mind as computer: information comes in, is being processed, and leads to certain outcomes. There are three popular theories to understand human learning process.

1. Information Processing Theory

The advent of the modern digital computer has provided a rich theoretical metaphor for theorizing about human information processing. Cognitivists have spent a lot of efforts developing accounts of mechanisms that control information processing. They question how humans process information, pick up information from the environment, store information in memory, retrieve information from memory, and send information back to the environment. The most widely accepted theory is labeled the "stage theory", assuming that the brain embodies a nervous system that processes the information from the time of the input to the time of storage in long-term memory (LTM). The system comprises three main stages that contain different physiological properties: the sensory registers, short-term memory and long-term memory.

The sensory registers briefly store representations of external stimuli from the environment until the information can be transferred further. There appears to be different sensory registers for each sense. In any case, the sensory registers can hold information for only a very brief period of time. The information is assumed to be lost from the registers unless it is passed along into short-term memory.

Short-term memory can be thought as conscious memory because, in addition to holding information, it allows information to be manipulated, interpreted and transformed. The new information in short-term memory, after being further processed, may be transferred to and made part of long-term memory.

Long-term memory is a relatively unlimited and permanent repository of information. Once the information is stored in the long-term memory, it can be retrieved for later use.

2. Cognitive Development Theory

Jean Piaget's[1] Cognitive Development Theory is a blueprint that describes the stages of normal intellectual development, from infancy through adulthood. This includes thought, judgment, and knowledge. Piaget's four stages of intellectual (or cognitive) development are:

Sensorimotor Stage: birth through toddlerhood (18–24 months)

During the early stage, infants are only aware of what is immediate in front of them. They focus on what they see, what they are doing, and physical interactions with their immediate environment. Because they don't yet know how things react, they're constantly experimenting with activities such as shaking or throwing things, putting things in their mouths, and learning about the world through trial and error. The later stage includes goal-oriented behavior which brings about a desired result.

Between 7 and 9 months, infants begin to realize that an object exists even if it can no longer be seen. This important milestone—known as object permanence—is a sign that memory is developing. After infants start crawling, standing, and walking, their increased physical mobility leads to increased cognitive development. Near the end of the sensorimotor stage (18–24 months), infants reach another important milestone—early language development, a sign that

---

1   Jean Piaget: 让·皮亚杰，瑞士心理学家。

they are developing some symbolic abilities.

Preoperational Stage: toddlerhood through early childhood (age 7)

During this stage, young children are able to think about things symbolically. Their language use becomes more mature. They also develop memory and imagination, which allows them to understand the difference between past and future, and engage in make-believe. However, their thinking is based on intuition and still not completely logical. They cannot yet grasp more complex concepts such as cause and effect, time, and comparison.

Concrete Operational Stage: ages 7 to 12

At this time, children demonstrate logical, concrete reasoning. Children's thinking becomes less egocentric and they are increasingly aware of external events. They begin to realize that one's own thoughts and feelings are unique and may not be shared by others or may not even be part of reality. During this stage, however, most children still can't think abstractly or hypothetically.

Formal Operational Stage: adolescence through early adulthood

Adolescents who reach this fourth stage of intellectual development are able to logically use symbols related to abstract concepts, such as algebra and science. They can think about multiple variables in systematic ways, formulate hypotheses, and consider possibilities. They can also ponder abstract relationships and concepts such as justice. Although Piaget believed in lifelong intellectual development, he insisted that the Formal Operational Stage is the final stage of cognitive development, and that continued intellectual development in adults depends on the accumulation of knowledge.

Piaget also suggested that learning process is iterative, in which new information is shaped to fit with the learner's existing knowledge, and existing knowledge itself is modified to accommodate the new information. The major concepts in this cognitive process include:

- Assimilation: It occurs when a child perceives new objects or events in terms of existing schemes. Children and adults tend to apply any mental structure that is available to assimilate a new event, and they will actively seek to use a newly acquired structure. This is a process of fitting new information into existing cognitive structures.

- Accommodation: It occurs when existing schemes or operations must be modified to account for a new experience. This is a process of modifying existing cognitive structures based upon new information.

- Equilibration: It is the master developmental process, encompassing both assimilation and accommodation. This concept implies a dynamic construction process of human's cognitive structure.

3. Schema Theory

One of the central issues that cognitive psychologists are interested in is mental structure. According to schema theory, the knowledge we have stored in memory is organized as a set of schemata, each of which incorporates all the knowledge of a given type of object or event that we have acquired from past experience. That is, they are mental templates that represent a person's

knowledge about people, situations or objects, and which originate from prior knowledge or experiences. A simple example is to think of your schema for dogs. Within that schema you most likely have knowledge about dogs in general (bark, four legs, teeth, hair, and tails) and probably information about specific dogs, such as collies (long hair, large, Lassie).

People make sense of new experiences and the world by activating the schemata stored in their memory. New experiences and information are interpreted according to how it fits into their schemata. This is useful, because if someone tells you a story about eating in a restaurant, he or she doesn't have to provide all of the details about being seated, giving his or her order to the server, leaving a tip at the end, etc. Your schema for the restaurant experience can fill in these missing details.

Three processes are proposed to account for the modification of schemata:

● Accretion: New information is remembered in the context of an existing schema, without altering that schema. For example, suppose you go to a bookstore, and everything you experience there is consistent with your expectations for a bookstore "experience", you can remember the details of your visit. But since they match your existing schema, they don't really alter that schema in any significant way.

● Tuning: New information or experience cannot be fully accommodated under an existing schema, so the schema evolves to become more consistent with experience. For example, when you first encountered a bookstore with a coffee bar, you probably had to modify your bookstore schema to accommodate this experience.

● Restructuring: When new information cannot be accommodated merely by tuning an existing schema, it results in the creation of a new schema. For example, your experience with World Wide Web-based bookstores may be so different from your experience with conventional ones that you are forced to create a new schema.

Cognitive psychologists, unlike behaviorists, believe that learning is a targeted internal process and focus on thinking, understanding, organizing, and consciousness. They say that this type of learning cannot be observed directly and it is associated with the change in capacity and capability of the person to respond. It is believed that the students should be equipped with questioning skills and problem-solving abilities. Therefore, by exploration and information processing, they will be able to learn actively, solve and search for new information, and review their previous experiences for better understanding.

New Words

cognitive ['kɒgnətɪv] *adj.* 认知的，认识的	rational ['ræʃənəl] *adj.* 理性的，理智的
retain [rɪ'teɪn] *v.* 保存，保留	complexity [kəm'pleksɪti] *n.* 复杂，复杂性
advocate ['ædvəkeɪt] *v.* 提倡，主张，拥护	indicator ['ɪndɪkeɪtə] *n.* 指标，指示器

foci ['fəusaɪ] *n.* 焦点；聚焦（focus的复数）

schema ['ski:mə] *n.* 图式，模式

schemata ['ski:mətə] *n.* 图式，模式（schema的复数）

metaphor ['metəfə] *n.* 暗喻，隐喻；比喻

retrieve [rɪ'tri:v] *v.* 提取，检索

label ['leɪbəl] *v.* 标注；贴标签于

manipulate [mə'nɪpjuleɪt] *v.* 操纵；操作

transform [træns'fɔ:m] *v.* 改变；转化

subjection [səb'dʒekʃən] *n.* 隶属，服从

repository [rɪ'pɒzətərɪ] *n.* 贮藏室，仓库；知识库

goal-oriented [gəʊl-'ɔ:rɪəntɪd] *adj.* 目标导向的

milestone ['maɪlstəʊn] *n.* 里程碑，划时代的事件

symbolic [sɪm'bɒlɪk] *adj.* 象征的；符号的；使用符号的

toddlerhood ['tɒdləhʊd] *n.* 学步期

make-believe [meɪk-bɪ'li:v] *n.* 假装，虚构

intuition [ˌɪntjʊ'ɪʃən] *n.* 直觉；直觉的知识

reasoning ['ri:zənɪŋ] *n.* 推理；论证

egocentric [ˌegəʊ'sentrɪk] *adj.* 自我中心的；利己主义的

abstractly ['æbstræktli] *adv.* 抽象地

hypothetically [ˌhaɪpə'θetɪkəli] *adv.* 假设地；假想地

adolescence [ˌædəʊ'lesəns] *n.* 青春期

ponder ['pɒndə] *v.* 仔细考虑；衡量

accumulation [əˌkju:mjʊ'leɪʃən] *n.* 积聚，积累

iterative ['ɪtərətɪv] *adj.* 迭代的；重复的，反复的

assimilation [əˌsɪmə'leɪʃən] *n.* 同化；吸收

accommodation [əˌkɒmə'deɪʃən] *n.* 顺应

equilibration [ˌi:kwɪlaɪ'breɪʃən] *n.* 平衡

incorporate [ɪn'kɔ:pəreɪt] *v.* 融合，吸收

template ['templeɪt] *n.* 模板，样板

modification [ˌmɒdɪfɪ'keɪʃən] *n.* 修改，修补

accretion [ə'kri:ʃən] *n.* 添加

tuning ['tju:nɪŋ] *n.* 调整

evolve [ɪ'vɒlv] *v.* 发展；进化

restructuring [ˌri:'strʌktʃərɪŋ] *n.* 重建

Phrases

be capable of 有能力，能够

long-term memory 长期记忆

sensory register 感觉寄存器

short-term memory 短期记忆

in addition to 除……之外（还有，也）

Sensorimotor Stage 感知运动阶段

be aware of 清楚，明白，意识到

trial and error 反复试验；试错法

object permanence 物体恒存性

preoperational stage 前运算阶段

engage in 从事，参与

cause and effect 因果关系；原因与结果

concrete operational stage 具体运算阶段

formal operational stage 正式运算阶段

schema theory 图式理论

in general 通常；一般而言

account for 解释说明

be consistent with 与……一致

Abbreviation

Long-Term Memory (LTM) 长期记忆

Exercises

Ex. 1 Give the English equivalents of the following Chinese expressions.

(1) 图式理论 _____

(2) 信息处理理论 _____

(3) 认知发展理论 _____

(4) 感觉寄存器 _____

(5) 同化 _____

(6) 清楚，明白 _____

(7) 从事，参与 _____

(8) 因果关系 _____

(9) 有能力，能够 _____

(10) 反复试验；试错法 _____

Ex. 2 Explain the following terminologies in English.

(1) sensory register _____

(2) formal operational stage _____

(3) equilibration _____

(4) tuning _____

(5) restructuring _____

Ex. 3 Answer the following questions according to Text A.

(1) How do behaviorism and cognitivism differ in terms of learning?

(2) What are the three major theories in explaining human learning process?

(3) Why is human information processing compared to computer?

(4) According to Information Processing Theory, what are the three main stages of information processing?

(5) According to Cognitive Development Theory, what are the four stages of intellectual development?

(6) How is new information shaped to fit with the learner's existing knowledge, and existing knowledge itself modified to accommodate the new information?

(7) What is schema?

(8) How is a schema modified?

Ex. 4 **Fill in the blanks with the words given below.**

brain	individual	viewpoint	extrinsic	implies
social	behavioral	mental	memory	processing

The Cognitive Learning Theory (CLT) explains why the brain is the most incredible network of information (1)_____ and interpretation in the body as we learn things. This theory can be divided into two specific theories: the (2)_____ Cognitive Theory (SCT), and the Cognitive (3)_____ Theory (CBT).

When we say the word "learning", we usually mean to think using the (4)_____. This basic concept of learning is the main (5)_____ in the Cognitive Learning Theory. The theory has been used to explain (6)_____ processes as they are influenced by both intrinsic and (7)_____ factors, which eventually bring about learning in an individual.

Cognitive Learning Theory (8)_____ that the different processes concerning learning can be explained by analyzing the mental processes first. It posits that with effective cognitive processes, learning is easier and new information can be stored in the (9)_____ for a long time. On the other hand, ineffective cognitive processes result in learning difficulties that can be seen anytime during the lifetime of an (10)_____.

Text B

Cognitivism in the Classroom

Learning involves the acquisition of knowledge. However, is remembering the same as learning? Put it another way: are knowledge and memory the same?

1. Learning

Learning, according to Cognitive Learning Theory, involves a change in one's cognitive structure. This change occurs when new information or experiences are combined with existing knowledge stored in the long-term memory. In this sense, new knowledge is constructed by learners. Learning becomes meaningful when it is connected to what you already know, that is, when new information is connected to old knowledge. This is called meaningful learning.

Effective teachers try to create learning experiences that result in this kind of learning. The opposite of meaningful learning is rote learning. This occurs when information is presented out of any knowledge context or when it is not connected with anything already known. For example, if you were to memorize a list of facts in order to pass an exam but made no conscious effort to understand, connect, or apply these facts, you would have engaged in rote learning, a pretty useless endeavor. It would be very hard to use or apply that information in the future.

Teachers are encouraged to use the following five strategies to make students' learning more meaningful.

The first is activating relevant schemata of students, that is, help students identify things they might already know about a subject. For example, Molly a third grade teacher, was teaching her students about reptiles. She began the lesson by showing students a picture of a snake and asking them to name characteristics or things they knew about snakes. She listed those facts on the board as students named them. She then showed a picture of lizard and did the same thing.

The second is using analogies, namely, comparing new things to known things. For example, in a computer class, the function of CPU is compared to human brain. Showing how the essential elements of a new concept are related to a familiar concept enhances students' ability to process and encode new information.

Third, information should be presented in an authentic context. This means presenting instruction within the context of real life situations. A common way to do this is to use problem-based or project-based learning. Here students are presented with real life situations or tasks that require them to use information or skills to solve a problem or create a project. Presenting new information in isolation or outside of any sort of meaningful context makes it more difficult for students to understand.

The fourth one is to make personal connections. Connect new information to students' lives or personal experiences. Look for ways in which new learning affects or is exemplified in the context of their lives. Create assignments and activities that invite students to connect new learning to what they have experienced or are experiencing.

Last, it is best to use kid language if you are teaching young children, and keep it concrete. Keep it simple when introducing new information. Too many words can be just as damaging as too few words when trying to introduce new information. Use words and concepts to explain things with which students are familiar.

2. Knowledge

Knowledge enhances learning. We use the knowledge we already have to help understand and interpret new information and construct new knowledge. Existing knowledge improves the ability to assimilate new information because there are more things to connect it to or associate it with in LTM. Put it another way: the more you know, the easier it is to know more. Thus, an important part of the job of a teacher is to present bodies of knowledge to students in an organized fashion in order to enable them to construct and expand their knowledge bases.

Current learning enhances future learning. Less knowledge means less learning. One of the reasons undergraduate students sometimes struggle with concepts in educational psychology is that they have little background knowledge with which to make sense of this new information. Without significant classroom experience, the knowledge they do have related to theories of learning and educational procedures is very shallow and disjointed. As more knowledge and experience are gained, these theories and other concepts make more sense. Students find that these theories of learning make much more sense after they have been teachers for two or three years because they have significant experiential knowledge to connect them to.

There are three different types of knowledge: declarative, procedural, and practical. All are important in any endeavor, especially teaching. Declarative knowledge is "knowing what" or knowing about something. It's information that can be declared or stated. It includes knowledge about the world, theories, ideas, or concepts. For example, you understand what operant conditioning is. Declarative knowledge, sometimes called propositional knowledge, is stored in LTM in the form of a series of propositions.

Procedural knowledge is "knowing how" or knowing how to do something. This is knowledge that is tied to specific steps, e.g., a skill, strategy, or technique. You know how to perform a specific task. In education, examples of procedural knowledge are knowing how to plan a lesson, using cooperative learning, constructing a PowerPoint presentation, or using specific questioning techniques.

Declarative and procedural knowledge are important for classroom teachers. However, without practical knowledge, they are of little use. Practical knowledge is "knowing how and when to use declarative and procedural knowledge". That is, you are able to make practical applications. For example, you know when to use a contingency contract in your classroom and are able to adopt and adapt it to meet the needs of a specific situation. Practical knowledge in education is understanding the theories, concepts, and various pedagogical strategies and knowing when and how to apply them in real life settings.

3. Memories

Learning involves both memory and knowledge, but is memory the same as knowledge? No. Knowledge has to be meaningful; memory does not. Memory is simply a storage tank for knowledge and experience. Within LTM, there are three other types of memory: episodic, semantic, and procedural. Episodic memory is the ability to recall the various episodes or events in your life. The word "semantic" refers to meaning; thus, semantic memory refers to your ability to recall meaningful data or knowledge. This type of memory is very important for school-related learning. Procedural memory, often called "how to" memory, is the ability to recall procedures, skills, or how to do things. Data related to each of these three types of memory are all stored differently in LTM. That is, how you store and retrieve semantic memory is different from how you store and retrieve the other types of memory. Learning is enhanced when all three types of memory are used in the learning process.

Moreover, memory has two levels. Explicit memory is the knowledge in LTM that can be recalled and consciously considered. For example, what did you have for breakfast today (episodic)? What is the capital of the USA (semantic)? How do I create a streaming video so that my students can access it (procedural)? Implicit memory is usually out of (our) awareness but can still influence our thoughts or behaviors. These are sometimes called unconscious memory

(memory of which we are not conscious but can be brought into awareness under the right circumstances) or subconscious memory (memory below our consciousness awareness that we are not able to access).

There are three types of implicit memory: procedural, conditioned, and priming. Implicit procedural memory involves those skills that have become automatic. For example, you know how to drive a car or ride a bike, so you don't have to think about it. Implicit procedural memory also includes habits you may have formed (you turn on TV as the first thing in the morning without thinking about it), or ways of doing things (you always put on the right sock and shoe first, and then put on the left sock and shoe). Implicit conditioned memory is related to classical condition. Here you unconsciously associate episodic memory to current environmental stimuli. For example, you become anxious when you're asked to bat in a baseball game because you remember getting hit in the head by a pitch before. Or you respond positively to a commercial with a dog in it because of your own pleasurable experiences with dogs. The third type of implicit memory involves priming or activating related information in LTM. Implicit priming memory is directly or closely related to something else you are retrieving. For example, in an education class that's studying lesson planning, your instructor uses a particular social studies lesson plan as an example. You suddenly remember such a lesson you had in middle school. The stimulus triggers something that was paired with it in LTM. That is, a similar thing triggers an associated memory.

Memory is an important part of learning, but is different from learning. Memory enables you to retrieve past knowledge, i.e., to activate relevant schemata, in order to interpret new information and construct new knowledge. However, sometimes old or new knowledge interferes with encoding and retrieval. Retrieval of knowledge from LTM can be enhanced by active learning, meaningful instruction, the use of authentic contexts, and frequent review and practice.

New Words

acquisition [ˌækwɪˈzɪʃən] n. 获得，习得

strategy [ˈstrætədʒi] n. 战略，策略

identify [aɪˈdentɪfaɪ] v. 确定；识别，辨认出

reptile [ˈreptaɪl] n. 爬行动物

lizard [ˈlɪzəd] n. 蜥蜴

analogy [əˈnælədʒi] n. 类比，类推；比喻

essential [ɪˈsenʃəl] adj. 必要的；本质的

enhance [ɪnˈhɑːns] v. 提高；加强

exemplify [ɪgˈzemplɪfaɪ] v. 例证；举例说明

fashion [ˈfæʃən] n. 方式，方法

expand [ɪkˈspænd] v. 拓展，发展

disjointed [dɪsˈdʒɔɪntɪd] adj. 脱节的；杂乱的

propositional [prɒpəˈzɪʃənl] adj. 命题的；建议的

application [ˌæplɪˈkeɪʃən] n. 应用；申请

pedagogical [ˌpedəˈgɒdʒɪkl] adj. 教学的，教学法的

tank [tæŋk] n. （储存液体或气体的）箱，罐

episodic [ˌepɪ'sɒdɪk] *adj.* 插曲式的；（故事或记忆）由松散片段组成的，不连贯的

semantic [sɪ'mæntɪk] *adj.* 语义的

procedural [prə'siːdʒərəl] *adj.* 程序上的

episode ['epɪsəʊd] *n.* 插曲；一段情节；有趣的事件

explicit [ɪk'splɪsɪt] *adj.* 明确的；清楚的

implicit [ɪm'plɪsɪt] *adj.* 隐式的，含蓄的，暗含的

awareness [ə'weənəs] *n.* 意识，认识；明白

subconscious [ˌsʌb'kɒnʃəs] *adj.* 潜意识的；下意识的

priming ['praɪmɪŋ] *n.* 引发，起爆

bat [bæt] *v.* 用球棒或球拍打球，击球

commercial [kə'mɜːʃəl] *n.* 商业广告

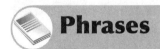

Phrases

be combined with 与……结合 / 联合

in this sense 从这个意义上来说

be connected to 连接到，与……有联系

rote learning 机械学习，死记硬背

problem-based learning 问题导向学习；基于问题的学习

project-based learning 项目教学法；基于项目的学习

in isolation 孤立地；绝缘

educational psychology 教育心理学

declarative knowledge 陈述性知识

procedural knowledge 程序性知识

practical knowledge 实践性知识，实用性知识

cooperative learning 小组合作学习

contingency contract 后效契约

episodic memory 情节记忆；情景记忆

semantic memory 语义记忆；语义存储器

procedural memory 程序记忆

explicit memory 外显记忆

implicit memory 内隐记忆

streaming video 流媒体；视频流

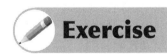

Exercise

Decide whether the following statements are true (T) or false (F) according to Text B. Give your reasons for the false ones.

(　　) (1) New knowledge is constructed when new information is connected to old knowledge.

(　　) (2) Rote learning is an effective way to acquire knowledge.

(　　) (3) It does not matter whether the examples a teacher presents in class is authentic or not.

(　　) (4) The more knowledge you have, the easier it is to know more.

(　　) (5) There are two types of knowledge: declarative and procedural.

(   ) (6) Within LTM, there are three other types of memory: episodic, semantic, and procedural.

(   ) (7) Semantic memory is the ability to recall the various episodes or events in your life.

(   ) (8) Explicit memory is the knowledge in LTM that can be recalled and consciously considered.

(   ) (9) Implicit procedural memory involves those skills that have become automatic, for example, you know how to ride a bike, so you don't have to think about it.

(   ) (10) Memory is learning.

 # Supplementary Reading

Text	Notes
Using Cognitive Psychology in the Classroom: Approach[1] with Caution[2] I've always thought it interesting how, as a profession, we teachers find the ideas of cognitive psychologists so beguiling[3] and persuasive[4]. I first heard of developmental psychologist Howard Gardner at an inset day[5] in the early 1990s. We were told that Gardner's[6] definition of intelligence—multiple intelligences[7]—along with various other discoveries, were going to revolutionize[8] teaching and learning. Schools were to become nirvanas[9] where each class would be transformed into an optimal[10] learning environment; Mozart was playing softly in the background, an infusion[11] of lovely smells was wafting[12] through the air and every activity perfectly matched to each student's individual learning styles and intelligences. Mostly it was nonsense. However, at the time, we didn't know any better. We were told these ideas were designed by brain experts, who conducted complicated[13] experiments and had hard evidence—lots of numbers and images of the brain—that proved what they were saying was true. We might think it was nonsense but really it was the future. So, we set to trial[14] the different approaches in our classrooms. Fortunately, in the school I worked in, we had a forward-thinking headteacher[15] who encouraged experimentation but was prepared to listen if we thought something wasn't working.	[1] approach *n.* 方法，途径；接近 [2] caution *n.* 小心，谨慎 [3] beguiling *adj.* 令人陶醉的；有趣的 [4] persuasive *adj.* 有说服力的 [5] inset day 培训日 [6] Gardner 加德纳，美国哈佛大学心理学教授 [7] multiple intelligences 多元智力；多元智力理论 [8] revolutionize *v.* 发动革命；彻底改革 [9] nirvana *n.* 涅槃；天堂 [10] optimal *adj.* 最佳的；最理想的 [11] infusion *n.* 灌输；注入；激励 [12] waft *v.* 使飘荡；吹送 [13] complicated *adj.* 难懂的，复杂的 [14] trial *v.* 试验；试用 [15] headteacher *n.* 中小学的校长

After a term most of the really wacky[16] stuff was gone. Brain gym[17]—a theory that promotes movement as a learning aid—held on for a while; the exercises seemed to calm down some of the hyperactive children. Nevertheless[18], I was never keen. One thing that stayed permanently[19] was bottled water, especially on hot days. I still carry a bottle around with me wherever I go so that my brain is constantly tuned[20] and fully hydrated[21].

Gardner was a conundrum[22], however. Unlike other ideas, which were practical (or rather impractical) applications of experiments, multiple intelligences was a respected theory written by a Harvard professor. While I felt confident to say "Brain Gym is stupid" after being told to rub[23] my "brain buttons"[24], I didn't feel qualified enough to call Howard Gardner an idiot. Therefore, I ordered his book, *Frames of Mind*[25].

I didn't enjoy reading it and couldn't say I understood everything; it wasn't written for teachers. I know this because I heard Gardner speak at a conference where he said something along those lines—that it was up to educators to explore whether his work has practical applications in the classroom. I liked him when he said that and wanted to shout out that it doesn't, but I didn't have the nerve[26].

After reading the book and exploring its implications in class, I came to two conclusions[27]: it was a theory that needed more evidence from the field it belonged to—cognitive psychology; it had little practical application in the classroom and was not a very helpful way of thinking about learning.

It was a lesson learned: be very cautious and test every idea you think will be useful in the classroom with real kids. As a teacher there is really only one question that matters: "does this help children learn better?"

I apply this principle to all the theories that come out of psychology, whether I sympathize[28] with the ideology or not. As a science, cognitive psychology is still in its infancy[29], and there are still much things that are unknown. In biology there are still some competing theories and ideas, still new discoveries to be made, but on the whole all biologists agree

[16] wacky *adj.* 乖僻的，古怪的
[17] brain gym 健脑操；健脑运动
[18] nevertheless *adv.* 然而，不过；虽然如此
[19] permanently *adv.* 永久地，长期不变地
[20] tune *v.* 调整；协调
[21] hydrate *v.* 与水化合
[22] conundrum *n.* 难解之谜

[23] rub *v.* 摩擦
[24] brain button 脑开关

[25] *Frames of Mind* 《智能结构》

[26] have the nerve 有胆量

[27] come to a conclusion 得出结论

[28] sympathize *v.* 同情；支持
[29] infancy *n.* 初期；婴儿期；幼年

on the way things work. Similarly, you won't find geologists fighting over plate tectonics[30]. These are mature sciences, where major theories are agreed on. By comparison, cognitive psychologists are still arguing if the world is flat or round.

This is not to say we have nothing to learn from cognitive psychology. As a teacher I have found many ideas from the field to be helpful and generative[31]. However, we should be cautious and critical, judging each idea on its merits[32] and remembering all the time that we are the experts in the classroom.

The following are three questions I find useful to ask when judging the merits of an idea that might have a practical application:

Is it believable? Ask yourself, based on your experience and thinking rationally[33], does this idea sound believable?

Is it practical? An idea might sound rational and useful in theory, but will it work in the classroom? When I first heard of multiple intelligences, it sounded reasonable[34], but it failed the test of practicality[35] when trialed in the classroom.

Does it improve what I'm doing already? All ideas should be tested against the need to improve practice. For example, it might sound like a very good idea to give every child in the class a written target for reading, writing and math. However, will the extra work and time away from the children writing them really improve learning? Although assessment for learning, especially oral feedback, becomes a major part of our practice, we resist writing up learning objectives and constructing layered[36] targets.

Over the years I've been to many conferences where I've heard expressions such as, "the latest research indicates...", "cognitive science tells us...", or "scans of the brain show..." I am always a little cynical[37] and wary[38] of experts telling me the answer. I get particularly annoyed when I read fellow teachers using the same strategies in their blogs. It is the main reason I liked Daniel Willingham's book, *Why Don't Students Like School?* Although it contained a lot of new thinking from the world of cognitive psychology, he never told me how to think or do my job as a teacher.

We should be very careful how we use research findings

[30] plate tectonics 板块构造论

[31] generative *adj.* 生产的，有产出的

[32] on its merits 根据事物本身的优缺点

[33] rationally *adv.* 理性地

[34] reasonable *adj.* 合理的，公道的

[35] practicality *n.* 实用性，可操作性

[36] layered *adj.* 分层的；层状的

[37] cynical *adj.* 愤世嫉俗的

[38] wary *adj.* 小心谨慎的

from cognitive psychology. Cognitive psychologists are a bit like those early explorers who set out to find a new route to India. Everything they discover is new and exciting, but it doesn't mean they know what is coming over the horizon, let alone[39] how the whole thing fits together.

Compared to mapping the human mind, mapping the globe was a skip through the park. So let's have a skeptical[40] view of the work cognitive scientists do, take what's useful and practical, and call their ideas what they are—theories rather than evidence. They won't mind.

[39] let alone 更不用说，更别提

[40] skeptical adj. 怀疑的；怀疑论的

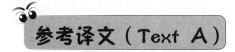

参考译文（Text A）

认知主义学习理论

学习理论描述的是知识如何在学习过程中被吸收、处理和保留。认知、情感、环境，以及先前的经验都在如何获得理解、改变世界观，保留知识等方面起着重要作用。行为主义者把学习看作是条件反射，并倡导学习中的刺激——反应系统。认知主义者认为，人不是只对环境刺激做出反应的"程序化的动物"。人是理性的，能够积极地参与学习，而且人的行为是思考的结果。接受认知理论的教育工作者认为，将学习定义为行为的变化过于狭隘，他们更倾向于研究学习者而不是他们的环境，特别是研究人类思维的复杂性。

持认知主义学习理论的学者认为，学习是通过信息的内部处理来实现的。认知主义学习范式更多地关注学习者头脑中发生的事情，关注的是心理过程而不是可观察到的行为。所观察到的行为变化可以看作是学习者头脑中发生的事情的指示器。也就是说，认知主义关注的是内在的精神活动——打开人类心灵的"黑盒子"对于理解人们如何学习非常有意义，也很有必要。思考、记忆、认知和解决问题等心理过程是其研究的重点。认知主义者视知识为图式，视学习为学习者图式的变化。认知主义者也将大脑比作计算机：信息输入，被处理，并产生一定的结果。三个主流理论分别解释了人类的学习过程。

1. 信息加工理论

现代数字计算机的出现为人处理信息的理论化提供了一个形象的比喻。认知主义者花费了大量的精力来开发控制信息处理的机制。他们探究人类如何处理信息，如何从环境中获取信息，如何在记忆中存储信息，如何在记忆中检索信息，以及如何将信息传回环境。最广为接受的理论被称为"阶段理论"，这个理论认为大脑包含一个神经系统，从输入时的信息到存储在长期记忆中的信息，它都会进行处理。该系统包含生理属性不同的三个主要阶段：感觉寄存器、短期记忆和长期记忆。

感觉寄存器会短暂地存储外部环境刺激所传递的信息，直到信息被进一步传输。每种感官似乎都有不同的感觉寄存器。在任何情况下，感觉寄存器只能在很短时间内保存信息。

如果不传递到短期记忆中，这些信息就会从寄存器中丢失。

短期记忆可以看作是有意识的记忆，因为除了保存信息之外，它还允许对信息进行操作、解释和转换。短期记忆中的新信息会被进一步处理，从而可以转移到长期记忆中并成为长期记忆的一部分。

长期记忆相对而言是一个无限量的和永久性的信息存储库。一旦信息存储在长期记忆中，就可供以后检索使用。

2. 认知发展理论

皮亚杰的认知发展理论是一个描述从婴儿到成年智力发展阶段的蓝图。这包括思维、判断和知识。皮亚杰的智力（或认知）发展的四个阶段是：

感觉运动阶段：从出生到18—24个月

在早期阶段，婴儿只能意识到眼前的、即时的东西。他们仅关注他们所看到的、他们正在做的事情，以及身体与环境的直接互动。因为他们还不知道事物是如何反应的，因此他们不断用各种活动做出尝试，比如摇晃或扔东西，把东西放进嘴里，通过反复试验或试错来了解这个世界。后期阶段包括目标导向的行为，这些行为会带来他们所期望的结果。

在7—9个月的时候，婴儿开始意识到，即使看不见，物体仍然是存在的。这个重要的里程碑——称为"物体恒存性"——是记忆发展的标志。当婴儿学会爬行、站立和行走后，更多的运动造就了他们认知的进一步发展。在感觉运动阶段晚期（18—24个月），婴儿会达到另一个重要的里程碑——早期语言发展，这表明他们开始发展使用符号的能力。

前运算阶段：幼儿期（18—24个月）到儿童早期（7岁）

在这个阶段，小孩们能够象征性地思考事物，他们的语言使用也变得更加成熟。他们的记忆力和想象力得到发展，这使得他们能够区别过去和未来，并学会假装。然而，他们的思维建立在直觉的基础上，并不完全合乎逻辑。他们还不能掌握更复杂的概念，比如因果关系、时间和比较。

具体运算阶段：7—12岁

在这个阶段，孩子们会展现出具体的、合乎逻辑的推理能力。孩子们的思维变得不那么以自我为中心，他们越来越能感知到外部事件。他们开始意识到自己的想法和感受是独一无二的，可能不被别人认同，也可能并非真实。然而，在这个阶段，大多数孩子仍然不具有抽象思维能力或假设能力。

正式运算阶段：青少年到成年早期

进入智力发展第四阶段的青少年能够合乎逻辑地使用与抽象概念相关的符号，例如代数和科学。他们可以以系统的方式思考多个变量，提出假设，并考虑可能性。他们也会思考抽象的关系和概念，如正义。尽管皮亚杰相信智力发展是终身的，但他坚持认为正式运算阶段是认知发展的最后阶段，成人后续的智力发展依赖于知识的积累。

皮亚杰也认为学习过程是迭代的，在这个过程中，新的信息会被整合以适应学习者现有的知识体系，同时现有的知识也会被修改以适应新的信息。这个认知过程的主要概念包括：

● 同化：当孩子以现有的知识体系来理解新的事物或事件时，就会发生这种情况。儿童和成人都倾向于使用已有的心理结构来吸收新事件，同时会积极地寻求使用新获得的结构。这是一个将新信息融入现有认知结构的过程。

- 顺应：当必须得修改现有的知识结构或操作以解释新的体验时，就会发生这种情况。这是一个根据新信息修改现有认知结构的过程。
- 平衡：它是一个同时包括同化与顺应的重要的发展过程。这一概念说明了人类认知结构的动态建构过程。

3. 图式理论

认知心理学家感兴趣的一个核心问题是心理结构。根据图式理论，我们存储在记忆中的知识是作为一组图式存在的，每一个图式都包含了我们从过去经验中获得的特定类型的物体或事件的所有知识。也就是说，这些图式代表了一个人对人类、情景或物体的知识的心理模板，这些模板源于先前的知识或经验。举个简单的例子，你可以想象一下狗的模板。据此模板，你很可能对狗有一般的了解（吠叫、四条腿、牙齿、毛发和尾巴），可能还有对特定犬种的信息，比如牧羊犬（长毛，巨大，灵犬莱西）。

人们通过激活存储在记忆中的图式来理解新的体验和世界，并根据新体验和信息如何融入既有图式来理解新的体验和信息。这很有用，因为如果有人给你讲一个在餐馆用餐的故事，他不必描述诸多细节，如领座、点菜、给小费等。你关于餐馆的图式会自动填补这些细节。

图式修补可用三个过程来解释：

- 增加：在不改变既有图式的情况下，新信息被写入既有图式。例如，假设你去了一家书店，你在那里所经历的一切都与你对书店体验的期望是一致的。你能记住你参观的细节，但是由于它们与你现有的图式相匹配，所以它们不会显著地改变你既有的图式。
- 调整：既有图式不能完全匹配新的信息或体验，因此既有图式会进化以适应新的体验。例如，当你第一次遇到一个有咖啡吧的书店时，你可能得修改你关于书店的原有图式以适应这种体验。
- 重建：当不能仅仅通过调整既有图式来适应新的信息时，就会产生新的图式。例如，你关于互联网书店的体验可能与你对传统书店的经历有很大的不同，所以你会被迫创建一个新的图式。

与行为主义者不同，认知心理学家认为学习是一个有目标的内在过程，它专注于思考、理解、组织和意识。他们认为这类学习不能被直接观察到，它与一个人的吸收能力和学习能力的变化有关。他们认为学生应该具备提出问题的能力和解决问题的能力。因此，通过探索和信息处理，学生能够积极地参与学习，解决并搜索新的信息，反思他们先前的经历以更好地理解知识。

Unit 3

Text A

Constructivist Learning Theory

Constructivism is first of all a theory of learning based on the idea that knowledge is constructed by the learners based on mental activity. Learners are considered to be active organisms seeking meaning. Constructivism is founded on the premise that, by reflecting on our experiences, we construct our own understanding of the world consciously we live in. Each of us generates our own "rules" and "mental models", which we use to make sense of our experiences. Learning, therefore, is simply the process of adjusting our mental models to accommodate new experiences. Constructions of meaning may initially bear little relationship to reality (as in the naive theories of children), but will become increasingly more complex, differentiated and realistic as time goes on.

Two names contribute greatly to the development of constructivism. Jean Piaget's theory stands under the umbrella of "Cognitive Constructivism". His theory has two major parts: the component of ages and stages that predicts what children can and cannot understand at different ages, and the theory of development that describes how learners develop cognitive abilities. Piaget's theory of cognitive development proposes that learners should not be given information, which they immediately understand and use. Instead, learners must construct their own knowledge. They build their knowledge through experience. Experiences enable them to create schemas—mental models of the world. These schemas are changed, enlarged, and made more sophisticated through two complimentary processes: assimilation and accommodation.

Lev Vygotsky[1] believes that knowledge is first constructed in a social context and collaborated with other individuals or groups. This is known as "Social Constructivism". Social

---

1　Lev Vygotsky：利维·维果斯基，苏联心理学家。

Constructivism emphasizes the collaborative nature of learning, which requires learners to develop teamwork skills and sees individual learning as essentially related to the success of group learning. He emphasizes the influences of cultural and social contexts in learning and supports a discovery model of learning. This type of model places the teacher in an active role while the students' mental abilities develop naturally through various paths of discovery.

Nevertheless, constructivists share the following principles about learning:

- Knowledge is constructed, not transmitted;
- Prior knowledge impacts the learning process;
- Initial understanding is local, not global;
- Building useful knowledge structures requires effortful and purposeful activity.

Typically, a constructivist teaching strategy is based on the belief that students learn best when they gain knowledge through exploration and active learning. Hands-on materials are used instead of textbooks, and students are encouraged to think and explain their reasoning instead of memorizing and reciting facts. Education is centered on themes and concepts and the connections between them, rather than isolated information.

Under the theory of Constructivism, instructors should focus on making connections between facts and fostering new understanding in students. Instructors tailor their teaching strategies to student responses and encourage students to analyze, interpret, and predict information. Teachers also rely heavily on open-ended questions and promote extensive dialogue among students. In terms of assessment, constructivism calls for the elimination of grades and standardized testing. Instead, assessment becomes part of the learning process so that students play a larger role in judging their own progress.

There are some guiding principles that we must keep in mind when we consider our role as educators. All are predicated on the belief that learning consists of individuals' constructed meanings.

First, learning is an active process in which the learner uses sensory input and constructs meaning out of it. The more traditional formulation of this idea involves the terminology of the active learner, stressing that the learner needs to do something, that learning is not the passive acceptance of knowledge which exists "out there" but it involves the learners' engaging with the world.

Second, people learn to learn as they learn. Learning consists of both constructing meaning and constructing systems of meaning. For example, if we learn the chronology of dates of a series of historical events, we are simultaneously learning the meaning of a chronology. Each meaning we construct makes us better able to give meaning to other sensations which can fit a similar pattern.

Third, the crucial action of constructing meaning is mental, i.e., it happens in the mind. Physical actions and hands-on experience may be necessary for learning, especially for children, but these are not sufficient. We need to provide activities which engage the mind as well as the hands, which can be called reflective activity.

Fourth, learning involves language. The language we use influences learning. On the empirical level, researchers have noted that people talk to themselves as they learn. On a more general level, there is a collection of arguments, presented most forcefully by Vygotsky, that language and learning are inextricably intertwined.

Fifth, learning is a social activity. Our learning is intimately associated with our connection with other human beings, our teachers, our peers, our family as well as casual acquaintances, including the people before us or next to us at the exhibit. We are more likely to be successful in our efforts to educate if we recognize this principle rather than try to avoid it. Much of traditional education is directed towards isolating the learner from all social interaction, and towards seeing education as a one-on-one relationship between the learner and the objective material to be learned. In contrast, constructivism education recognizes the social aspect of learning and uses conversation, interaction with others, and the application of knowledge as an integral aspect of learning.

Sixth, learning is contextual. We do not learn isolated facts and theories in some abstract ethereal land of the mind separate from the rest of our lives. We learn in relationship to what else we know, what we believe, our prejudices and our fears. On reflection, it becomes clear that this point is actually a corollary of the idea that learning is active and social. We cannot divorce our learning from our lives.

Seventh, we need knowledge to learn. It is not possible to assimilate new knowledge without having some structure developed from previous knowledge to build on. The more we know, the more we can learn. Therefore, any effort to teach must be connected to the state of the learner, and provide a path into the subject for the learner based on the learner's previous knowledge.

Eighth, it takes time to learn. Learning is not instantaneous. For significant learning, we need to revisit ideas, ponder them, try them out, play with them and use them. If we reflect on anything we have learned, we soon realize that it is the product of repeated exposure and thought. Even, or especially, moments of profound insight can be traced back to longer periods of preparation.

In the constructivist classroom, the focus tends to shift from the teacher to the students. The classroom is no longer a place where the teacher ("expert") pours knowledge into passive students, who wait like empty vessels to be filled. In the constructivist model, the students are urged to be actively involved in their own process of learning. Both the teacher and the students think of knowledge as a dynamic, ever-changing view of the world we live in and the ability to successfully stretch and explore that view, rather than as inert factoids to be memorized. The educators usually assume that:

- What the student currently believes, whether correct or incorrect, is important.
- Despite having the same learning experience, each individual will base his or her learning on the understanding and meaning personal to him or her.
- Understanding or constructing a meaning is an active and continuous process.
- Learning may involve some conceptual changes.
- When students construct a new meaning, they may not believe it but may give it

provisional acceptance or even rejection.

● Learning is an active, not a passive, process and depends on the students taking responsibility to learn.

The main activity in a constructivist classroom is solving problems. Students use inquiry methods to ask questions, investigate a topic, and use a variety of resources to find solutions and answers. As students explore the topic, they draw conclusions, and, as exploration continues, they revisit those conclusions. Exploration of questions leads to more questions.

There is a great deal of overlap between a constructivist and social constructivist classroom, with the exception of the greater emphasis placed on learning through social interaction, and the value placed on cultural background in a social constructivist classroom. For Vygotsky, culture gives the child the cognitive tools needed for development. Adults in the learner's environment are conduits for the tools of the culture, which include language, cultural history, social context, and more recently, electronic forms of information access. In a social constructivist classroom, collaborative learning is a process of peer interaction that is mediated and structured by the teacher. Discussion can be promoted by the presentation of specific concepts, problems or scenarios, and is guided by means of effectively directed questions, introduction and clarification of, and references to previously learned material.

New Words

constructivist [kən'strʌktɪvɪst] *n.* 建构主义者

constructivism [kən'strʌktɪvɪzəm] *n.* 建构主义，结构主义

generate ['dʒenəreɪt] *v.* 生成，产生

complex ['kɒmpleks] *adj.* 复杂的

differentiate [ˌdɪfə'renʃɪeɪt] *v.* 使有差别

realistic [rɪə'lɪstɪk] *adj.* 现实的；现实主义的

sophisticated [sə'fɪstɪkeɪtɪd] *adj.* 复杂的；精致的

collaborate [kə'læbəreɪt] *v.* 合作；勾结

transmit [træns'mɪt] *v.* 传授，传播

impact ['ɪmpækt] *v.* 影响

global ['gləubəl] *adj.* 总体的，全局的

hands-on ['hændz-ɒn] *adj.* 亲身实践的，亲自动手的

foster ['fɒstə] *v.* 培养，养育

tailor ['teɪlə] *v.* 剪裁；使合适

assessment [ə'sesmənt] *n.* 评价，考核

elimination [ɪˌlɪmɪ'neɪʃən] *n.* 消除，取消

formulation [ˌfɔ:mjʊ'leɪʃən] *n.* 表述，提法

terminology [ˌtɜ:mɪ'nɒlədʒi] *n.* 术语

chronology [krə'nɒlədʒi] *n.* 年表；年代学

simultaneously [ˌsɪməl'teɪnɪəsli] *adv.* 同时地

sufficient [sə'fɪʃənt] *adj.* 足够的；充分的

empirical [ɪm'pɪrɪkəl] *adj.* 实证的

argument ['ɑ:gjumənt] *n.* 论点，论据

inextricably [ˌɪnɪk'strɪkəbli] *adv.* 密不可分地，难分难解地

intertwined [ˌɪntɜ:'twaɪnd] *adj.* 缠绕的；错综复杂的

intimately ['ɪntɪmɪtli] *adv.* 密切地，亲密地

contextual [kən'tekstʃuəl] *adj.* 情境的；上下文的；前后关系的

ethereal [ɪ'θɪərɪəl] *adj.* 缥缈的；优雅的

prejudice ['predʒudɪs] *n.* 偏见

corollary [kə'rɒləri] *n.* 推论；必然的结果

instantaneous [ˌɪnstən'teɪnɪəs] *adj.* 瞬间的；即时的

exposure [ɪk'spəʊʒə] *n.* 暴露；接触

vessel ['vesl] *n.* 容器，器皿

dynamic [daɪ'næmɪk] *adj.* 动态的；动力的

stretch [stretʃ] *v.* 伸展，张开

inert [ɪ'nɜːt] *adj.* 惰性的；迟缓的

factoid ['fæktɔɪd] *n.* 仿真陈述

provisional [prə'vɪʒənəl] *adj.* 临时的，暂时的；暂定的

rejection [rɪ'dʒekʃən] *n.* 抛弃；拒绝

overlap [ˌəʊvə'læp] *n.* 重叠；重复

conduit ['kɒndjuɪt] *n.* 管道，渠道

mediate ['miːdɪeɪt] *v.* 调解，斡旋

scenario [sə'nɑːrɪəʊ] *n.* 情境，场景，情节

clarification [ˌklærəfɪ'keɪʃən] *n.* 澄清，说明

reference ['refərəns] *n.* 参考，参照；涉及

Phrases

on the premise that 在……前提下

reflect on 仔细考虑，反思

adjust to 适应；调整以适应

bear relationship to 和……有关

naive theory 朴素理论

contribute to 有助于；贡献

Cognitive Constructivism 认知建构主义

Social Constructivism 社会建构主义

open-ended question 开放式问题

keep in mind 记住，牢记

sensory input 感官输入

casual acquaintance 点头之交，泛泛之交

try out 试验，试用，尝试

trace back to 追溯到

tend to 趋向于；有……的倾向

collaborative learning 合作性学习

Exercises

Ex. 1 **Give the English equivalents of the following Chinese expressions.**

(1) 认知建构主义　　　　_____

(2) 社会建构主义　　　　_____

(3) 合作性学习　　　　　_____

(4) 朴素理论　　　　　　_____

(5) 感官输入　　　　　　_____

(6) 追溯到　　　　　　＿＿＿＿＿＿＿＿＿＿＿＿＿＿＿＿＿＿＿＿＿＿＿＿＿＿

(7) 在……前提下　　　＿＿＿＿＿＿＿＿＿＿＿＿＿＿＿＿＿＿＿＿＿＿＿＿＿＿

(8) 调整以适应　　　　＿＿＿＿＿＿＿＿＿＿＿＿＿＿＿＿＿＿＿＿＿＿＿＿＿＿

(9) 开放式问题　　　　＿＿＿＿＿＿＿＿＿＿＿＿＿＿＿＿＿＿＿＿＿＿＿＿＿＿

(10) 点头之交，泛泛之交　＿＿＿＿＿＿＿＿＿＿＿＿＿＿＿＿＿＿＿＿＿＿＿＿＿

Ex. 2 **Explain the following terminologies in English.**

(1) Cognitive Constructivism　＿＿＿＿＿＿＿＿＿＿＿＿＿＿＿＿＿＿＿＿＿＿＿＿

(2) Social Constructivism　＿＿＿＿＿＿＿＿＿＿＿＿＿＿＿＿＿＿＿＿＿＿＿＿＿

(3) active learner　＿＿＿＿＿＿＿＿＿＿＿＿＿＿＿＿＿＿＿＿＿＿＿＿＿＿＿＿

(4) inquiry method　＿＿＿＿＿＿＿＿＿＿＿＿＿＿＿＿＿＿＿＿＿＿＿＿＿＿＿

(5) social interaction　＿＿＿＿＿＿＿＿＿＿＿＿＿＿＿＿＿＿＿＿＿＿＿＿＿＿

(6) collaborative learning　＿＿＿＿＿＿＿＿＿＿＿＿＿＿＿＿＿＿＿＿＿＿＿＿＿

Ex. 3 **Decide whether the following statements are true (T) or false (F) according to Text A. Give your reasons for the false ones.**

(　　) (1) Learning is a process adjusting our mental models to accommodate new experiences.

(　　) (2) According to Piaget's cognitive constructivism, learners should be given information that they can immediately understand and use.

(　　) (3) Lev Vygotsky believes that knowledge is mainly constructed by individual learning.

(　　) (4) The more knowledge a teacher transmits, the more students learn.

(　　) (5) A constructivist classroom prefers hands-on teaching materials, and students are encouraged to think and explain their reasoning instead of memorizing facts.

(　　) (6) Students are passive receivers of knowledge.

(　　) (7) Language and learning have no direct connection.

(　　) (8) Teachers are the experts who transmit knowledge to students in a classroom.

(　　) (9) The main activity in a constructivist classroom is solving problems.

(　　) (10) The social constructivist classroom puts emphasis on learning through social interaction, and values cultural background.

Ex. 4 **Fill in the blanks with the words given below.**

discarding	practices	assess	reconcile	conceptions
theory	expert	construct	encouraging	creators

　　Constructivism is basically (1)＿＿＿＿＿— based on observation and scientific study— about how people learn. It says that people (2)＿＿＿＿＿ their own understanding and knowledge of the world, through experiencing things and reflecting on those experiences. When we encounter something new, we have to (3)_____ it with our previous ideas and experience, maybe changing what we believe, or maybe (4)_____ the new information as irrelevant. In any case, we are active (5)_____ of our own knowledge. To do this, we must ask questions, explore, and assess what we know. In the classroom, the constructivist view of learning can point towards a number of different teaching (6)_____. In the most general sense, it usually means (7)_____ students to use active techniques (experiments, real-world problem solving) to create more knowledge and then to reflect on and talk about what they are doing and how their understanding is changing. The teacher makes sure he or she understands the students' preexisting (8)_____, and guides the activity to address them and then build on them.

Constructivist teachers encourage students to constantly (9)_____ how the activity is helping them gain understanding. By questioning themselves and their strategies, students in the constructivist classroom ideally become (10)_____ learners. This gives them ever-broadening tools to keep learning. With a well-planned classroom environment, the students learn how to learn.

Text B

Constructivism Teaching Approaches

Constructivist teaching is based on the belief that learning occurs as learners are actively involved in the process of meaning and knowledge construction as opposed to passively receiving information. Learners are the makers of meaning and knowledge. The following three are among the popular instruction approaches in the constructivism classroom.

1. Scaffolding Instruction

In building construction, scaffolding is used in the process of building something in order to support the pieces that aren't yet firmly in place. In education, scaffolding is used in much the same way. The concept of scaffolding is based on the work of Vygotsky, who proposed that with an adult's assistance, children could accomplish tasks that they ordinarily could not perform independently. Like constructing a building, conveying information to students is never done all at once and without support. Scaffolding Instruction is the support given during the learning process which is tailored to the needs of the students with the intention of helping the students achieve their learning goals. It allows teachers to present information to their students piece by piece, building with each lesson upon a lesson already learned. This learning process is designed to promote a deeper level of learning.

In essence, Scaffolding Instruction means to break knowledge up into chunks of knowledge that can be more easily learned. Doing so allows teachers to naturally support their students' absorption of knowledge. With Scaffolding Instruction, students are able to master skills or ideas that are required for further learning.

Breaking up large lessons into smaller bits allows the teacher to see which students are having trouble and with which concepts. If a student is struggling on a particular chunk of new knowledge, the teacher may briefly backtrack to make sure the student has a proper grasp on relevant background information (i.e., their scaffolding). Whether by reviewing a lesson chunk with the whole class or by providing an individual with tools to better understand the information, the teacher has the opportunity to provide more support to students not yet ready to move on to the next knowledge point. As students demonstrate their comprehension of lesson chunks, the teacher begins to remove support from already-mastered concepts and introduces new concepts. This process is repeated until a whole concept, unit, or book is mastered by the students and they're able to work without the support in place.

Scaffolding Instruction has three essential features. The first has to do with the interaction between the learner and the teacher. This interaction should be collaborative for it to be effective. The second, learning should take place in the learner's Zone of Proximal Development (ZPD). To do that, the teacher needs to be aware of the learner's current level of knowledge and then work to a certain extent beyond that level. The third is that the scaffolding, the support and guidance provided, is gradually removed as the learner becomes more proficient.

The scaffolds may include models, cues, prompts, hints, partial solutions, think-aloud modeling, and direct instruction. In order to provide young learners with an understanding of how to link old information with new knowledge, the teacher must guide learners through verbal and nonverbal communication and model behaviors. Teachers can facilitate this advancement through ZPD by providing activities and tasks that:

- motivate the child's interest related to the task;
- simplify the task to make it more manageable and achievable for a child;
- provide some direction in order to help the child focus on achieving the goal;
- clearly indicate differences between the child's work and the standard or desired solution;
- reduce frustration and risk;
- model and clearly define the expectations of the activity to be performed.

This type of instruction has been praised for its ability to engage most learners because they are constantly building on prior knowledge and forming associations between new information and concepts. Additionally, scaffolding presents opportunities for students to be successful before moving into unfamiliar territory. This type of instruction minimizes failure, which decreases frustration, especially for students with special learning needs.

2. Anchored Instruction

Anchored Instruction is a technology-centered learning approach, which falls under the social constructionism paradigm. While many people have contributed to the theory and research of Anchored Instruction, John Bransford[1] is the principal spokesperson and hence the theory is attributed to him. Anchored Instruction has been developed by the Cognition &

---

1 John Bransford：约翰·布兰斯福德，美国范德堡大学心理学教授。

Technology Group at Vanderbilt (CTGV) under the leadership of Bransford.

Anchored Instruction is usually anchored (situated) in videodisc-based, problem-solving environments that teachers and students can explore. The ultimate goals of Anchored Instruction are to foster learners' problem-solving skills and to help students to become independent thinkers and learners. The instruction demands the material to be learned in the context of an authentic event that serves to anchor or situate the material and, further, allows it to be examined from multiple perspectives.

The focus is on the development of interactive videodisc tools that encourage students and teachers to pose and solve complex, realistic problems. The video materials serve as "anchors" (macro-contexts) for all subsequent learning and instruction. As explained by CTGV: "The design of these anchors is quite different from the design of videos that are typically used in education. The goal is to create interesting, realistic contexts that encourage the active construction of knowledge by learners. The anchors are usually stories rather than lectures and are designed to be explored by students and teachers." The use of interactive videodisc technology makes it possible for students to easily explore the content.

The primary application of Anchored Instruction has been to elementary reading, language arts and mathematics skills. The CTGV has developed a set of interactive videodisc programs called "Jasper Woodbury Problem Solving Series"[1]. These programs involve adventures in which mathematical concepts are used to solve problems. In essence, learners are immersed in a story or scenario that allows them not only to explore a particular problem, but also to acquire skill sets that can be used in the real world. Anchored Instruction is used in a wide variety of subject matters, particularly those designed to encourage the development of reasoning skills. Two principal elements of Anchored Instruction educational model are:

(1) Video-based macro-contexts as anchors. All lessons should be centered around what is known as an "anchor". This anchor is typically a problem-solving scenario. That is, the instruction is situated in the rich context of meaningful authentic problem-solving environment, which provides kinds of problems and opportunities that experts in various areas encounter, as well as helps students explore the knowledge that the experts use as tools.

(2) Discovery learning. Another basic principle is that the curriculum that is used should always allow learners to explore and delve into the problem or scenario. The activities should turn learners into active participants in the scenario, rather than passive overlookers.

In addition, in order to be effective, "anchors" should enable learners to identify critical elements of the learning situation that need further investigation or activation of their previous knowledge. Anchored Instruction must also intrinsically motivate learners by providing interesting activities within context, challenging enough to initiate the discovery learning process.

1　此系列是一套由趣味冒险小故事组成的影碟，学生要利用自己所学的知识思考并解决故事里出现的问题。

3. Random Access Instruction

Rand Spiro[1] is the professor of education and psychology in Pennsylvania State University. He sees that complexity is an inevitable part of advanced knowledge and a particularly thorny problem for teaching and learning. In the domain of complex and advanced knowledge, he has pioneered Cognitive Flexibility Theory, and sought to refashion teaching and learning for an ever-changing and complex world.

Cognitive Flexibility Theory is about preparing people to select, adapt, and combine knowledge and experience in new ways to deal with situations that are different from the ones they have encountered before. It is the flexible application of knowledge in new contexts. With cognitive flexibility, Spiro makes the case for a different kind of instruction. Among the tenets of this new approach are that instruction needs to provide students with multiple representations of content, and should be case-based. The instruction should emphasize knowledge construction instead of transmission of information, and knowledge sources should be highly interconnected. Application of these principles will help students to use knowledge in new ways to suit the purposes of different situations.

For example, in the domain of history, where multiple perspectives and even competing contexts and facts are often present, cognitive flexibility can allow students to gain a deeper understanding. In many situations, it is found that the old linear, more mechanistic, single-perspective approaches don't work. Learners need interconnected knowledge and knowledge in context. They need to be able to apply multiple perspectives, multiple knowledge sources, and multiple points of view.

It turns out that technology (the World Wide Web, CD-ROMs, digital video) is uniquely suited to this type of learning. Spiro and his colleagues have developed electronic learning environments that allow students to get away from the chapter-by-chapter approach, and use the new media to easily access different cases and gain multiple perspectives. This is called Random Access Instruction. Learners can jump from here to there, and look at information in varying contexts of new or previous knowledge, thereby demonstrating the subtleties and nuances that experts appreciate. The goal is to accelerate the acquisition of experience so learners are better prepared to apply their knowledge.

It is believed that cognitive flexibility must be nurtured early in the learning process. Learning shouldn't begin with massive complexity because it leads to confusion that will overwhelm and discourage learners. By starting small, students can avoid oversimplification and learn the underlying habits of mind necessary to acquire complex knowledge. Each "mini-case" is a microcosm of the larger world of practice, with its complexities represented initially in cognitively manageable proportions. Showing students a minute-long digital video clip of a teacher teaching a lesson, for instance, allows them to focus on only two or three complex issues. They can then build up to longer clips as they learn new perspectives on teaching, knowing

---

1　Rand Spiro：兰德·斯皮罗，美国宾夕法尼亚州立大学教育心理学教授。

that they have a more secure foundation that includes ways of looking for and understanding complexity.

As soon as students start thinking in terms of multiple perspectives, they've switched things around. They are not looking for the single best answer, or the best way of looking at things. They realize that there is an interaction of factors, and they can learn about it in those introductory stages because it isn't full-blown complexity.

 **New Words**

scaffolding ['skæfəldɪŋ] *n.* 脚手架

assistance [ə'sɪstəns] *n.* 援助，帮助

accomplish [ə'kʌmplɪʃ] *v.* 完成；实现；达到

ordinarily ['ɔ:dənərɪli] *adv.* 通常地；一般地

independently [ˌɪndɪ'pendəntli] *adv.* 独立地；自立地

intention [ɪn'tenʃən] *n.* 意图；目的

chunk [tʃʌŋk] *n.* 组块，大块

absorption [əb'sɔ:pʃən] *n.* 吸收；全神贯注

backtrack ['bæktræk] *v.* 回溯，返回

proximal ['prɒksɪməl] *adj.* 最接近的，邻近的

facilitate [fə'sɪlɪteɪt] *v.* 促进；帮助；使容易

simplify ['sɪmplɪfaɪ] *v.* 简化；使简易

manageable ['mænɪdʒəbl] *adj.* 易管理的；易控制的

achievable [ə'tʃi:vəbl] *adj.* 可完成的；可取得成就的

frustration [frʌ'streɪʃən] *n.* 挫折

expectation [ˌekspek'teɪʃən] *n.* 期望值，期望

territory ['terətri] *n.* 领土，领域

minimize ['mɪnɪmaɪz] *v.* 使最小化，使减到最小

decrease [dɪ'kri:s] *v.* 减少，减小

anchor ['æŋkə] *v.* 抛锚；固定

ultimate ['ʌltɪmət] *adj.* 最终的；根本的

multiple ['mʌltɪpl] *adj.* 多重的；多个的

perspective [pə'spektɪv] *n.* 观点；远景

subsequent ['sʌbsɪkwənt] *adj.* 后来的，随后的

adventure [əd'ventʃə] *n.* 冒险；冒险精神

immerse [ɪ'mɜ:s] *v.* 沉浸；使陷入

delve [delv] *v.* 钻研；探究

overlooker [əuvə'lukə] *n.* 看客；检查员

intrinsically [ɪn'trɪnzɪkəli] *adv.* 本质地；内在地

initiate [ɪ'nɪʃieɪt] *v.* 开始，发起

inevitable [ɪn'evɪtəbl] *adj.* 必然的，不可避免的

thorny ['θɔ:ni] *adj.* 棘手的；令人苦恼的

domain [də'meɪn] *n.* 领域；域名

refashion [ri:'fæʃən] *v.* 重制；重新设计

tenet ['tenɪt] *n.* 原则；信条；教义

case-based [keɪs-'beɪst] *adj.* 基于案例的，基于实例的

transmission [træns'mɪʃən] *n.* 传播，传输，传授

interconnected [ˌɪntəkə'nektɪd] *adj.* 关联的；有联系的

linear ['lɪnɪə] *adj.* 线型的；直线的

mechanistic [ˌmekə'nɪstɪk] *adj.* 机械论的；机械的

subtlety ['sʌtlti] *n.* 微妙；敏锐；精明

nuance ['njuːɑːns] *n.* 细微差别

accelerate [ək'seləreɪt] *v.* 加速；促进；增加

nurture ['nɜːtʃə] *v.* 培育，养育，培养

overwhelm [ˌəʊvə'welm] *v.* 受打击；压倒；压垮

underlying [ˌʌndə'laɪɪŋ] *adj.* 潜在的；根本的

microcosm ['maɪkrəʊkɒzəm] *n.* 微观世界；小宇宙；缩图

proportion [prə'pɔːʃən] *n.* 比例，规模

full-blown [ˌfʊl-'bləʊn] *adj.* 成熟的；充分发展的

Phrases

Scaffolding Instruction 支架式教学

piece by piece 逐渐地；一点一点地

in essence 本质上；其实

Anchored Instruction 抛锚式教学

be immersed in 全身心投入，沉浸于

center around 以……为中心

Cognitive Flexibility Theory 认知灵活性理论，认知弹性理论

Random Access Instruction 随机进入教学，随机通达教学

video clip 视频剪辑

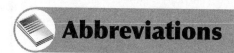
Abbreviations

Zone of Proximal Development (ZPD) 最近发展区

Cognition & Technology Group at Vanderbilt (CTGV) 范德堡认知和技术项目组

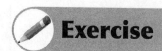
Exercise

Answer the following questions according to Text B.

(1) Whose theory is Scaffolding Instruction based on?

(2) Could you define Scaffolding Instruction?

(3) What are the three essential features of Scaffolding Instruction?

(4) Could you elaborate Anchored Instruction?

(5) How do you understand "anchor" in terms of Anchored Instruction?

(6) Could you elaborate "Cognitive Flexibility Theory"?

(7) What is Random Access Instruction according to your understanding?

(8) How should cognitive flexibility be developed?

Supplementary Reading

Text	Notes
Instruction Design of Behaviorism, Cognitivism and Constructivism As one moves along the behaviorist-cognitivist-constructivist continuum[1], the focus of instruction shifts from teaching to learning, from the passive transfer of facts and routines[2] to the active application of ideas to problems. Both cognitivists and constructivists view the learner as being actively involved in the learning process, yet the constructivists look at the learner as more than just an active processor[3] of information; the learner elaborates[4] upon and interprets[5] the given information. It is apparent that students exposed to these three instructional approaches would gain different competencies[6]. This leads instructors to ask two significant questions: Is there a single "best" approach and is one approach more efficient than the others? Given that learning is a complex, drawn-out[7] process that seems to be strongly influenced by one's prior knowledge, perhaps the best answer to these questions is "it depends". Because learning is influenced by many factors from many sources, the learning process itself is constantly changing, both in nature[8] and diversity[9], as it progresses. What might be most effective for novice[10] learners encountering a complex body of knowledge for the first time would not be effective, efficient or stimulating for a learner who is more familiar with the content. Typically, one does not teach facts the same way that concepts or problem-solving are taught. Likewise[11], one teaches differently depending on the	[1] continuum *n.* 连续统一体 [2] routine *n.* 惯例；常规；程序 [3] processor *n.* 加工者；处理器 [4] elaborate *v.* 详细阐述；周密发展 [5] interpret *v.* 解释，解读 [6] competency *n.* 能力；资格 [7] drawn-out *adj.* 延长的；持续很久的 [8] nature *n.* 性质；本性 [9] diversity *n.* 多样性；差异 [10] novice *n.* 初学者，新手 [11] likewise *adv.* 同样地；也

proficiency level of the learners involved. Both the instructional strategies employed and the content addressed (in both depth and breadth) would vary based on the level of the learners.

So how does an instructor facilitate a proper match between learners, content, and strategies? Consider, first of all, how learners' knowledge changes as they become more familiar with a given content. As people acquire more experience with a given content, they progress along a low-to-high knowledge continuum from being able to recognize and apply the standard rules, facts, and operations of a profession (knowing what), to thinking like a professional[12] to extrapolate[13] from these general rules to particular, problematic cases (knowing how), to developing and testing new forms of understanding and actions when familiar categories and ways of thinking fail (reflection-in-action). In a sense, the points along this continuum mirror[14] the points of the learning theory continuum described earlier.

Depending on where the learners "sit" on the continuum in terms of the development of their professional knowledge (knowing what vs. knowing how vs. reflection-in-action), the most appropriate instructional approach for advancing the learners' knowledge at that particular level would be the one advocated by the theory that corresponds to that point on the continuum. That is, a behavioral approach can effectively facilitate mastery of the content of a profession (knowing what); cognitive strategies are useful in teaching problem-solving tactics[15] where defined facts and rules are applied in unfamiliar situations (knowing how); and constructivist strategies are especially suited to dealing with complex problems through reflection-in-action.

A second consideration depends upon the requirements of the task to be learned. Based on the level of cognitive processing required, strategies from different theoretical perspectives may be needed. For example, tasks requiring a low degree of processing (e.g., basic paired associations[16], discriminations[17], rote memorization) seem to be facilitated by strategies most frequently associated with a behavioral outlook (e.g., stimulus-response, contiguity[18] of reinforcement). asks requiring an increased level of processing (e.g., classifications[19],

[12] **professional** *n.* 专业人员

[13] **extrapolate** *v.* 外推；推断

[14] **mirror** *v.* 反射；反映

[15] **tactic** *n.* 策略；战术

[16] **paired association** 配对联想

[17] **discrimination** *n.* 区别，辨别

[18] **contiguity** *n.* 邻近，接触

[19] **classification** *n.* 分类，类别

rule or procedural executions[20]) are primarily associated with strategies having a stronger cognitive emphasis (e.g., schematic[21] organization, analogical[22] reasoning, algorithmic[23] problem solving). Tasks demanding high levels of processing (e.g., heuristic[24] problem solving, personal selection and monitoring of cognitive strategies) are frequently best learned with strategies advanced by the constructivist perspective (e.g., situated learning[25], cognitive apprenticeships[26], social negotiation[27]).

We believe what the critical question instructional designers must ask is not "Which is the best theory?" but "Which theory is the most effective in fostering mastery of specific tasks by specific learners?". Prior to[28] strategy selection, consideration must be made of both the learners and the task. This means that when integrating any strategies into the instructional design process, the nature of the learning task (i.e., the level of cognitive processing required) and the proficiency level of the learners involved must both be considered before selecting one approach over another. Depending on the demands of the task and where the learners are in terms of the content to be delivered, different strategies based on different theories appear to be necessary. Powerful frameworks[29] for instruction have been developed by designers inspired by each of these perspectives. In fact, successful instructional practices have features[30] that are supported by virtually all three perspectives (e.g., active participation and interaction, practice and feedback).

For this reason, we have consciously chosen not to advocate one theory over the others, but to stress instead the usefulness of being well-versed[31] in each. This is not to suggest that one should work without a theory, but rather that one must be able to intelligently choose the appropriate methods for achieving optimal[32] instructional outcomes, on the basis of information gathered about the learners' present level of competence and the type of learning task.

Reasoned[33] and validated[34] theoretical eclecticism[35] has been a key strength of our field because no single theoretical base provides complete prescriptive principles for the entire

---

[20] execution *n.* 执行，实行

[21] schematic *adj.* 图式的，图解的

[22] analogical *adj.* 类推的，相似的

[23] algorithmic *adj.* 算法的；规则系统的

[24] heuristic *adj.* 启发式的；探索的

[25] situated learning 情境学习，情境性学习

[26] cognitive apprenticeship 认知学徒，认知学徒策略

[27] social negotiation 社会协商

[28] prior to 在……之前；居先

[29] framework *n.* 框架，构架

[30] feature *n.* 特色，特征

[31] well-versed *adj.* 精通的；熟知的

[32] optimal *adj.* 最佳的；最理想的

[33] reasoned *adj.* 理由充分的；合乎逻辑的

[34] validated *adj.* 经过验证的

[35] eclecticism *n.* 兼收并蓄，折中主义

design process. Some of the most crucial design tasks involve being able to decide which strategy to use, for what content, for which students, and at what point during the instruction. Knowledge of this sort is an example of conditional knowledge, where "thinking like" a designer becomes a necessary competency. It should be noted, however, that to be eclectic[36], one must know a lot, not a little, about the theories being combined. A thorough understanding of the learning theories presented above seems to be essential for professional instructors who must constantly make decisions for which no design model provides precise rules. Being knowledgeable about each of these theories provides instructors with the flexibility needed to be spontaneous[37] and creative when a first attempt doesn't work or when they find themselves limited by time, budget, or personnel constraints[38].

The practitioner[39] cannot afford to ignore any theories that might provide practical implications. Given the myriad[40] of potential design situations, the designer's "best" approach may not ever be identical[41] to any previous approach, but will truly "depend upon the context". This type of instructional "cherry-picking" has been termed "systematic eclecticism" and has had a great deal of support in the instructional design literature.

In closing, we need the behaviorist's triad[42] of practice-reinforcement-feedback to enlarge learning and memory. We need purpose, decision, values, understanding—the cognitive categories—lest[43] learning be mere behavioral activities rather than action.

[36] eclectic *adj.* 兼收并蓄的，折中的

[37] spontaneous *adj.* 自发的，自然的

[38] constraint *n.* 约束，束缚

[39] practitioner *n.* 从业者

[40] myriad *n.* 无数，极大数量

[41] identical *adj.* 同一的，完全相同的

[42] triad *n.* 三人组合；三种事物的组合

[43] lest *conj.* 以免；唯恐，担心

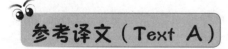

建构主义学习理论

建构主义首先是一种认为知识是由学习者心理活动构建的学习理论。该理论认为学习者是积极寻求意义的生物。建构主义的建立是基于这样一个前提：通过反思我们的经历，我们有意识地构建自己对所生活的这个世界的理解。我们每个人都建立了自己的"规则"和"心理模型"，并用它来诠释我们的经历。因此，学习就是调整我们的心理模型以适应新体验的过程。意义的建构最初可能与现实没有什么关系（如孩子们的朴素理论），但随

着时间的推移，它会变得更加复杂化、差异化和现实化。

两位学者对结构主义的发展贡献巨大。让·皮亚杰的理论置身于"认知建构主义"这一概念之下。他的理论主要分为两个部分：预测不同年龄的孩子理解知识的年龄和阶段因素，和描述学习者如何提高认知能力的发展理论。皮亚杰的认知发展理论认为，教师不应传授学习者立刻就能理解和应用的知识，相反，学习者必须构建自己的知识。他们通过经历来构建自己的知识。经验使他们能够构建出自己的图式——关于世界的心理模型。通过同化与顺应这两个互补的过程，这些图式会变化、扩大，并变得愈发复杂。

利维·维果斯基认为，知识首先是在社会环境中构建的，并与他人或团体协作。这被称为"社会建构主义"。社会建构主义强调学习的协作性，它要求培养学习者团队合作技能，并认为个人学习与小组学习的成功有着必然联系。他强调文化和社会背景对学习的影响，并支持发现式的学习模式。这种模式强调教师的积极作用，而学生的心智能力则通过各种发现途径自然地发展。

尽管如此，建构主义者认为学习遵循以下原则：

- 知识是构建的，而不是传授的；
- 先验知识影响学习过程；
- 最初的理解是局部的，不全面的；
- 建立有用的知识结构需要努力和有目的的活动。

一般来说，建构主义教学策略是基于这样一种理念：当学生通过探索和主动学习来获得知识时，学习效果最好。用实践材料代替教科书，鼓励学生去思考和解释他们的推理，而不是死记硬背。教育应以主题和概念以及它们之间的联系为中心，而不是孤立的信息。

根据建构主义理论，教师应注重在事实之间建立联系，培养学生全新的理解力。教师应根据学生的反应调整教学策略，鼓励学生分析、解释和预测信息。教师也应注重开放式问题，并促进学生之间的广泛对话。在评估方面，建构主义主张取消评分和标准化测试。相反，评估应成为学习过程的一部分，这样学生在评判自己的进步时就能发挥更大的作用。

作为教育者，我们必须牢记一些指导原则。这些原则都基于这样一个理念：学习是学习者自己建构意义的过程。

第一，学习是一个积极的过程，在这个过程中，学习者使用感觉输入并构造意义。这个观点更传统的表述涉及主动学习者这个术语，强调学习者需要动手做事情。学习不是被动地接受固有的知识，而是涉及学习者与世界的互动。

第二，人们在学习的过程中学会了学习。学习包括建构意义和建构意义系统。例如，当我们学习一系列历史事件的时间顺序时，我们同时掌握了年表的意义。我们所建构的每一个意义都能让我们更好地赋予其他类似模式的感觉以意义。

第三，建构意义的关键活动是精神上的，即发生在大脑中。肢体活动、动手体验可能是学习所必要的，尤其是对儿童而言，但这并不充分。我们需要提供一些让脑和手都参与进来的活动，也就是所说的反思性活动。

第四，学习需要语言。我们使用的语言影响学习。在实证层面上，研究人员注意到，人们在学习的过程中会自言自语。在更一般的层面上，维果斯基提出了一组非常有说服力的观点，认为语言和学习是不可分割地交织在一起的。

第五，学习是一种社会活动。学习与我们和其他人的关系紧密相连，比如我们的老师、同辈、家人以及点头之交的人，甚至包括展览会上在我们前后左右的人。如果我们认识到这一原则，而不是试图回避它，那么我们进行教育时就可能会更成功。许多传统教育将学习者从社会交往中分离出来，并把教育看作是学习者和学习材料之间的一对一关系。与此相反，建构主义教育观认识到学习的社会层面，并把对话、与他人互动及知识的应用作为学习不可分割的一部分。

第六，学习是有情境的。我们不是在与生活隔绝的抽象缥缈的思维中学习孤立的事实和理论，我们的学习与我们的其他知识、信念、偏见和恐惧都息息相关。经过深思熟虑后，很明显，我们可以推断出：学习是主动的、社会的。我们不能把学习与生活隔离开来。

第七，我们需要学习知识。如果没有从以前的知识结构作基础，吸收新知识是不可能的。我们懂得越多，就能学到更多。因此，任何教学都必须与学习者的状态相联系，并基于学习者先前的知识为他们学习这个科目提供一条路径。

第八，学习需要时间。学习不是瞬时的。为了更有意义地学习，我们需要重新审视想法，思考它们，尝试它们，把玩它们，并使用它们。如果你反思自己学过的东西，你很快就会意识到它是反复接触和思考的产物。甚至，深刻的见解往往源于长时间的准备。

在建构主义课堂中，重心往往从老师转向学生。教室不再是教师（"专家"）向被动接受的学生传递知识的地方，学生不再是等待被填满的容器。在建构主义教学模式中，学生要积极地参与学习过程。教师和学生都认为知识是动态的、不断变化的世界观，是成功地大展手脚并探索这一观点的能力，而不是需要记忆的惰性的仿真论述。教育工作者通常认为：

- 学生当前所想，无论正确与否，都是重要的；
- 尽管有类似的学习经历，但每个人的学习都是基于他们个人的领悟和意义建构；
- 领悟和意义建构是一个主动的、持续的过程；
- 学习可能涉及一些概念上的改变；
- 当学生建构新的意义时，他们可能并不认同它，也可能会暂时接受或拒绝它；
- 学习是一种积极的，而不是被动的过程，学生要承担学习的责任。

建构主义课堂的主要活动是解决问题。学生使用探究法提出问题、调查问题，并使用各种资源来寻找解决方案和答案。当学生们探究话题时，他们会得出结论。而且，随着探究的继续，他们会重新审视这些结论，对问题的探究会引出更多的问题。

建构主义和社会建构主义课堂之间有很多相同的做法，但社会建构主义课堂更强调社会互动和文化背景在学习中的作用。对于维果斯基来说，文化给孩子提供了发展所需的认知工具。在学习者的环境中，成年人是文化传播的载体，包括语言、文化历史、社会背景，以及最新的电子方式的信息获取。在社会建构主义课堂中，合作学习是一种由教师协调组织、同伴互动的过程，可以通过提出具体的概念、问题或场景来引发讨论，并以导向明确的问题、概念的介绍和澄清，以及对先前学习材料的引申来指导讨论。

Unit

Text A

Intrinsic and Extrinsic Motivation

1. Types of Motivation

To be motivated means to be moved to do something. A person who feels no impetus or inspiration to act is thus characterized as unmotivated, whereas someone who is energized or activated toward an end is considered motivated. People have not only different amounts, but also different kinds of motivation. That is, they vary not only in level of motivation (i.e., how much motivation), but also in the orientation of that motivation (i.e., what type of motivation).

Motivation concerns the underlying attitudes and goals that give rise to action—that is, it concerns the reason of actions. As an example, a student can be highly motivated to do homework out of curiosity and interest or, alternatively, because he or she wants to gain the approval of a teacher or parent. A student could be motivated to learn a new set of skills because he or she understands his or her potential utility or value or because learning the skills will yield a good grade and the privileges a good grade affords. In these examples the amount of motivation does not necessarily vary, but the nature of the motivation being evidenced certainly does.

The most basic distinction is between intrinsic motivation, which refers to doing something because it is inherently interesting or enjoyable, and extrinsic motivation, which refers to doing something because it leads to a separable outcome. Research has shown that the quality of experience and performance can be very different when one is behaving for intrinsic versus extrinsic reasons.

Intrinsic motivation has emerged as an important phenomenon for educators—a natural wellspring of learning and achievement that can be systematically catalyzed or undermined by parent and teacher practice. Because intrinsic motivation results in high-quality learning and creativity, it is especially important to detail the factors and forces that engender versus undermine it. However, what's equally important is the very different types of motivation that fall into the category of extrinsic motivation. In the classic literature, extrinsic motivation has typically been characterized as pale and impoverished. However, there are varied types of extrinsic motivation, some of which do, indeed, represent impoverished forms of motivation and some represent active, agentic states.

2. Intrinsic Motivation

Intrinsic motivation is defined as the doing of an activity for its inherent satisfactions rather than for some separable consequence. When intrinsically motivated, a person is moved to act for the fun or challenge entailed rather than because of external prods, pressures, or rewards.

In humans, intrinsic motivation is not the only form of motivation, but a pervasive and important one. From birth onward, humans, in their healthiest states, are active, inquisitive, curious, and playful creatures, displaying a ubiquitous readiness to learn and explore, and they do not require extraneous incentives to do so. This natural motivational tendency is a critical element in cognitive, social, and physical development because it is through acting on one's inherent interests that one grows in knowledge and skills. The inclinations to take interest in novelty, to actively assimilate, and to creatively apply our skills are not limited to childhood, but is a significant feature of human nature that affects performance, persistence, and well-being across life time.

Although, in one sense intrinsic motivation exists within individuals; in another sense intrinsic motivation exists in the relation between individuals and activities. People are intrinsically motivated for some activities and not for others, and not everyone is intrinsically motivated for any particular task. Because intrinsic motivation exists in the relation between a person and a task, some authors have defined intrinsic motivation in terms of the task being interesting while others have defined it in terms of the satisfactions a person gains from intrinsically motivated task engagement.

Feelings of competence will not enhance intrinsic motivation unless they are accompanied by a sense of autonomy. That is, people must not only experience perceived competence, but also experience their behavior to be self-determined, if intrinsic motivation is to be maintained or enhanced. Stated differently, for a high level of intrinsic motivation people must experience satisfaction of the needs both for competence and autonomy.

Classroom and home environments can facilitate or forestall intrinsic motivation by supporting versus thwarting the needs for autonomy and competence. However, it is critical to remember that intrinsic motivation will occur only for activities that hold inner interest for an individual—those that have the appeal of novelty, challenge, or aesthetic value for that individual. To understand the motivation for activities that are not experienced as inherently interesting, we need to look more deeply into the nature and dynamics of extrinsic motivation.

3. Extrinsic Motivation

Although intrinsic motivation is clearly an important type of motivation, most of the activities people do are not, strictly speaking, intrinsically motivated. This is especially the case after early childhood, as the freedom to be intrinsically motivated becomes increasingly reduced by social demands and roles that require individuals to assume responsibility for non-intrinsically interesting tasks. In schools, for example, it appears that intrinsic motivation becomes weaker with each advancing grade.

Extrinsic motivation is a concept that pertains whenever an activity is done in order to attain some separable outcome. Extrinsic motivation thus contrasts with intrinsic motivation, which refers to doing an activity simply for the enjoyment of the activity itself, rather than its instrumental value. However, unlike some perspectives that view extrinsically motivated behavior as invariantly non-autonomous, others propose that extrinsic motivation can vary greatly in the degree to which it is autonomous. For example, a student who does his homework only because he fears parental sanctions for not doing it is extrinsically motivated, because he is doing the work in order to attain the separable outcome of avoiding sanctions. Similarly, a student who does the work because he or she personally believes it is valuable for his or her chosen career is also extrinsically motivated because he or she too is doing it for its instrumental value rather than because he or she finds it interesting. Both examples involve instrumentalities, yet the latter case entails personal endorsement and a feeling of choice, whereas the former involves mere compliance with an external control. Both represent intentional behavior, but the two types of extrinsic motivation vary in their relative autonomy.

Given that many of the educational activities prescribed in schools are not designed to be intrinsically interesting, a central question concerns how to motivate students to value and self-regulate such activities, and to carry them out on their own without external pressure. This problem pertains to fostering the internalization and integration of values and behavioral regulations. Internalization is the process of taking in a value or regulation, and integration is the process by which individuals more fully transform the regulation into their own so that it will emanate from their sense of self. Thought of as a continuum, the concept of internalization describes how one's motivation for behavior can range from unwillingness, to passive compliance, to active personal commitment. With increasing internalization (and its associated sense of personal commitment), come greater persistence, more positive self-perceptions, and better quality of engagement. Integration is to integrate the different forms of extrinsic motivation and the contextual factors that promote the regulation of their behaviors.

Because extrinsically motivated behaviors are not inherently interesting, they thus must initially be externally prompted. The primary reason people are likely to be willing to do the behaviors is that they are valued by significant others to whom they feel connected, whether that be a family, a peer group, or a society. This suggests that the groundwork for facilitating internalization is providing a sense of belongingness and connectedness to the persons, group, or culture. In classrooms this means that students' feelings respected and cared for by the teacher are essential for their willingness to accept the proffered classroom values. Research has found that relatedness to teachers (and parents) was associated with greater internalization of school-related behavioral regulation.

A second issue concerns perceived competence. Adopting an extrinsic goal on one's own requires that one feel efficacious with respect to it. Students will be more likely to adopt and internalize a goal if they understand it and have the relevant skills to succeed at it. Thus, we theorize that supports for competence (e.g., offering optimal challenges and effectance-relevant feedback) facilitate internalization.

In summary, intrinsically motivated behaviors, which are performed out of interest and satisfy the innate psychological needs for competence and autonomy, are the prototype of self-determined behavior. Extrinsically motivated behaviors—those that are executed because they are instrumental to some separable consequence—can vary in the extent to which they represent self-determination. Internalization and integration are the processes through which extrinsically motivated behaviors become more self-determined.

New Words

intrinsic [ɪn'trɪnsɪk] *adj.* 内在的，固有的，本质的

extrinsic [eks'trɪnsɪk] *adj.* 外在的，外来的，非固有的

motivation [ˌməʊtɪ'veɪʃən] *n.* 动机；激励；动力

motivate ['məʊtɪveɪt] *v.* 刺激；使有动机

impetus ['ɪmpɪtəs] *n.* 动力；促进；冲力

inspiration [ˌɪnspə'reɪʃən] *n.* 鼓舞；灵感

characterized ['kærɪktəraɪzd] *adj.* 以……为特点的，以……为特征

unmotivated [ˌʌn'məʊtɪveɪtɪd] *adj.* 无动机的

energize ['enədʒaɪz] *v.* 激励；使活跃

activate ['æktɪveɪt] *v.* 刺激；使活动；使活泼

orientation [ˌɔːrɪən'teɪʃən] *n.* 方向；定向

alternatively [ɔː'lɜːnətɪvli] *adv.* 或者；二者择一地

approval [ə'pruːvəl] *n.* 认可，赞成

utility [juː'tɪləti] *n.* 实用；效用

privilege ['prɪvəlɪdʒ] *n.* 好处；特权

distinction [dɪ'stɪŋkʃən] *n.* 区别，差别；特性

wellspring ['welsprɪŋ] *n.* 源泉；水源

catalyze ['kætəlaɪz] *v.* 催化；刺激，促进

undermine [ˌʌndə'maɪn] *v.* 破坏；挖掘地基

engender [ɪn'dʒendə] *v.* 产生，引起

literature ['lɪtrətʃə] *n.* 文献；文学

impoverished [ɪm'pɒvərɪʃt] *adj.* 用尽了的，无创造性的；穷困的

agentic ['eɪdʒəntɪk] *adj.* 能动的；代理的

prod [prɒd] *n.* 刺激；刺针

pervasive [pə'veɪsɪv] *adj.* 普遍的；流行的

inquisitive [ɪn'kwɪzətɪv] *adj.* 好奇的，好问的

ubiquitous [juː'bɪkwɪtəs] *adj.* 普遍存在的，无所不在的

extraneous [ɪk'streɪnɪəs] *adj.* 外来的；来自体外的

tendency ['tendənsi] *n.* 倾向，趋势；癖好

inclination [ˌɪnklɪ'neɪʃən] *n.* 倾向，爱好

novelty ['nɒvəlti] *n.* 新奇；新奇的事物

well-being [wel-'bɪːɪŋ] *n.* 幸福；康乐

engagement [ɪn'geɪdʒmənt] *n.* 参与；婚约；交战；诺言

accompany [ə'kʌmpəni] *v.* 陪伴，伴随

autonomy [ɔː'tɒnəmi] *n.* 自治，自治权

perceived [pə'siːvd] *adj.* 感知到的；感观的

self-determined [ˌself-dɪ'tɜːmɪnd] *adj.* 自我决定的，自主的

instrumentality [ˌɪnstrʊmen'tælɪti] *n.* 工具；手段

endorsement [ɪn'dɔːsmənt] *n.* 认可，支持；背书

compliance [kəm'plaɪəns] *n.* 顺从，服从

internalization [ɪnˌtɜːnəlaɪ'zeɪʃən] *n.* 内化；内在化

integration [ˌɪntɪ'greɪʃən] *n.* 整合，融合，一体化

regulation [ˌregju'leɪʃən] *n.* 规则，法规，调节

emanate ['eməneɪt] *v.* 发出，流出，发源

commitment [kə'mɪtmənt] *n.* 承诺，保证；承担义务

associated [ə'səʊʃɪeɪtɪd] *adj.* 相关的，相关联的

self-perception [self-pə'sepʃən] *n.* 自我知觉，自我认知

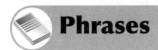
Phrases

give rise to 使发生，引起

not necessarily 未必，不一定

intrinsic motivation 内在动机

extrinsic motivation 外在动机

in terms of 依据，按照；在……方面

instrumental value 工具性价值

on one's own 独立地，独自地；主动地

pertain to 关于；从属于

emanate from 发源于；出自

range from... to 从……到……

sense of belongingness 归属感

care for 关心，照顾；喜欢

with respect to 关于，至于

Exercises

Ex. 1 **Give the English equivalents of the following Chinese expressions.**

(1) 文献；文学 _____

(2) 动机；激励；动力 _____

(3) 归属感 _____

(4) 内化；内在化 　　　　_____

(5) 自治，自治权 　　　　_____

(6) 最佳的；最理想的 　　_____

(7) 引起，使发生 　　　　_____

(8) 独立地，独自地 　　　_____

(9) 依据；在……方面 　　_____

(10) 未必，不一定 　　　　_____

Ex. 2 **Explain the following terminologies in English.**

(1) intrinsic motivation 　　_____

(2) extrinsic motivation 　　_____

(3) instrumental value 　　　_____

(4) internalization 　　　　_____

(5) integration 　　　　　　_____

(6) self-determination 　　　_____

Ex. 3 **Answer the following questions according to Text A.**

(1) Linda is motivated to do homework because she wants to gain the approval of her teachers and parents. What type of motivation is exerting influence here?

(2) Mary makes a lot of efforts to learn English because she really enjoys it. What type of motivation is exerting influence here?

(3) Is intrinsic motivation more important than extrinsic motivation? Why or why not?

(4) Are students in the same class equally motivated for any particular task?

(5) Will feelings of competence enhance intrinsic motivation?

(6) Are most of human activities intrinsically or extrinsically motivated?

(7) How can we motivate students to value school activities, and carry them out on their own without external pressure?

(8) Many activities are not inherently interesting. Why are people still willing to do them?

Ex. 4 **Fill in the blanks with the words given below.**

needs	recognition	utilize	backward	obstacles
self-actualization	psychological	unmet	potential	basic

Humanistic theory is one of the most well-known theory of motivation. According to this theory, humans are driven to achieve their maximum (1)_____ and will always do so unless (2)_____ are placed in their way. These obstacles include hunger, thirst, financial problems, safety issues, or anything else that takes our focus away from maximum (3)_____ growth.

The best way to describe this theory is to (4)_____ the famous pyramid developed by Abraham Maslow called the "Hierarchy of Needs". Maslow believed that humans have specific (5)_____ that must be met and that if lower level needs go (6)_____, we cannot possible strive for higher level needs. The "Hierarchy of Needs" shows that at the lower level, we must focus on (7)_____ issues such as food, sleep, and safety. Without food, without sleep, how could we possible focus on the higher level needs such as respect, education, and (8)_____?

Throughout our lives, we work toward achieving the top of the pyramid, (9)_____, or the realization of all of our potential. As we move up the pyramid, however, things get in the way that slow us down and often knock us (10)_____. Imagine working toward the respect and recognition of your colleagues and suddenly finding yourself out of work and homeless. Suddenly, you are forced backward and can no longer focus your attention on your work due to the need for finding food and shelter for you and your family.

Text B

Theories of Motivation

Motivation is the force that initiates, guides, and maintains goal-oriented behaviors. It is what causes us to take action, whether to grab a snack to reduce hunger or enroll in college to earn a degree. The forces that lie beneath motivation can be biological, social, emotional, or cognitive in nature. Motives are the "whys" of behavior—the needs or wants that drive behavior and explain what we do. In everyday usage, the term motivation is frequently used to describe why a person does something. We don't actually observe a motive; rather, we infer that it exists based on the behavior we observe.

Researchers have developed a number of theories to explain motivation. Each individual theory tends to be rather limited in scope. However, by looking at the key ideas behind each theory, we can gain a better understanding of motivation as a whole.

1. Instinct Theory of Motivation

According to the instinct theory, people are motivated to behave in certain ways because they are evolutionarily programmed to do so. An example of this in the animal world is seasonal migration. These animals do not learn to do this, it is, instead, an inborn pattern of behavior. Instincts motivate some species to migrate at certain times each year.

There are a list of human instincts that include such things as attachment, play, shame, anger, fear, shyness, modesty, and love. The main problem with this theory is that it does not really explain behavior. Instead, it just describes it. By the 1920s, the instinct theory were pushed aside in favor of other motivational theories, but contemporary evolutionary psychologists still study the influence of genetics and heredity on human behavior.

2. Incentive Theory of Motivation

The incentive theory suggests that people are motivated to do things because of external rewards. For example, you might be motivated to go to work each day for the monetary reward of being paid. Behavioral learning concepts such as association and reinforcement play an important role in this theory of motivation. This theory shares some similarities with the behaviorist concept of operant conditioning. In operant conditioning, behaviors are learned by forming associations with outcomes. Reinforcement strengthens a behavior while punishment weakens it.

While the incentive theory is similar, it proposes that people intentionally pursue certain courses of action in order to gain rewards. The greater the perceived rewards, the more strongly people are motivated to pursue those reinforcements.

3. Drive Theory of Motivation

According to the drive theory of motivation, people are motivated to take certain actions in order to reduce the internal tension that is caused by unmet needs. For example, we might be motivated to drink a glass of water in order to reduce the internal state of thirst.

This theory is useful in explaining behaviors that have a strong biological component, such as hunger or thirst. The problem with the drive theory of motivation is that these behaviors are not always motivated purely by physiological needs. For example, people often eat even when they are not really hungry.

4. Arousal Theory of Motivation

According to the arousal theory of motivation, each of us has a unique arousal level that is right for us. When our arousal levels drop below these personalized optimal levels, we seek some sort of stimulation to elevate them. For example, if our levels drop too low we might seek stimulation by going out to a nightclub with friends. If these levels become too high and we become overstimulated, we might be motivated to select a relaxing activity such as going for a walk or taking a nap.

One of the key assumptions of the arousal theory is that we are motivated to pursue actions that help us maintain an ideal balance. When we become overly aroused, we seek soothing activities that help calm and relax us. If we become bored, we head in search of more invigorating activities that will energize and arouse us. It's all about striking the right balance, but that balance is unique to each individual.

5. Humanistic Theory of Motivation

The humanistic theory of motivation is based on the idea that people also have strong cognitive reasons to perform various actions. This is famously illustrated in Abraham Maslow's Hierarchy of Needs, which presents different motivations at different levels.

People are firstly motivated to fulfill basic biological needs for food and shelter, as well as those of safety, love, and esteem. Once the lower level needs have been met, the primary motivator becomes the need for self-actualization, or the desire to fulfill one's individual potential.

6. Expectancy Theory of Motivation

The expectancy theory of motivation suggests that when we are thinking about the future, we formulate different expectations about what we think will happen. When we predict that there will most likely be a positive outcome, we believe that we are able to make that possible future a reality. This leads people to feel more motivated to pursue those likely outcomes.

The theory proposes that motivations consist of three key elements: valence, instrumentality, and expectancy. Valence refers to the value people place on the potential outcome. Things that seem unlikely to produce personal benefit have a low valence, while those that offer immediate personal rewards have a higher valence.

Instrumentality refers to whether people believe that they have a role to play in the predicted outcome. If the event seems random or outside of the individual's control, people will feel less motivated to pursue that course of action. If the individual plays a major role in the success of the endeavor, however, people will feel more instrumental in the process.

Expectancy is the belief that one has the capabilities to produce the outcome. If people feel like they lack the skills or knowledge to achieve the desired outcome, they will be less motivated to try. People who feel capable, on the other hand, will be more likely to try to reach that goal.

7. Three Major Components of Motivation

There are three major components of motivation: activation, persistence, and intensity.

- Activation involves the decision to initiate a behavior, such as enrolling in a psychology class.

- Persistence is the continued effort toward a goal even though obstacles may exist. An example of persistence would be taking more psychology courses in order to earn a degree although it requires a significant investment in time, energy, and resources.

- Intensity can be seen in the concentration and vigor that go into pursuing a goal. For example, one student might coast by without much effort, while another student will study regularly, participate in discussions, and take advantage of research opportunities outside of class. The first student lacks intensity, while the second pursues his educational goals with greater intensity.

While no single theory can adequately explain all human motivation, looking at the individual theories can offer a greater understanding of the forces that cause us to take action. In reality, there are likely many different forces that interact to motivate our behavior.

New Words

motive ['məʊtɪv] *n.* 动机，目的	elevate ['elɪveɪt] *v.* 提升；举起
scope [skəʊp] *n.* 范围；视野；眼界	overly ['əʊvəli] *adv.* 过度地；极度地
instinct ['ɪnstɪŋkt] *n.* 本能，直觉；天性	soothing [su:ðɪŋ] *adj.* 抚慰的；使人宽心的
evolutionarily [i:və'lu:ʃənərɪli] *adv.* 在进化上	invigorating [ɪn'vɪɡəreɪtɪŋ] *adj.* 激发精神的；令人振奋的
programme ['prəʊɡræm] *v.* 编程序；计划，安排	esteem [ɪ'sti:m] *n.* 尊重，尊敬
migration [maɪ'ɡreɪʃən] *n.* 迁移；移民	valence ['veɪləns] *n.* 效价；价值
attachment [ə'tætʃmənt] *n.* 附件，依附物	expectancy [ɪk'spektənsi] *n.* 期望，期待
modesty ['mɒdəsti] *n.* 谦逊；稳重	activation [ˌæktɪ'veɪʃən] *n.* 激活；活化作用
genetics [dʒə'netɪks] *n.* 遗传学	intensity [ɪn'tensəti] *n.* 强度；强烈
heredity [hə'redəti] *n.* 遗传，遗传性	concentration [ˌkɒnsn'treɪʃən] *n.* 专注；注意力
strengthen ['streŋθn] *v.* 加强；巩固	vigor ['vɪɡə] *n.* 活力，精力
tension ['tenʃən] *n.* 紧张，不安	

Phrases

enroll in 参加；选课	arousal theory 激活论，唤醒理论
instinct theory 本能论，本能理论	humanistic theory 人本论，人本主义理论
incentive theory 激励理论；诱因论	expectancy theory 期望理论，期望值理论
drive theory 驱力理论，驱动理论	coast by 得过且过；随波逐流

Exercise

Decide whether the following statements are true (T) or false (F) according to Taxt B. Give your reasons for the false ones.

(   ) (1) Motives are the result of behavior.

(   ) (2) According to the instinct theory, people are motivated to behave in certain ways because they find the inner pleasure in doing so.

(   ) (3) The incentive theory suggests that people are motivated to do things to avoid external punishments.

(   ) (4) According to the drive theory of motivation, people are motivated to take certain actions in order to reduce the internal tension that is caused by unmet needs.

(   ) (5) One of the key assumptions of the arousal theory is that we are motivated to pursue actions that help us maintain an ideal balance.

(   ) (6) Without fulfilling the basic biological needs such as food and shelter, humans will not look for the higher level needs such as self-actualization and respect.

(   ) (7) Things that seem unlikely to produce personal benefit have a high valence.

(   ) (8) Students choosing the same course have the same intensity of motivation for learning it.

(   ) (9) Motivation is the force that initiates, guides, and maintains goal-oriented activities.

(   ) (10) If people feel like they are not capable of achieving the desired outcome, they will be less likely to try.

Supplementary Reading

Text	Notes
Motivating Students in the Foreign Language Classroom 　　Teacher's skills in motivating learners are central to teaching effectiveness. The following briefly examines a variety of techniques and strategies that teachers can employ[1] in order to motivate their students. 　　Until recently, teachers were forced to rely on their "bag-of-tricks"[2] to manage their classroom and motivate their learners. These approaches have been influenced by two contradictory[3] views: a) learning should be fun and any motivation problems that may appear should be ascribed to[4] the teacher's attempt to convert[5] an enjoyable activity to drudgery[6]; and b) school activities are inherently boring and unrewarding[7], so that we must rely on extrinsic rewards and punishment with a view to forcing students to engage in these unpleasant tasks. 　　Rewards and punishments may be a mainstay[8] of the teaching-learning process, but they are not the only tools in teachers' arsenal[9]. The central question in designing a framework of motivational strategies is to decide how to organize	[1] employ *v.* 使用，采用 [2] bag of tricks　种种妙计，各种花招 [3] contradictory *adj.* 矛盾的，对立的 [4] ascribe to　归因于；认为……是 [5] convert *v.* 使转变；转换 [6] drudgery *n.* 苦差事，辛苦乏味的工作 [7] unrewarding *adj.* 无成就感的，无报酬的 [8] mainstay *n.* 支柱；主要的依靠 [9] arsenal *n.* （设备、方法等的）宝库；武器库

them into separate themes. The following taxonomy[10] is based on the process-oriented model to motivate students:

- Creating the basic motivational conditions, which involves setting the scene for the use of motivational strategies.

- Generating[11] student motivation, which roughly corresponds to[12] the pre-actional phase in the model.

- Maintaining and protecting motivation, which corresponds to the actional phase.

- Encouraging positive self-evaluation[13], which corresponds to the post-actional phase.

1. Creating the Basic Motivational Conditions

Motivational strategies cannot work in a vacuum[14], nor are they set in stone[15]. There are certain preconditions to be met before any attempts to generate motivation can be effective. Some of these conditions are the following:

- Appropriate teacher behavior and good teacher-student rapport[16].

- A pleasant and supportive classroom atmosphere.

- A cohesive[17] learner group characterized by appropriate group norms[18].

1.1　Appropriate Teacher Behavior and Good Teacher-student Rapport

Whatever is done by a teacher has a motivational, formative[19] influence on students. In other words, teacher behavior is a powerful "motivational tool". Teacher influences are manifold[20], ranging from the rapport with the students to teacher behaviors which "attract" students to engage in tasks. A key element is to establish a relationship of mutual trust and respect with the learners by means of talking with them on a personal level. This mutual trust could lead to enthusiasm[21]. At any rate, enthusiastic teachers impart[22] a sense of commitment[23] to, and interest in the subject matter, not only verbally but also non-verbally. These are cues[24] that students take from them about how to behave.

1.2　A Pleasant and Supportive Classroom Atmosphere

It stands to reason[25] that a tense classroom climate can undermine learning and demotivate[26] learners. On the other hand, learner motivation will reach its peak in a safe classroom

[10] taxonomy n. 分类学；分类法

[11] generate v. 使形成，产生

[12] correspond to
与……一致，相当于……

[13] self-evaluation n. 自我评价，自我评估

[14] vacuum n. 真空

[15] set in stone 一成不变

[16] rapport n. 密切关系，和谐一致

[17] cohesive adj. 凝聚的；有结合力的

[18] norm n. 规范，标准，准则

[19] formative adj. 形成的；格式化的

[20] manifold adj. 多方面的；各式各样的

[21] enthusiasm n. 热心，热情

[22] impart v. 传授；告知，透露

[23] commitment n. 投入；承诺；献身

[24] cue n. 提示，暗示；线索

[25] stand to reason 显而易见；合乎道理

[26] demotivate v. 使失去动力；使变得消极

climate in which students can express their opinions and feel that they do not run the risk of being ridiculed[27]. To be motivated to learn, students need both ample[28] opportunities to learn and steady encouragement and support of their learning efforts. Because such motivation is unlikely to develop in a chaotic[29] classroom, it is important that the teacher organize and manage the classroom as an effective learning environment. Furthermore, because anxious or alienated[30] students are unlikely to develop motivation to learn, it is important that learning occur within a relaxed and supportive atmosphere.

1.3   A Cohesive Learner Group Characterized by Appropriate Group Norms

Fragmented[31] groups, characterized by lack of cooperativeness, can easily become ineffective, thus putting paid to[32] the individual members' commitment to learn. There are several factors that promote group cohesiveness[33], such as the time spent together, shared group history, learning about each other, interaction, intergroup competition, common threat, and active presence of the leader. As for group norms, they should be discussed and adopted by members in order to be constructive and long-lasting. If a norm mandated[34] by a teacher fails to be accepted as proper by the majority of the class members, it will not become a group norm.

2. Generating Student Motivation

Ideally, all learners exhibit an inborn curiosity to explore the world, so they are likely to find the learning experience per se[35] intrinsically pleasant. In reality, however, this "curiosity" is weakened by such inexorable[36] factors as compulsory school attendance[37], curriculum content, and grades, most importantly, the premium[38] placed on them. Apparently, unless teachers increase their learners' goal-orientedness, make curriculum relevant for them, and create realistic learner beliefs, they will come up against a classroom environment fraught with[39] lack of cohesiveness and rebellion[40].

2.1   Increasing the Learners' Goal-orientedness

In an ordinary class, many, if not most, students do not understand why they are involved in an activity. It may be the

[27] ridicule *v.* 嘲笑；嘲弄；愚弄

[28] ample *adj.* 丰富的；足够的

[29] chaotic *adj.* 混乱的，无秩序的

[30] alienated *adj.* 疏远的；被疏远的

[31] fragmented *adj.* 支离破碎的；成碎片的

[32] put paid to   毁坏，破坏

[33] cohesiveness *n.* 凝聚力；内聚力

[34] mandate *v.* 强制执行

[35] per se   本身，自身

[36] inexorable *adj.* 无情的；无法改变的

[37] attendance *n.* 出席，到场；考勤

[38] premium *n.* 溢价；额外费用

[39] fraught with   充满

[40] rebellion *n.* 反抗；不服从

case that the goal set by outsiders[41] (i.e., the teacher or the curriculum[42]) is far from being accepted by the group members. Thus, it would seem beneficial to increase the group's goal-orientedness, that is, the extent to which the group tunes in[43] to the pursuit of its official goal. This could be achieved by allowing students to define their own personal criteria[44] for what should be a group goal.

2.2 Making the Curriculum Relevant for the Learners

Many students do their homework and engage in all sorts of learning activities, even when a subject is not very interesting. Obviously, these students share the belief of the curriculum makers that what they are being taught will come in handy[45]. In order to inspire learners to concern themselves with most learning activities, we should find out their goals and the topics they want to learn, and try to incorporate[46] them into the curriculum. If a teacher is to motivate pupils to learn, then relevance[47] has to be the red thread permeating[48] activities.

2.3 Creating Realistic Learner Beliefs

It is widely acknowledged that learner beliefs about how much progress to expect, and at what pace, can, and do, lead to disappointment. Therefore, it is important to help learners get rid of their preconceived[49] notions[50] that are likely to hinder[51] their attainment[52]. To this end, learners need to develop an understanding of the nature of second language learning, and should be cognizant[53] of the fact that the mastery of L2 can be achieved in different ways, using a diversity of strategies. The key factor is for learners to discover for themselves the optimal methods and techniques.

3. Maintaining and Protecting Motivation

Unless motivation is sustained[54] and protected when action has commenced[55], the natural tendency to get tired or bored of the task and succumb to[56] any attractive distractions[57] will result in demotivation. Therefore, there should be a motivational repertoire[58] including several motivation maintenance[59] strategies. Here we will introduce two of them: increasing the learners' self-confidence, and creating learner autonomy.

[41] outsider *n.* 局外人

[42] curriculum *n.* 课程；课程体系

[43] tune in 调谐；使……协调

[44] criteria *n.* 标准，条件（criterion 的复数形式）

[45] come in handy 迟早有用，派得上用处

[46] incorporate *v.* 包含；吸收；融入

[47] relevance *n.* 相关性，相关

[48] permeate *v.* 渗透；弥漫

[49] preconceived *adj.* 预想的；事先形成的

[50] notion *n.* 观念，概念，想法

[51] hinder *v.* 阻碍，妨碍

[52] attainment *n.* 学识；成就

[53] cognizant *adj.* 认识的，知道的

[54] sustain *v.* 维持，保持

[55] commence *v.* 开始，着手

[56] succumb to 屈服于，屈从于

[57] distraction *n.* 干扰；使人分心的事

[58] repertoire *n.* 全部技能

[59] maintenance *n.* 保持，维护

3.1　Increasing the Learners' Self-confidence

In an inherently face-threatening[60] context, as the language classroom is likely to be, it is important to find out how to maintain and increase the learners' self-confidence. There are five approaches that purport to help to this end:

- Teachers can foster[61] the belief that competence is a changeable aspect of development.

- Favorable self-conceptions[62] of L2 competence can be promoted by providing regular experiences of success.

- Everyone is more interested in a task if they feel that they make a contribution.

- A small personal word of encouragement is very helpful.

- Teachers can reduce classroom anxiety by making the learning context less stressful[63].

3.2　Creating Learner Autonomy

Many educationists and researchers agree that taking charge of one's own learning, that is, becoming an autonomous learner, is beneficial to learning. This assumption[64] is premised[65] on humanistic psychology, namely that "the only kind of learning which significantly affects behavior is self-discovered, self-appropriated[66] learning". Five types of practice may foster the development of autonomy:

- Resource-based approaches, which emphasize independent interaction with learning materials.

- Technology-based approaches, which emphasize independent interaction with educational technologies.

- Learner-based approaches, which emphasize the direct production of behavioral and psychological changes in the learner.

- Classroom-based approaches, which emphasize changes in the relationship between learners and teachers in the classroom.

- Curriculum-based approaches, which extend the idea of learner control over the planning and evaluation of learning to the curriculum as a whole.

The simplest way to ensure that people value what they are doing is to maximize[67] their free choice and autonomy.

[60] face-threatening *adj.* 损面子的

[61] foster *v.* 培养；养育

[62] self-conception *n.* 自我概念，自我观念

[63] stressful *adj.* 紧张的；有压力的

[64] assumption *n.* 假设，设想

[65] premise *v.* 以……为前提

[66] self-appropriated *adj.* 适合自己的

[67] maximize *v.* 使最大化

Self-motivation is a question of thinking effectively and meaningfully about learning experience and learning goals. It is a question of applying positive thought patterns and belief structures so as to[68] optimize[69] and sustain one's involvement in learning.

[68] so as to 以便；以致

[69] optimize *v.* 使最优化，使完善

4. Encouraging Positive Self-evaluation

Research has shown that the way learners feel about their accomplishments[70] and the amount of satisfaction they experience after task completion will determine how teachers approach and tackle[71] subsequent learning tasks. By employing appropriate strategies, the teachers can help learners to evaluate themselves in a positive light, encouraging them to take credit for[72] their advances. Three areas of such strategies are presented here:

[70] accomplishment *n.* 成就；完成；技能

[71] tackle *v.* 处理

[72] take credit for 因……而获得荣誉

- Promoting attributions[73] to effort rather than to ability.
- Providing motivational feedback.
- Increasing learner satisfaction.

[73] attribution *n.* 归因

We briefly discuss the third one. The feeling of satisfaction is a significant factor in reinforcing achievement behavior, which renders[74] satisfaction, a major component of motivation. Motivational strategies aimed at increasing learner satisfaction usually focus on allowing students to display their work, encouraging them to be proud of themselves and celebrate success, as well as using rewards.

[74] render *v.* 给予，提供

In general, motivation is often the "neglected heart" of our understanding of how to design instruction. Many teachers believe that by sticking to the language materials and trying to discipline[75] their students, they will manage to create a classroom environment that will be conducive[76] to learning. Nevertheless, these teachers seem to lose sight of[77] the fact that, unless they accept their students' personalities and work on those minute details that constitute their social and psychological make-up[78], they will fail to motivate them. What is more, they will not be able to form a cohesive and coherent group, unless they succeed in turning most "curriculum goals" (goals set by outsiders) into "group goals" (goals accepted by the group members, that is, students).

[75] discipline *v.* 训练，管教

[76] conducive *adj.* 有益的；有助于……的

[77] lose sight of 忘记；忽略

[78] make-up *n.* 性格；构成

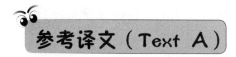

内在动机和外在动机

1. 动机的类型

有动机意味着有动力去做某事。没有动力或未受鼓舞的人被认为是缺乏动机的，而那些受到激励为某一目标奋斗的人被认为是有动机的。人的动机不仅强度不同，而且有不同的种类。也就是说，人不仅在动机水平上有所不同（如动机的大小），而且在动机的定向上有差异（如动机的类型）。

动机涉及引发行动的基本态度和目标——也就是说，它涉及行动的原因。举个例子，某学生有完成作业的强烈动机，这可能是出于好奇和兴趣，也可能是因为他／她想获得老师或家长的认可。某学生学习一套新技能的动机可能是因为他／她懂得其潜在的效用或价值，或因为学习这些技能会获得好的成绩，且好成绩能带来其他好处。在这些例子中，动机的强度不一定有差异，但动机的性质是不同的。

内在动机和外在动机具有最基本的区别。内在动机指做某件事是因为它本质上是有趣的或令人愉快的，而外在动机指做某件事是因为它会导致一个脱离事件本身的结果。研究表明，一个人的行为是出于内在还是外在原因，其体验和表现的性质会有很大的不同。

内在动机对教育者来说是一个重要现象——这是学习和成绩的自然源泉，家长和老师的做法可能慢慢激发或破坏内在动机。因为内在动机能够产生高质量的学习和创造力，所以详述激发或破坏它的因素和力量就显得尤其重要。然而，同等重要的还有另外一种不同类型的动机，即外在动机。在经典文献中，外在动机通常被认为是苍白乏力的。然而，外在动机多种多样，其中一些确实苍白乏力，有些则呈现积极能动的状态。

2. 内在动机

内在动机可以定义为从事某个活动是由于内在的满足感，而不是脱离事件本身的结果。当由内在动机驱动时，人的行为是因为活动所蕴含的乐趣或挑战，而不是因为外在的刺激、压力或回报。

对人而言，内在动机不是唯一的激励形式，而是一种普遍而重要的动机。人从出生开始，在健康状态下，就是活跃好奇、喜欢探究的生物，随时准备学习和探索，这些行为并不需要外界的刺激。这种自然的动机倾向是认知、社会和身体发展的一个关键因素。正是有内在兴趣的行为，人才能在知识和技能上成长。对新奇事物感兴趣、积极吸收并创造性地运用技能的倾向并不局限于童年时期，而是人类本性的一个重要特征，它影响一个人一生的表现、毅力和幸福。

不过，在某种意义上，内在动机存在于个体内部；在另一种意义上，内在动机存在于个体与活动的关系中。人们对某些活动有内在的动机，对某些活动却没有，而且并非每个人都对某个特定的任务有内在动机。由于内在动机存在于人与任务之间的关系中，有些学者按照任务的趣味性来定义内在动机，而另一些学者则根据参与活动所获得的满足感来定义内在动机。

除非伴有自主感，否则感到有能力并不会增强内在动机。也就是说，如果要保持或增强内在动机，人们不仅要体验到所感知的能力，还要体验到他们的行为是自我决定的。换言之，要获得高水平的内在动机，人们必须对能力和自主的需求都感到满足。

课堂和家庭环境是支持还是妨碍自主学习和能力培养会促进或抑制内在动机。然而，重要的是要记住，内在动机只会发生在那些能激发人内在兴趣的活动中——那些对人在新奇、挑战或审美价值方面有吸引力的活动。要理解那些不能体验到内在趣味的活动动机，我们需要更深入地研究外在动机的本质和动态。

3. 外在动机

尽管内在动机是一种重要的动机类型，但严格来说，人们所参与的大部分活动并不是受内在动机驱使的。在儿童阶段之后尤其如此，因为社会需求和社会角色要求个人承担起无内在趣味性的任务，所以受内在动机驱使的自由变得越来越少。例如，在学校里，升入更高的年级后，学生的内在动机似乎变得越来越弱。

外在动机这个概念是指为了获得一些脱离事件本身的结果而从事的活动。外在动机与内在动机相反，后者是指仅仅为了活动本身的愉悦而做这项活动，而不是因为它的工具性价值。有些观点认为外在动机的行为是不自主的，而另一些观点则认为外在动机在自主度上有很大差异。例如，一个学生做作业仅仅是因为他担心不做的话父母会惩罚他，这是出于外在动机，因为他做作业是为了获得不被惩罚这个脱离事件本身的结果。同样地，认为对他／她所选择的职业有意义而完成作业的学生，也是出于外在动机，因为他／她做作业也是出于工具性价值，而不是因为他／她觉得这样很有趣。这两个例子都涉及工具性动机，但后一种情况包含了个人的认可和选择，而前者只涉及服从外部控制。两者都是有目的的行为，但这两种外在动机在自主性上有所不同。

考虑到学校的许多教学活动从本质上说并无多少趣味，一个核心问题就是如何激励学生重视和自我调节这些活动，并在没有外部压力的情况下独立完成这些活动。这个问题涉及促进价值观和行为规范的内化和整合。内化是一个吸收价值或规则的过程，整合是一个将规则充分转化为自身的过程，这样规则就会源于自我意识。如将内化这个概念看成一个连续体，它描述了一个人的行为动机可介于从不愿意到被动服从，再到主动认同之间。内化的增强（以及随之产生的个人认同）会带来更强的毅力、更积极的自我认知，以及更高质量的投入。整合是将不同形式的外在动机和情境因素整合在一起以促进对行为的调节。

因为受外在动机驱使的行为本身并不是很有趣，所以它们首先必须被外部激励。人们愿意做某些事情的主要原因是，这些行为会受到与他们相关的一些重要的人的重视，如家人、同伴、社会。这表明，促进内化的基础是提供与他人、群体或文化的归属感和关联感。在课堂上，这意味着受到老师的尊重和关心对于学生是否愿意接受所提出的课堂价值观至关重要。研究发现，学生与教师（和家长）的关系和学校行为规范的内化有关。

第二个问题涉及对自己能力的认识。自主选择的一个外在目标是一个人认为自己有能力完成它。如果学生理解了这个目标，并且掌握了相关的技能，那么他们就更有可能选择并内化这个目标。因此，我们提出的理论是，对能力的支持（如提供最优的挑战和有效的反馈）有助于内化。

　　总之，受内在动机驱使的行为是出于兴趣而表现出来的，满足了对能力和自主的内在心理需求，是自我决定行为的原型。受外在动机驱使的行为——因为可以带来工具性的、脱离事物本身的结果而被执行的行为——在自决权的程度上可能有所不同。通过内化和整合这个过程，受外在动机驱使的行为会变得更加自主。

Unit

Text A

Effective Learning Strategies

When learners intentionally use a certain approach to learning and remembering something, they are using a learning strategy. As children grow older, they increasingly discover the benefits of learning strategies and use them more frequently. Children gradually acquire additional strategies as well. For example, consider the simple idea that when you do not learn something the first time you try, you need to study it again. This is a strategy that 8-year-olds use but 6-year-olds do not. With age and experience, children also become more aware of which strategies are effective in different situations.

Even so, many students of all ages, including college students, seem relatively uninformed about effective learning strategies. As we discovered, rehearsal is usually not the best way to learn and remember new information. Truly effective learning requires thinking actively about and elaborating on classroom material. The followings are seven basic learning strategies.

1. Identifying Important Information

Because the human memory system is not set up to remember everything presented in class or a textbook, students must be selective when studying classroom material. The things they choose to study—whether main ideas and critical pieces of information or, instead, isolated facts and trivial details—inevitably affect their learning and school achievement.

Students often have trouble identifying the most important information in a lesson or reading assignment. Many are apt to zero in on superficial characteristics, such as what a teacher writes on the chalkboard or what are written in italics or boldface by the author. As teachers, we can help students learn more effectively by letting them know what are the most important ideas to be gained from lectures and reading materials. We can, of course, simply tell them exactly what to study. However, we can also get the same message across through more subtle means. For example,

- Provide a list of objectives for a lesson.
- Write key concepts and relationships on the chalkboard.
- Ask questions that focus students' attention on important ideas.

Students, especially low-achieving ones, are more likely to learn the important points of a lesson when such prompts are provided for them. As students become better able to distinguish important from unimportant information on their own, we can gradually phase out our guidance.

2. Retrieving Relevant Prior Knowledge

Students can engage in meaningful learning only when they have previous knowledge to which they can relate new information and when they are aware of the potential relationship. Although we can certainly remind students of prior knowledge that is relevant to the topic they are studying, we must also encourage them to retrieve relevant knowledge on their own as they study. One approach is to model this strategy for students. For example, we might read aloud a portion of a textbook, stopping occasionally to tie an idea in the text to something previously studied in class or to something in their own personal experience. We can then encourage students to do likewise, giving suggestions and guiding their efforts as they proceed. Especially when working with students in the elementary grades, we might also want to provide specific questions that remind students to reflect on their existing knowledge and beliefs as they read and study:

- What do you already know about the topic?
- What do you hope to learn about the topic?
- Do you think what you learn by reading the books will change what you already know about the topic?

With time and practice, students should eventually get in the habit of retrieving relevant prior knowledge with little or no assistance from us.

3. Taking Notes

By the time students reach the upper elementary or middle school grades, note-taking skills begin to play a role in their classroom achievement. In general, students who take more notes learn and remember classroom subject matter better. However, the quality of the notes is equally important. Useful notes typically reflect the main ideas of a lesson or reading assignment. Good notes seem to be especially important for students who have little prior knowledge about the subject matter they are studying.

When students are first learning how to take notes in class, we should scaffold their efforts by giving them an idea about which things are most important to include. One approach is to provide a specific structure of notes for students to use. Another strategy to consider, especially if students are novice note takers, is to occasionally check their notebooks for accuracy and appropriate emphasis and then give constructive feedbacks.

4. Organizing Information

Students learn more effectively when they engage in activities that help them organize what they are studying. One useful strategy is outlining the material, which may be especially helpful for low-achieving students. Another approach is to make a concept map, a diagram that depicts the concepts of a unit and their interrelationships.

Students derive numerous benefits from constructing their own concept maps for classroom material. By focusing on how key concepts relate to one another, students organize material better. They are also more likely to notice how new concepts are related to the concepts they already know; thus, they are more likely to learn the material meaningfully. Furthermore, when students construct a concept map from verbal material (e.g., a lecture), they can encode the material visually as well as verbally. In addition, the very process of concept mapping may promote a more sophisticated perspective of what learning is. Specifically, students may begin to realize that learning is not just a process of absorbing information, but instead, involves actively making connections among ideas.

5. Elaborating on Information

As a strategy that children intentionally use to help them learn and make sense of new information, elaboration appears relatively late in development (usually around puberty) and gradually increases throughout the teenage years. There are a variety of things we can do to teach students—even those in the elementary grades—to elaborate on classroom topics. When we model retrieval of relevant prior knowledge, we can model elaboration as well. For example, we can identify our own examples of a new concept, consider the implications of a new principle, and so on. We can also give students questions such as the following to consider as they listen to a lecture or read a textbook:

- Explain why...
- How would you use... to...?
- What is a new example of...?
- What do you think would happen if...?
- What is the difference between... and...?

Another approach is to have students work in pairs or small groups to formulate and answer their own elaborative questions. Such group questioning is called elaborative interrogation or guided peer questioning.

6. Creating Summaries

Another effective learning strategy is summarizing the material being studied. Creating a good summary is a fairly complex process, however. At a minimum, it includes distinguishing between important and unimportant information, synthesizing details into more general ideas, and identifying important relationships among the ideas. It is not surprising, then, that even many high school students have difficulty developing good summaries.

Probably the best way to help students acquire this strategy is to ask them on a regular basis to summarize what they hear and read. For example, we might occasionally give assignments asking students to write a summary of a textbook chapter. Alternatively, we might ask them to work in cooperative groups to develop a brief oral presentation that condenses information they have learned about a topic. At first, we should restrict summarizing assignments to short, simple, and well-organized passages involving material with which students are familiar. We can assign more challenging material as students become more proficient summarizers.

7. Monitoring Comprehension

One especially powerful learning strategy is comprehension monitoring, a process of periodically checking oneself for recall and understanding. Successful learners continually monitor their comprehension both while they study something and at some point after they have studied it. Furthermore, when they realize they do not understand, they take steps to correct the situation, perhaps by rereading a section of a textbook or asking a question in class.

Many children and adolescents engage in little, if any, comprehension monitoring. When they do not monitor their learning and comprehension, they do not know what they know and what they do not know; consequently, they may think they have mastered something when they really have not. Although this illusion of knowing is especially common in young children, it is seen in learners at all levels, even college students. When paper-and-pencil exams become common at upper grade levels, an illusion of knowing can lead students to overestimate how well they will perform on these assessments.

Comprehension monitoring does not have to be a solitary activity, of course. If students work in small study groups, they can easily test one another on material they are studying and may detect gaps or misconceptions in one another's understandings. Yet to be truly effective learners, students must ultimately learn how to test themselves as well. One effective strategy is self-explanation, in which students frequently stop to explain to themselves what they have learned. Another, similar approach is self-questioning, in which students periodically stop to ask themselves questions. Their self-questions should, of course, include not only simple, fact-based questions but also the elaborative questions described earlier.

Some of the strategies just described, such as taking notes and making outlines, are behaviors we can actually see. Others, such as retrieving relevant prior knowledge and monitoring comprehension, are internal mental processes that we often cannot see. It is probably the latter set of strategies—internal mental processes—that ultimately affect students' learning. As we help students develop learning strategies, we must remember that behavioral strategies (e.g., taking notes) will be useful only to the extent that they promote more effective cognitive processing.

 **New Words**

intentionally [ɪn'tenʃənəli] *adv.* 有意地，故意地

increasingly [ɪn'kri:sɪŋli] *adv.* 越来越多地；渐增地

uninformed [ˌʌnɪn'fɔ:md] *adj.* 不了解情况的；无知的

rehearsal [rɪ'hɜ:səl] *n.* 练习；排演

isolated ['aɪsəleɪtɪd] *adj.* 孤立的；单独的

trivial ['trɪvɪəl] *adj.* 不重要的，琐碎的

inevitably [ɪn'evɪtəbli] *adv.* 不可避免地；必然地

superficial [ˌsu:pə'fɪʃəl] *adj.* 表面的；肤浅的

italics [ɪ'tælɪks] *n.* 斜体字，斜体

boldface ['bəʊldfeɪs] *n.* 黑体字；粗体字

low-achieving [ləʊ-ə'tʃi:vɪŋ] *adj.* 成绩差的，水平低的

distinguish [dɪ'stɪŋgwɪʃ] *v.* 区别，区分

novice ['nɒvɪs] *n.* 初学者，新手

accuracy ['ækjərəsi] *n.* 精确度，准确性

constructive [kən'strʌktɪv] *adj.* 建设性的；有助益的

feedback ['fi:dbæk] *n.* 反馈；回复

depict [dɪ'pɪkt] *v.* 描述；描画

interrelationship [ˌɪntərɪ'leɪʃənʃɪp] *n.* 相互关系

derive [dɪ'raɪv] *v.* 源于；得自；获得

encode [ɪn'kəʊd] *v.* 编码，译码

visually ['vɪʒʊəli] *adv.* 形象化地；视觉上

verbally ['vɜ:bəli] *adv.* 口头地，非书面地

perspective [pə'spektɪv] *n.* 观点；远景；透视图

puberty ['pju:bəti] *n.* 青春期；开花期

retrieval [rɪ'tri:vl] *n.* 检索；恢复

implication [ˌɪmplɪ'keɪʃən] *n.* 含义；暗示；影响

formulate ['fɔ:mjuleɪt] *v.* 制定；明确地表达

elaborative [ɪ'læbəˌrətɪv] *adj.* 阐释性的；仔细的

synthesize ['sɪnθəsaɪz] *v.* 合成；综合

proficient [prə'fɪʃənt] *adj.* 熟练的，精通的

monitor ['mɒnɪtə] *v.* 监控

periodically [ˌpɪərɪ'ɒdɪkəli] *adv.* 定期地；周期性地

adolescent [ˌædə'lesənt] *n.* 青少年

consequently ['kɒnsɪkwəntli] *adv.* 因此；结果；所以

illusion [ɪ'lu:ʒən] *n.* 幻觉，错觉；错误的观念或信仰

overestimate [ˌəʊvə'estɪmeɪt] *v.* 估计过高；评价过高

solitary ['sɒlətri] *adj.* 孤独的；孤立的

detect [dɪ'tekt] *v.* 察觉；发现；探测

misconception [ˌmɪskən'sepʃən] *n.* 误解；错觉；错误想法

ultimately ['ʌltɪmətli] *adv.* 最后；根本

Phrases

learning strategy 学习策略
elaborate on 详细说明，阐释
be apt to 倾向于，易于
zero in 集中火力，瞄准
get across 解释清楚，使被理解
distinguish from 区别，区分
phase out 逐步淘汰；逐渐停止
prior knowledge 先前知识，先验知识
concept map 概念图

make sense of 理解，搞清……的意思
elaborative interrogation 阐释性询问
peer guided questioning 朋辈互相提问
at a minimum 最低限度
at some point 在某一时刻
take steps 采取措施，采取行动
to the extent that 达到……的程度以致；在这个意义上

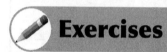

Exercises

Ex. 1 Give the English equivalents of the following Chinese expressions.

(1) 评价，考核 _____

(2) 合成；综合 _____

(3) 阐释性的；仔细的 _____

(4) 检索；恢复 _____

(5) 在这个意义上 _____

(6) 最低限度 _____

(7) 概念图 _____

(8) 先验知识 _____

(9) 详细说明，阐释 _____

(10) 学习策略 _____

Ex. 2 Decide whether the following statements are true (T) or false (F) according to Text A. Give your reasons for the false ones.

(   ) (1) With age and experience, children will become more aware of which strategies are effective in different situations.

(   ) (2) College students usually know the effective learning strategies.

(   ) (3) Rehearsal is usually the most effective way to learn new knowledge.

(   ) (4) It is best that students remember everything a teacher lectures in class.

(   ) (5) Prior knowledge helps meaningful learning.

(   ) (6) Note-taking skills become more important when students reach the upper elementary grades.

(   ) (7) Elaboration ability appears quite early in children's development.

(   ) (8) Comprehension monitoring is a solitary activity.

(   ) (9) Learners should monitor their comprehension while they study, but not after that.

(   ) (10) Behavioral learning strategies, such as taking notes are usually effective.

Ex. 3   **Answer the following questions according to Text A.**

(1) What is learning strategy?

(2) How do you distinguish important information from unimportant one in a lesson?

(3) How can we help students to retrieve prior knowledge when they learn?

(4) What are high quality notes?

(5) How do you define a concept map?

(6) What skills can we teach students to elaborate on information?

(7) How can students monitor their comprehension?

(8) Could you give some examples of internal mental process concerning learning strategies?

Ex. 4   **Fill in the blanks with the words given below.**

recall	kinesthetic	tackle	grouped	instructor
benefit	regarding	category	transfer	construct

Learning strategies can vary by subject matter, student learning styles, instruction styles, and more. Many strategies (1)_____ across subjects and styles, while others will work specifically for one area of study only. A teacher or (2)_____ may want to consider narrowing his or her focus to determine what, exactly, he or she needs to know to (3)_____ an instructional or learning issue. An English teacher, for example, may need to know about learning strategies (4)_____ vocabulary, while a science teacher may need to know about strategies for information retention and application.

Grouping is one of the most common learning strategies that transfers across subject matter. This process involves placing information into logical groups for easier (5)_____ of information later on. For example, a person learning a complex vocabulary list may group the words according to (6)_____. Words like "genus" and "species" might be (7)_____ subconsciously in the "zoo" category, while "simile" and "metaphor" may be grouped in the "poem" category.

Hands-on and (8)_____ learning strategies involve movement and practice by doing. These strategies are especially useful in the math and science fields. Students who are hands-on learners (9)_____ from activities rather than lectures. A student learning about sentence structure may not understand the concept written on the board, but when given paper cut-outs of various words, he or she may be able to (10)_____ the sentence by manipulating the pieces of paper.

Text B

Thinking About Thinking: Metacognition

1. Metacognition

Often we hear that one of the most important tasks of education is to teach students how to learn on their own throughout their lifetimes. However, how do we learn how to learn? How do we know what we've learned and how to direct our own future learning? These are all questions addressed by the concept of metacognition. Simply put, metacognition means "thinking about one's own thinking". There are two aspects of metacognition: reflection—thinking about what we know; and self-regulation—managing how we go about learning.

Research has shown that one of the key traits good problem-solvers possess is highly developed metacognitive skills. They know how to recognize flaws or gaps in their own thinking, articulate their thought processes, and revise their efforts. As adults, we actively engage in these skills in our everyday thinking. We decide what method to use to solve a problem or when to ask for help. We use metacognitive skills to help us decide which elements we understand and which we do not understand. In short, we direct our own learning. Students and novices often lack these skills or fail to recognize when to use them. As educators, it is important for us to help foster the development of metacognitive skills in students. These are skills that will help students learn how to learn.

Sometimes people use the phrase "going meta" when talking about metacognition, referring to the process of stepping back to see what you are doing, as if you were someone else observing it. "Going meta" means becoming an audience for your own performance—in this case, your own intellectual performance. When a person is learning to play golf, for example, seeing a video of his or her own swing can help his or her to understand what he or she is doing well and what he or she is doing poorly. It is very hard to improve a process that we are engaged in if we do not have a sense of what we are doing in the moment. Even a skilled professional ballet dancer relies on mirrors to help him understand what he looks like and what he is doing as he dances. He has to be able to see his performance as others might see it before he can begin to improve it.

2. Components of Metacognition

Metacognition is most commonly broken down into two distinct but interrelated areas. John Flavell, one of the first researchers in metacognition and memory, defined these two areas as metacognitive knowledge—awareness of one's thinking, and metacognitive regulation—

the ability to manage one's own thinking processes. These two components are used together to inform learning theory.

2.1 Metacognitive Knowledge—Reflecting on What We Know

Students have thoughts, notions, and intuitions about their own knowledge and thinking. Flavell describes three kinds of metacognitive knowledge:

- Awareness of knowledge—understanding what one knows, what one does not know, and what one wants to know. For example, "I know that plants need sunlight but I do not know why."

- Awareness of thinking—understanding cognitive tasks and the nature of what is required to complete them. For example, "I know that reading this newspaper article will be easier for me than reading my textbook."

- Awareness of thinking strategies—understanding approaches to directing learning. For example, "I am having difficulty reading this article. I should summarize what I just read before going on."

Children are not initially very accurate at describing what they know, but as they get older their skills improve, especially if they have been taught and have had practice in how to think about and discuss their own thinking. Children can be guided to develop an understanding of what they know and what they do not know. Teachers can also help students develop an appreciation for what learning tasks might demand, as well as an awareness of the particular knowledge and strategies they can bring to these tasks. In a writing class, for example, students use mind maps to organize their thinking before writing an essay. They also articulate their ideas and peer review each other's writing before revising their essays.

Students can be encouraged to develop a sense of their own knowledge by asking questions such as, "What do I know? What do I not know? What do I need to know?" Teachers can help students to reflect on what they know and what they want to know as they embark on the study of a new topic. Students can reflect again on what they know as they conclude a lesson or unit. During the course of their work, teachers can encourage a reflective stance toward learning that helps students assess and direct their own emerging understandings. By asking students to consider what they might do to learn something they want to know, and then providing a range of resources (materials, peers, and information) for them to pursue it, teachers can help students learn how to learn with greater independence. Students can play an increasingly active role in monitoring what they know and what they don't know, and how they can find out what they need to know to further their own learning.

Students can also be prompted to ask more general questions about a task or problem that help them become aware of their existing resources and needs. Reflective questions can help students become aware of what they can do and make connections to the tasks at hand. A student might reflect on her work and conclude, "I understand what I want to say in my essay, but I'm having trouble figuring out how to get into it," or "I have lots of ideas about ways to test my hypothesis, but I don't know how I'll know if I've proved or disproved it." Identifying the challenging aspects of complex cognitive tasks can help students narrow down what they need as they seek assistance. This process of being aware of one's own knowledge state is called self-monitoring.

Teachers can help their students learn how to ask self-monitoring questions as they are learning. These questions might differ depending on the developmental level of the learner. For very young children, the focus of the question might serve to self-test. For instance, while they are reading a story, young students might be encouraged to ask, "Do I know who this character is? What problem he is trying to solve, or the sequence of events in this story?" As students enter the middle grades, the nature of the questions increasingly shifts to "What inferences can I draw? What is the meaning of this symbol in the story, or what is the relevance of this information to a problem that I'm trying to solve?" High school teachers might encourage their students to evaluate the stand an author is taking "What is the author's perspective? Is the author's evidence sufficient to support the stand that he has taken?"

One common approach to developing metacognitive skills involves teaching study strategies that ask students to think about the way they learn best. Students must learn to become aware of their capabilities, strengths, and weaknesses as learners in order to develop as learners. The questions that explicitly help students think about, "How do I study best?" or "What kinds of tools help me learn?" All engage metacognitive knowledge.

2.2　Metacognitive Regulation—Directing Our Learning

When a student has information about his or her thinking (metacognitive knowledge), he or she is able to use this information to direct or regulate her learning. This kind of metacognition is also referred to as "executive control". Just as a business executive manages and oversees activities in a company, executive control can be thought as managing and overseeing one's own thinking. Metacognitive regulation involves the ability to think strategically and to problem-solve, plan, set goals, organize ideas, and evaluate what is known and what is not known. It also involves the ability to teach to others and make the thinking process visible.

Ann Brown and her colleagues describe three ways we direct our own learning:

● Planning approaches to tasks—identifying the problem, choosing strategies, organizing our thoughts, and predicting outcomes.

● Monitoring activities during learning—testing, revising, and evaluating the effectiveness of our strategies.

● Checking outcomes—evaluating the outcomes against specific criteria of efficiency and effectiveness.

Learning how to be mindful of one's learning process and how to think strategically about a task can make problem solving more efficient. A strategic essay writer knows how to plan his central thesis and supporting points, rather than simply writing thoughts in a stream of consciousness, just as a strategic mathematics student is able to step back and consider different approaches to a problem, rather than trying all the possible numbers that might give a correct answer. Such learners are accustomed to monitoring their work as they are working, "Am I making my points clear and understandable? Am I getting closer to a solution or farther away?"

They also look back on their work to evaluate their own success, "Have I convinced my reader? Does this solution make sense?" Learning how to monitor one's own thinking process can enable the learner to self-correct, rather than always relying on others to be the audience and sounding board for one's work.

Teachers can also help students become better at selecting strategies. They can help students ask and answer questions such as "How can I keep track of what I know?" or "How do I decide which paths to go down?" and "How long should I try this approach? When should I switch to another strategy?" or "What should I try next?" All of these questions help students explore new subject areas, and assist them in transferring what they know from one problem to the next.

Good metacognitive thinkers are also good intentional learners. That is, they are able to direct their learning in proper ways to build understanding. They know when to use strategies and how to use them. They are able to redirect the normal frustration that occurs when things are confusing or are not initially productive into further learning and research strategies. Teachers can help students become intentional learners by helping them manage uncertainty, redirect their efforts productively, and persevere when they get frustrated. Teachers can do this by modeling and discussing their thinking process aloud when they themselves approach uncertain tasks ("I am thinking I could try this approach or that approach. Let's see what happens if I try this one."), as well as what they do when they hit a snag or dead end. They can also monitor students as they work to catch them at points when they need encouragement or are becoming frustrated and need a new strategy. The ability to work strategically can be taught and must be learned if students are to succeed at being self-directed learners throughout their lives.

 **New Words**

metacognition [me'tækɔ:gnɪʃən] *n.* 元认知	hypothesis [haɪ'pɒθəsɪs] *n.* 假设
self-regulation [self-ˌregju'leɪʃən] *n.* 自我调节	disprove [ˌdɪs'pruːv] *v.* 反驳，证明……是虚假的
flaw [flɔ:] *n.* 瑕疵，缺点	inference ['ɪnfərəns] *n.* 推断；推论；推理
articulate [ɑ:'tɪkjuleɪt] *v.* 明确有力地表达；清晰地发音	stand [stænd] *n.* 立场；观点
distinct [dɪ'stɪŋkt] *adj.* 不同的，有区别的	explicitly [ɪk'splɪsɪtli] *adv.* 明确地；明白地
accurate ['ækjərət] *adj.* 精确的	oversee [ˌəʊvə'siː] *v.* 监督；俯瞰；无意中看到
stance [stæns] *n.* 立场；姿态	efficiency [ɪ'fɪʃənsi] *n.* 效率；效能；功效
independence [ˌɪndɪ'pendəns] *n.* 独立性，自立性；自主	persevere [ˌpɜ:sə'vɪə] *v.* 坚持；不屈不挠
further ['fɜ:ðə] *v.* 促进，助长；增进	

Phrases

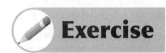

rely on 依靠，依赖

mind map 思维导图；思维图

embark on 着手，开始；从事

at hand 在手边；即将到来

figure out 想出，理解；解决

be mindful of 关注；注意，留心

stream of consciousness 意识流

be accustomed to 习惯于，适应于

sounding board 回响板；被用作试探意见之人

keep track of 记录；明了；追踪

switch to 切换到，转到，转变成

hit a snag 遇到意外困难，碰钉子

dead end 死胡同；死路

Exercise

Answer the following questions according to Text B.

(1) Could you briefly explain metacognition?

(2) What does "going meta" mean?

(3) What are the two areas of metacognition?

(4) What are three kinds of metacognitive knowledge described in the text?

(5) What is self-monitoring in terms of learning?

(6) Could you define metacognitive regulation?

(7) How can we direct our learning?

(8) What is the benefit of learning how to monitor one's thinking process?

Supplementary Reading

Text	Notes
Six Learning Strategies You Should Share with Students Yana Weinstein and Megan Smith are cognitive psychological scientists who have done a lot of researches on how people learn. They proposed six learning strategies. If we can work these strategies into our instruction, and teach students how to use them on their own, our students stand a much better chance of actually remembering our learning materials.	

Although performance assessments and project-based learning[1] allow students to show what they know with more depth and authenticity[2], most content areas still need to measure some learning with tests. When we are teaching that kind of content, these six strategies will help our students perform better on the test and retain that information long after the test is over.

1. Spaced Practice: Space out[3] Your Studying over Time.

Far too many students wait until the night before a test to study for it. Similarly, teachers often wait until the day before a test to review. When enough students score well on the test, it appears they have learned the material. However, a few weeks later, most of that information has vanished[4] from students' minds. Cramming[5] does not work! You learn the information quickly, and then you forget it just as quickly as you learned it. Therefore, if you stay up all night cramming before an exam, you might do fine on that exam, but then, you know, that information is not going to be available to you next time when you are trying to learn more complicated information.

For more durable[6] learning, the studying has to take place in smaller chunks[7] over time. What we recommend is what's called spaced practice, where you break up that studying that you might do at the end right before an exam. You space it out across a number of days or even weeks or months, and so then you're doing a little bit at a time, and it all adds up. What happens is that every time you leave a little space, you forget a bit of the information, and then you kind of relearn it, because that forgetting actually helps you to strengthen the memory.

Teachers can help students apply this strategy by helping them create a studying calendar to plan out how they will review chunks of content, and by carving out[8] small chunks of class time every day for review. In both cases, teachers need to plan to include current concepts and previously learned material. This is known as "spiraling[9]".

2. Retrieval Practice: Practice Bringing Information to Mind Without the Help of Materials.

Many people think of studying as simply re-reading notes,

[1] project-based learning 基于项目的学习，项目教学法

[2] authenticity *n.* 真实性

[3] space out 使间隔开；均匀分配

[4] vanish *v.* 消失，突然不见

[5] cramming *n.* 死记硬背，填鸭式教育

[6] durable *adj.* 持久的，耐用的

[7] chunk *n.* 大块；组块

[8] carve out 留出；开拓

[9] spiraling *n.* 螺旋式上升

textbooks, or other materials. However, having the information right in front of us does not force us to retrieve it from memory. Instead, it allows us to trick ourselves into thinking we know the knowledge. Recalling information without supporting materials helps us learn it much more effectively.

"Put your class materials away, and then write out or maybe sketch or speak everything you know and try to be as thorough as possible, and then check your materials for accuracy," Smith advises. "You're bringing information to mind almost like you're testing yourself. Though it can be a practice test, it does not have to be. You can just sort of go through and explain what you know, or teach a friend or a pet or even an inanimate[10] object everything that you learned in school. By bringing that information to mind, you're changing the way that information is stored so that it's easier for you to retrieve later on."

This is the approach to teach students to do retrieval practice in class. Have them turn off their devices, put all their notes and books away, then ask them to write everything they know about a particular term or topic, or share their thoughts in a think-pair-share[11]. When the practice is done, have students check their understanding by revisiting their materials and discussing misconceptions as a class. Once they learn how to do this in school, they can then apply it at home.

3. Elaboration: Explain and Describe Ideas with Many Details.

More specifically, this should be called "elaborative interrogation". The idea behind this is that you need to ask yourself how and why question while you are studying. For example, if you are studying Pearl Harbor Attack in a history class, you might ask yourself, "Well, why did this attack happen? How exactly did it happen? What were the results of this? How did this relate to other events?" This method asks students to go beyond simple recall of information and start making connections within the content. Students should ask themselves open-ended questions[12] about the material, answer in as much detail as possible, and then check the materials to make sure their understanding is correct.

[10] inanimate *adj.* 无生命的

[11] think-pair-share 思考—分组—分享

[12] open-ended question 开放式问题

4. Interleaving: Switch Between Ideas While You Study.

Common knowledge tells us that to learn a skill, we should practice it over and over again. While repetition is vital, research says we will actually learn that skill more effectively if we mix our practice of it with other skills. This is known as interleaving[13].

"Take math for example," Weinstein says. "What's fairly typical is that students often do the same type of math problem. That is, after they learn a particular strategy or formula[14], they might do five even ten of the same problem as homework. Interleaving would involve trying different problems in different orders. Therefore, if students are learning to calculate the area of a triangle, instead of having them do ten problems with triangles, have them do one of a triangle, then one of a circle, then a triangle, then a square."

Weinstein notes, "The thing is that it's actually harder. They'll make more errors, but they'll also learn something very important, which is how to choose a particular strategy for each problem, as opposed to[15] just repeatedly doing the same thing."

When planning exercises for students, resist the temptation[16] to have them repeat the exact same process multiple times in a row[17]. Instead, have them do a few of the new process, then weave in[18] other skills, so that the repetitive behavior is interrupted and students are forced to think more critically.

5. Concrete Examples: Use Specific Examples to Understand Abstract Ideas.

Most teachers already use this strategy in their own teaching. It is a natural part of explaining a new concept. However, what we do not necessarily do is to help students extend their understanding by coming up with examples of their own.

Teachers can apply this strategy by using concrete examples when teaching abstract concepts, then asking students to come up with their own, correcting any examples that are not quite right, and looking for more. Encourage students to continue this practice when they study.

[13] interleaving *n.* 交叉，交叉存取

[14] formula *n.* 公式

[15] as opposed to 与……相反，而不是

[16] temptation *n.* 引诱

[17] in a row 连续；成一长行

[18] weave in 编织在一起；穿插

6. Dual Coding[19]: Combine Words and Visuals.

When information is presented to us, it is often accompanied by some kind of visual: an image, a chart or graph. When students are studying, they should make it a habit to pay attention to those visuals and link them to the text by explaining what they mean in their own words. Then, students can create their own visuals of the concepts they are learning. This process reinforces[20] the concepts in the brain through two different paths, making it easier to retrieve later.

"And when we say visuals," Smith explains, "We don't necessarily mean anything specific, because it depends on the types of materials. You could have an infographic[21], a cartoon strip[22], a diagram, a graphic organizer, timeline[23], anything that makes sense to you so long as you're sort of depicting the information both in a way with words and a way with pictures."

"This isn't just for students who are good at drawing," Weinstein adds, "It's not about the quality of the drawing. It really just needs to be a visual representation as you can depict it."

In class, regularly turn students' attention to the visuals used in textbooks, on websites, and even in your own slideshow presentations. Have students describe the visuals to each other and make connections with what they're learning. Then have students create their own visuals of the content to further reinforce it. Remind students to include diagramming, sketching, and creating graphic organizers when they study at home.

Below are two pieces of advice on how to maximize these strategies:

- Combine them.

These strategies do not necessarily work in isolation[24]. You can space out your retrieval practice, and when doing retrieval practice, try to recall concrete examples, elaborate, or sketch out[25] a concept. When doing retrieval practice, you can also interleave between different concepts.

- Make them part of your class vocabulary.

If you just use these strategies in your teaching, you'll see improvement. However, if you actually explain the research to students, teach them the terminology, and use that terminology when teaching—"Okay, we're going to spend a few minutes

[19] dual coding 双重编码

[20] reinforce v. 加强，强化

[21] infographic n. 信息图
[22] cartoon strip 连环漫画
[23] timeline n. 时间轴，时间线；大事年表

[24] isolation n. 孤立；隔离

[25] sketch out 概述，草拟

on retrieval practice"—students will not only have a clearer understanding of why you're doing what you do, but they may be more likely to carry those skills with them into future classes.

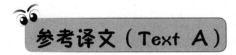

参考译文（Text A）

有效的学习策略

当学习者有意识地使用某种方法来学习和记忆某事时，他们就是在使用学习策略。随着年龄的增长，孩子们会愈发发现学习策略的益处，并更频繁地使用它们。孩子们也会慢慢掌握更多的策略。例如，简单地设想下，当你第一次尝试却没有学会某事的时候，你会再次去学习它。这是一个8岁孩子使用的策略，但6岁的孩子却不会使用。随着年龄和经验的增长，孩子们会愈发意识到在不同情况下哪些策略是有效的。

即便如此，许多不同年龄阶段的学生，包括大学生，似乎对有效的学习策略并不熟悉。我们发现，练习通常不是学习和记忆新信息的最好方法。真正有效的学习需要积极思考并详细阐释课堂材料。下述是七种基本学习策略。

1. 识别重要信息

因为人类的记忆系统并不能记住课堂上或课本上的所有信息，所以学生在学习课堂材料时必须要有选择性。他们所选择学习的东西——不管是主题思想和关键信息，还是孤立的事实和不重要的细节——会不可避免地影响他们的学习和学业成就。

学生往往不能在课堂或阅读中识别出最重要的信息。许多学生倾向于把注意力放在非常肤浅的事情上，比如老师的板书，或者作者用斜体或粗体写的东西。作为老师，我们可以帮助学生更有效地学习，让他们学会如何从讲座和阅读材料中获得最重要的信息。当然，我们可以直接告诉他们应该学习什么，但也可以通过更巧妙的方式来传达同样的信息。例如：

- 列出本堂课的学习目标。
- 在黑板上写下关键概念以及它们之间的关系。
- 问一些能让学生把注意力放在重要知识上的问题。

当得到这样的提示时，学生，尤其是成绩较差的学生，更有可能学到课程要点。当学生能够更好地将重要信息与次要信息区分开来时，我们就可以逐步停止引导。

2. 检索相关的先验知识

学生只有在掌握了与新信息相关的先验知识，并意识到它们的潜在关系时，才能进行有意义的学习。尽管我们可以提醒学生，他们正在学习的主题与某个先验知识相关，但我们也必须鼓励他们在学习的过程中自己检索相关的先验知识。一种方法是为这种学习策略建立模型。例如，我们可以朗读课本的一部分，间或停顿一下，把课文中的知识点和以前在课堂上所学的，或与个人亲身经历的东西联系起来。然后我们鼓励学生也这样做，并在他们做的过程中给予建议和指导。特别是在我们教小学生时，当他们阅读和学习时，我们可以提出一些具体的问题，来引导他们对已有的知识和观念进行反思：

- 关于此话题你已经了解到了什么？
- 关于此话题你希望学到什么？
- 你认为通过阅读这些书籍所学到的东西会改变你对此话题的既有知识吗？

有了足够的时间和练习，学生最终应该能养成这种习惯，即在没有我们帮助的情况下，也会检索先验知识。

3. 记笔记

当学生升至小学高年级或中学时，记笔记的技能开始在他们的课堂学习中发挥作用。一般来说，记较多笔记的学生能更好地学习和记住所学的主题。但是，笔记的质量同样重要。有用的笔记通常反映了一节课或阅读作业的主要思想。对于那些对他们正在学习的主题知之甚少的学生来说，好的笔记显得尤为重要。

当学生开始学习如何记课堂笔记的时候，我们应给给予他们指导，让他们明白哪些东西是最重要的，应该记下。方法之一是给学生提供一个具体的笔记模式。另一个可以考虑的策略是，尤其是当学生是新手的时候，间或检查他们的笔记是否准确，是否记录下了重点，然后给出建设性的反馈。

4. 组织信息

当学生参与到能够帮助他们组织所学到的知识的活动时，他们的学习会更有效。一个有用的策略是列出所学材料的大纲，这对成绩不佳的学生尤其有帮助。另一种方法是制作概念图，即一个描述本单元所学概念及其相互关系的图表。

通过对课堂资料构建自己的概念图，学生获益颇多。通过关注核心概念之间的关系，学生可以更好地组织材料。他们也更有可能注意到新概念和已知概念之间的联系，由此，更有可能对这些材料进行有意义的学习。此外，当学生从口头材料（如讲座）中构建概念图时，他们可以通过视觉和语言来对材料进行编码。而且，构建概念图的过程可以让学生对什么是学习有更加精准的理解。具体而言，学生可能开始意识到学习不仅仅是一个吸收信息的过程，更是一个在概念之间积极地建立联系的过程。

5. 阐释信息

作为一种学生可有意识地运用以帮助他们学习和理解新信息的策略，"阐释"这一技能在学生的能力发展过程中出现较晚（通常在青春期），并在青少年时期逐步发展。我们可以做很多事情来教会学生——甚至是小学生——阐释课堂上的话题。我们在对相关的先验知识的检索建立模型的同时，也可以对阐释进行建模。例如，我们可以把新概念联系到自己身边的实例，思索新原理的意义等。当他们听讲座或阅读课本时，我们可以让学生思考以下问题：

- 解释为什么……
- 你如何将……应用到……？

- ……新的实例是什么？
- 如果……你认为将会产生什么结果？
- ……和……的不同之处是什么？

另一种方法是让学生两人或多人一组，提出并回答阐释性的问题。这种小组问答被称为阐释性询问或朋辈互相提问。

6. 总结

另一个有效的学习策略是对所学的材料进行总结。不过，做出好的总结是一个相当复杂的过程。其基本要素至少应包括区分重要和次要信息，将细节整合成主体思想，并确定这些概念之间的重要关系。然而，即使是大学生也很难做出好的总结，这不足为奇。

或许帮助学生掌握这一策略的最好方法是定期让他们总结听到和读到的内容。例如，我们有时候可以布置这样的作业，让学生写一篇课本某章节的摘要。或者，我们可以让他们以合作小组的形式做一个简短的口头报告，来浓缩他们所学的某个话题的信息。开始时，总结作业应局限于简短、结构清晰、内容熟悉的文章。当学生熟练掌握了总结技能时，我们可以布置更具挑战性的作业。

7. 理解监控

理解监控是一个特别强大的学习策略，是一个定期检查自己的记忆和理解的过程。成功的学习者会在学习的同时，或者在学习后的某个时刻，持续监控自己的理解。而且，当他们意识到自己不理解的时候，他们会采取措施来纠正这种情况，或通过重读教材的特定章节，或通过课堂提问。

许多儿童和青少年很少进行理解监控。如果不监控自己的学习和理解，就不知道自己学会了什么，没有学会什么。因此，他们可能认为自己已经掌握了某些知识，实际上却并非如此。尽管这种认知错觉在儿童中非常常见，但各个层次的学习者都存在这种现象，甚至大学生也是如此。高年级往往以书面的形式进行考试，这种认知错觉会导致学生高估自己的考评成绩。

当然，理解监控并不一定是一项单独的活动。如果有学习小组的话，学生就可以方便地对所学的材料进行互测，从而发现理解上的缺口或误解。然而，要成为真正有效的学习者，学生最终得学会如何自测。一个有效的策略是自我诠释，即学生要经常停下来向自己解释学过的知识。另一个类似的方法是自我提问，即学生要经常停下来向自己提问。当然，他们的自我提问不仅要包括那些简单、事实性的问题，还应包括前面所描述的阐释性问题。

上述的部分学习策略，如记笔记和做提纲，是我们看得见的行为。其他的，如检索相关的先验知识和监控理解，是我们无法看到的内部心理过程。后一种策略——内部心理过程——可能会最终影响学生的学习。当我们培养学生的学习策略时，我们必须牢记，行为性策略（如记笔记）只有在能有效促进认知处理时才有用。

Unit

6

Learner Autonomy as an Educational Goal

1. Defining Learner Autonomy

Henri Holec defines learner autonomy as the ability to take charge of one's own learning. This indicates the learner holds the responsibility for decisions concerning all aspects of learning, i.e.:

- Determining the objectives;
- Defining the contents and progressions;
- Selecting methods and techniques to be used;
- Monitoring the procedure of learning (rhythm, time, place, etc.);
- Evaluating what has been learned.

Traditionally, the teacher is in charge of learning, usually on behalf of some higher agency—school, educational authority, examining board, government department. In that case, the curriculum is not only imposed on learners from outside, but has been drawn up without specific regard to their individual experience, needs, interest, and aspiration. The transfer of responsibility for learning from the teacher to the learner has far-reaching implications not simply for the way in which education is organized but for power relationships that are central to our social structure. The learners are supposed to generate their own purposes for learning. In pursuit of those purposes, they determine not only the content of learning but the way in which learning will take place and they are responsible for deciding how successful learning is, both as process and as goal-attainment. In other words, the curriculum should come from the learners as a product of their past experience and present and future needs. Holec does not, of course, imagine that the capacity for autonomous learning is inborn. On the contrary, he insists that it must be developed with expert help. Inevitably, the need for such help becomes a central factor in redefining the role of teachers.

2. Autonomy and Schooling

One of the most powerful attacks against traditional educational structure is that school institutionalizes values, and thus teaches students to confuse process with substance. The student is "schooled" to confuse teaching with learning, grade advancement with education, a diploma with competence, and fluency with the ability to say something new. The traditional school "removes things from everyday use by labelling them education tools". This means that even if it offers learners new information and new experience, school erects a barrier between students and the intended content and process of their learning. Traditional schooling is based on the illusion that most learning is the result of teaching. In fact, most learning happens casually, and even most intentional learning is not the result of programmed instruction. For example, children learn their mother tongue casually.

Learning is self-motivated, and undertaken in order to fulfil a personal need. The benefits that should come from the development of learner autonomy may be summarized as follows:

● Because the learner sets the agenda, learning should be more focused and more purposeful, and thus more effective both immediately and in the longer term.

● Because the responsibility for learning lies in the learner, the barriers between learning and living that are often found in traditional teacher-led educational structures should not arise.

● If there are no barriers between learning and living, learners should have little difficulty in transferring their capacity for autonomous behavior to all other areas of their lives, and this should make them more useful members of society and more effective participants as well.

Formal education at all levels usually claims that it promotes the kind of learning that will enhance the life of the individual and thus enrich society. As we have seen, one of the chief reasons for promoting learner autonomy is the desire to remove the barriers between learning and living.

3. Misconceptions About Autonomous Learning

Like any other powerful ideas, the concept of learner autonomy arouses strong hostility in some quarters. However, more often than not such hostility seems to be based on one or another false assumption about what autonomy is and what it entails. Perhaps the most widespread misconception is that autonomy is synonymous with self-instruction, which is essentially a matter of learning without a teacher. Certainly, some learners who follow the path of self-instruction achieve a high degree of autonomy, but many do not. Autonomy is not exclusively or even primarily a matter of how learning is organized.

Misconception emerges again in the assumption that in the classroom context learner autonomy somehow requires the teacher to relinquish all initiative and control. This assumption has two principal sources. The first is a belief that autonomous learners make the teacher redundant, which is closely related to our first misconception. The second source is a belief that any intervention on the part of the teacher may destroy whatever autonomy the learners have managed to attain.

Another misconception that arises in relation to classroom learning is that autonomy is something teachers do to their learners. In other words, it is a new methodology. This is not entirely false, for learners are unlikely to become autonomous without active encouragement from their teachers, but it is certainly not the case that the development of learner autonomy can be programmed in a series of lesson plans.

A fourth misconception is that autonomy is a single, easily described behavior. It is true that we recognize autonomous learners by their behavior, but it can take numerous different forms, depending on learners' age, how far they have progressed with their learning, what they perceive their immediate learning needs to be, and so on. Autonomy, in other words, can manifest itself in very many different ways.

Fifthly, closely related to our fourth misconception, it is sometimes mistakenly believed that autonomy is a steady state achieved by certain learners. This may well emerge in a teacher's boast that all her learners are autonomous, which seems to set them far apart from ordinary learners. The fact is that autonomy is likely to be hard-won and its permanence cannot be guaranteed. The learner who displays a high degree of autonomy in one area may be non-autonomous in another.

4. Fostering Learner Autonomy

Autonomy is defined as the ability to take charge of one's own learning. In this case, a student is the one who takes responsibility for their own learning. This model of learning is so-called student-centered learning in which the focus of learning is the student, not the teacher. This idea has changed the old paradigm from teaching process into learning process. An autonomous learner is not dependent solely on the role of teacher in the classroom. The learner has to set their own goal, strategies and style, make decisions and solve the problem. The role of teacher is as facilitator. In the same vein, an autonomous learner solves problems or develops new ideas through a combination of divergent and convergent thinking and functions with minimal external guidance in selected areas of endeavor. That is, the role of teaching should be minimized in the classroom in order to promote learning autonomy.

In a classroom with autonomous learners, it is no longer assumed that the teacher is the only one who possesses knowledge and answers questions. The students can possibly access information and produce satisfying answers. By applying this style of learning, the learning activities do not have to always take place in schools, but also at home or somewhere outdoors. However, it does not suggest that the teacher enacts less important role. The teacher becomes an organizer and facilitator of learning activities. He or she goes beyond teaching to raise the students' awareness of independent learning.

To foster the ability of autonomous learning is to transform and release responsibility gradually to learners. In the following learning model (Figure 6-1), Douglas Fisher and Nancy Frey dig deep into the hows and whys of the instructional framework of gradual release of responsibility. To gradually release responsibility is to equip students with what they need to be engaged and self-directed learners. On a day-to-day level, it means delivering lessons purposefully planned to incorporate four essential and interrelated instructional phases:

- Focused Instruction: Preparing students for learning by establishing lesson purpose, modeling strategies and skills, thinking aloud, and noticing how students respond.

- Guided Instruction: Strategically using prompts, cues, and questions to lead students to new understanding.

- Collaborative Learning: Allowing students to consolidate their understanding through exploration, problem-solving, discussion, and thinking with their peers.

- Independent Learning: Requiring students to use the skills and knowledge they have acquired to create authentic products and ask new questions.

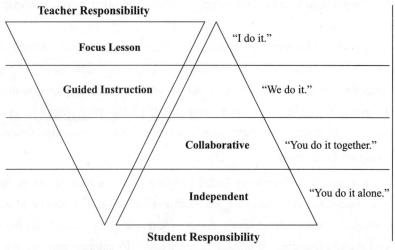

Figure 6-1   The Instructional Framework of the Gradual Release of Responsibility

Autonomous learning does not directly get the teacher free of their charge. Instead, the teacher is to enact a role of an instructor. The students who evolve their strategies are called reactive autonomous learners. This is the initial phase. Soon after, when the students are aware to collaborate with each other, they actually have shown the manifestation of their responsibility. Eventually, the teacher can take breath witnessing the fact that students become individually proactive and capable of deciding goals, planning learning strategies, experiencing learning activities, and evaluating their progress.

 **New Words**

concerning [kən'sɜːnɪŋ] *prep.* 关于；就……而言
progression [prə'greʃn] *n.* 前进；进度

rhythm ['rɪðəm] *n.* 节奏；韵律
aspiration [ˌæspə'reɪʃn] *n.* 抱负，志向；渴望

transfer [træns'fɜ:] *n.* 转让；转移

goal-attainment [gəʊl-ə'teɪnmənt] *n.* 目标达到

inborn [ˌɪn'bɔ:n] *adj.* 天生的；先天的

institutionalize [ˌɪnstɪ'tju:ʃənəlaɪz] *v.* 使制度化或习俗化

erect [ɪ'rekt] *v.* 竖立；建造

agenda [ə'dʒendə] *n.* 议程；日程表

hostility [hɒ'stɪləti] *n.* 敌对，敌意，敌视

synonymous [sɪ'nɒnɪməs] *adj.* 同义的；同义词的

exclusively [ɪk'sklu:sɪvli] *adv.* 仅仅；唯一地

relinquish [rɪ'lɪŋkwɪʃ] *v.* 放弃；放手

initiative [ɪ'nɪʃətɪv] *n.* 主动权；首创精神

redundant [rɪ'dʌndənt] *adj.* 多余的，累赘的

intervention [ˌɪntə'venʃn] *n.* 介入；干预

manifest ['mænɪfest] *v.* 显现；证明

boast [bəʊst] *v.* 自夸，吹牛

hard-won [hɑ:d-wʌn] *adj.* 来之不易的；难得的

paradigm ['pærədaɪm] *n.* 模式，范式，范例

solely ['səʊlli] *adv.* 仅仅；单独地，唯一地

divergent [daɪ'vɜ:dʒənt] *adj.* 相异的，有分歧的

convergent [kən'vɜ:dʒənt] *adj.* 趋同的；会聚性的

endeavor [ɪn'devə] *n.* 努力，尽力

enact [ɪ'nækt] *v.* 扮演；颁布

phase [feɪz] *n.* 阶段

prompt [prɒmpt] *n.* 提示；（给演员）提白

cue [kju:] *n.* 提示，暗示；线索

consolidate [kən'sɒlɪdeɪt] *v.* 巩固，加强

authentic [ɔ:'θentɪk] *adj.* 真正的，真实的

evolve [ɪ'vɒlv] *v.* 发展，进化

manifestation [ˌmænɪfe'steɪʃn] *n.* 表现；显示

proactive [ˌprəʊ'æktɪv] *adj.* 有前瞻性的；积极主动的

Phrases

learner autonomy 自主学习，学习者自主性
in charge of 负责，掌管
on behalf of 代表；为了
impose on 强加于
in pursuit of 追求，寻求
confuse... with... 混淆……，搞乱……
mother tongue 母语；本国语言

in the longer term 从长远来看，在较长的时间内
autonomous learning 自主学习；自主性学习
more often than not 常常，通常
in relation to 关于；涉及
in the same vein 同样地
think aloud 有声思维，思考并讲述思维过程
take breath 歇口气，喘口气

✏ Exercises

Ex. 1 Give the English equivalents of the following Chinese expressions.

(1) 转让；转移　_____

(2) 深远的；广泛的　_____

(3) 误解；错觉　_____

(4) 仅仅；唯一的　_____

(5) 有前瞻性的；积极主动的　_____

(6) 同样地　_____

(7) 常常，通常　_____

(8) 母语；本国语言　_____

(9) 追求，寻求　_____

(10) 自主学习，学习者自主性　_____

Ex. 2 Decide whether the following statements are true (T) or false (F) according to Text A. Give your reasons for the false ones.

(　　) (1) The transfer of responsibility for learning from the teacher to the learner is one of the demonstrations of autonomous learning.

(　　) (2) The capacity for autonomous learning is inborn.

(　　) (3) Traditional schooling is based on the illusion that most learning is the result of teaching.

(　　) (4) One of the chief reasons for promoting learner autonomy is the desire to remove the barriers between learning and living.

(　　) (5) Learner autonomy is synonymous with self-instruction.

(　　) (6) Autonomous learning makes the teacher redundant.

(　　) (7) The learner who displays a high degree of autonomy in one area may be non-autonomous in another.

(　　) (8) In an autonomous learning classroom, the teacher is the only one who possesses knowledge and knows the question answers.

(　　) (9) To foster the ability of autonomous learning is to release responsibility gradually to learners.

(　　) (10) Autonomous learning may directly get the teacher free of charge.

Ex. 3 Answer the following questions according to Text A.

(1) Could you define learner autonomy?

(2) What are the roles of teachers and learners in terms of autonomous learning?

(3) What is one of the most powerful attacks against traditional educational structure?

(4) What are benefits of developing learner autonomy?

(5) What is the most widespread misconception about learner autonomy?

(6) Should teachers relinquish all initiative and control in an autonomous learning context?

(7) What is the instructional framework of gradual release of learning responsibility to students?

(8) What are reactive autonomous learners?

Ex. 4 **Fill in the blanks with the words given below.**

contrasts	evaluating	linguistic	scale	responsibility
proficiency	Autonomous	objectives	components	preferences

Learner autonomy refers to the principle that learners should take a maximum amount of (1)_____ for what they learn and how they learn it. They should be involved in decisions concerning setting (2)_____ for learning, determining ways and means of learning, and reflecting on and (3)_____ what they have learned. (4)_____ learning is said to make learning more personal and focused and consequently achieve better learning outcomes since learning is based on learners' needs and (5)_____. It (6)_____ with the traditional teacher-led approach in which most decisions are made by the teacher. The use of self-directed learning in a self-access center is one application of this approach.

An example of application of the principles of learner autonomy is the Council of Europe's European Language Portfolio (ELP), which is intended to help support autonomous learning on a wide (7)_____. The ELP has three (8)_____: alanguage passport, which summarizes the owners' (9)_____ identity; a language biography, which provides for a reflective account of the learners experience in learning and using the foreign language, and a dossier, in which the learner collects evidence of his or her developing (10)_____ in the language. The ELP involves regular goal-setting and self-assessment.

Text B

Autonomy in the Foreign Language Classroom

1. The Sequence of Developing Learner Autonomy

No school, or even university, can provide its pupils with all the knowledge and the skills they will need in their adult lives. Adult life, in its personal as well as its vocational aspects, is far too diverse and too subjective to change for any educational curriculum to attempt to provide a detailed preparation. It is more important for a young person to have an understanding of himself/herself, an awareness of the environment and its workings, and to learn how to think and how to learn.

Apart from enabling the learners to take charge of their own learning, the biggest hurdle when developing learner autonomy is to make the learners willing to take over the responsibility for doing so. An autonomous classroom is an institutional teaching and learning environment in its broadest sense, from ordinary classrooms to self-access centers, where the learners are given the chance to act independently. What we are aiming at is a move from an exclusively teacher-directed teaching environment with a focus on teaching to a possible learner-directed learning environment with a focus on learning, as illustrated in Figure 6-2.

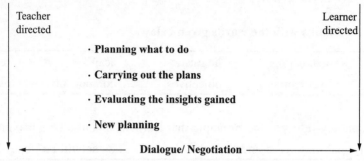

Figure 6-2   Developing Learner Autonomy

In the center of the illustration are the three elements generally involved in any teaching and learning sequence:

- Planning, based on previous teaching and learning experiences;
- Carrying out the plans;
- Evaluating the work undertaken and insights gained, leading on to a new planning phase.

This sequence can, of course, be directed solely by a teacher without involving the learners. However, developing learner autonomy, which is supporting students in their awareness and consciousness of being autonomous learners, is a matter of getting the learners actively involved in the three phases of this teaching and learning sequence. This involvement is a prerequisite if we, the teachers, eventually want them to be capable of and thus co-responsible for carrying out the sequence on their own—to be in charge of their own learning—even outside the institutional context.

Helping the learners to administer and take care of their own learning is a matter for the teacher to move from an exclusive focus on his or her teaching to a focus on how best he or she can support his or her learners in being actively involved in their own learning. However, it is not an either/or, but a both/and. Furthermore, the move demands close cooperation, negotiation, and openness between the participants in the learning process, and at the same time it demands clear definitions of the power given to the various participants in the process of learning. What are the teacher's rights? What are her responsibilities? What are the rights and responsibilities of the individual learner? What is expected of peers? Well, let us enter an autonomous classroom.

2. The Features of an Autonomous Classroom

2.1   The Physical Settings

In the foreign language teaching and learning classroom, then, as now, learners are placed in groups. There is an intensive student activity and engagement which creates what could be called a "continuous humming". That is, learners are engaged in many different activities. Logbooks, which, in reality, are just extended exercise books, can be seen lying open next to the learners who make notes or drawings in them as the lesson proceeds. The teacher is moving around or sitting down, engaged in discussions with individual learners or groups of learners. On the wall, posters display requirements as well as help in the form of guidelines for work. In some cases, the written text on the posters is supported by drawings or symbols, such as a book for reading, a pencil for writing, or an ear for listening. Examples of student products are also posted on the wall. Various materials to be used by the learners on their own, such as dictionaries, extra readers, newspapers and magazines, and learner-produced games, can be found on the shelves.

2.2　The Role of Teachers and Learners

The role of teachers and learners can be summarized as:

- A changed teacher role, i.e., the teacher's role as a consultant and a partner;
- Student's taking hold and teacher's letting go;
- Shared decision making;
- Student's more definite awareness about aims;
- Reduced teacher dependence and increased student independence;
- The knowledge of the learners and the importance and value of the teachers;
- Responsibility transfer.

The role of the teacher in an autonomous classroom differs markedly from his role in a traditional teacher- or teaching-directed environment. There has often been the misconception that in the autonomous classroom the teacher is superfluous; that "autonomy is synonymous with self-instruction, and that it is essentially a matter of deciding to learn without a teacher". Nothing could be more wrong. Getting the learners actively involved in their own learning is primarily the teacher's responsibility. This change cannot be effected in one go. The teacher has to think of ways in which he can gradually get his learners engaged in decisions to be made and actions to be taken in the three phases of a teaching and learning sequence for them to be able to take over.

2.3　Learner's Awareness of the Demands and Conditions When Planning

The teacher has got certain information about what is expected of him as a teacher, such as an insight into curricular guidelines and requirements (what should be learned), i.e., information that is normally kept from the learners. In the autonomous classroom, the teacher is responsible for making these insights public and known to the learners. This can be done on posters or in the learners' logbooks. It can begin with "You must be able to…" followed by possible objectives or requirements taken from the guidelines for the specific learner group in question. Again, this process, of course, presupposes that the teacher himself is fully aware of these objectives and can formulate them in a language understandable to her learners. The followings are some examples taken from classroom work with different levels of learners:

- You must be able to say a nursery rhyme.

- You must be able to say at least 10 words in English beginning with "b".
- You must be able to explain new words from the text in English and use them in a sentence.
- You must be able to carry on a conversation for two minutes with your partner.
- You must be able to rewrite a newspaper article in 50 words.

It is not until the learners are aware of what is expected of them that they can be precise about their own aims and objectives within the overall curricular demands. Here is an example from one learner of English, "I want to improve my pronunciation. I will do it by using 'two minutes' talk' as suggested by Leni and by talking to a mirror at home."

2.4 Structure in Connection with Carrying out the Plans

It is important that the teacher gives his learners an insight into and an awareness of possible ways in which a task or a lesson can be structured and carried out. This is likely to happen if the learners have experienced a transparent structure of a task or a lesson run by the teacher before they are to carry out any plans themselves. This demand may sound obvious and easy enough. However, when asked, many language teachers are not able to describe the structure of their lessons, either because they have followed a course book or have no in-detail thought about it.

The problem is, of course, that if this is the case, then it will be extremely difficult, almost impossible, for the learners to take over the work on their own. The teacher has to present his structure for a task or a lesson, or if using a course book, he has to make the structure in the book clear to the learners. When introducing a task to be done, he has to tell his learners what he expects them to do, why he has chosen this task, how he wants it done in detail, and what results might come out of the work. In this way, he provides his learners with a model for carrying out a specific task, a model that they can relate to and eventually use or change for their own purposes. Similarly to aims and objectives, the model can be written on a poster—open for discussions and changes. And/or it can be placed in the learners' logbooks. When the learners have taken hold, then it is time for the teacher to "be consultant and a partner".

2.5 Evaluation

Evaluation and, in that connection, reflection are the pivot of the whole process in an autonomous classroom. Unfortunately many teachers feel that evaluation detracts time from the "real" teaching and learning—it is too time-consuming. This opinion is fundamentally flawed because evaluation is an integrated and important part of the learning process. Furthermore, their attitude often implies that evaluation is hardly integrated into the teacher-directed sessions and is, therefore, very difficult for the learners to take over. This is extremely unfortunate, especially because the results from evaluations seem to be a good starting point for discussions and negotiations between teachers and learners or between learners. This interaction is a good place to cross the water, so to speak, to move from teacher direction to possible learner direction. However, here as in connection with planning, it is essential that the teacher take the first step and use evaluation himself. By doing so, he can provide his learners with an insight into different approaches to evaluation and make them aware of evaluative criteria. Only in this way will the learners be capable of successfully taking over evaluation themselves. Moreover, evaluation becomes an activity in its own right and gives scope for authentic communication and reflection, two crucial criteria for a good activity in the autonomous classroom.

2.6　Reduction of Teacher's Talking Time

It must be emphasized that big difference exists between a traditional classroom and the autonomous classroom: the teacher's talking time. A prerequisite for active learner interaction and communication is that the teacher stops talking in front of the whole class for a longer period of time and makes space for the learners to talk among themselves. Unfortunately, this is extremely difficult for teachers. In some autonomous classrooms, for example, the teacher takes over when participating in a group discussion. Therefore, reduction of teacher's talking time must be at the back of every teacher's head when he enters the autonomous classroom.

3. Conclusion

If the teacher succeeds in showing the way as well as letting go, then we can rely on the learners' ability to take hold. An autonomous classroom will and should always be open to new demands and possibilities in its educational as well as social surroundings and change accordingly.

However, the situation has not changed for the teacher who decides to develop learner autonomy in his class. He will enter a long and often troublesome journey. He might, like so many teachers before him, experience the "octopus syndrome" when trying to help his learners (a feeling of being everywhere and nowhere). He might also be overwhelmed with a feeling of insecurity: "Do my learners learn enough when I am not in charge all the time?" Then he has to remember that "Rome was not built in one day.".

In addition, he has to remember that an autonomous classroom gives scope for "interested, happy, engaged and satisfied learners, for personal development of teachers and students, for a feeling of security". Moreover, it develops good language learners who "have an understanding of himself or herself, an awareness of the environment and its workings, and have learned how to think and how to learn". What else can a teacher ask for? Perhaps the following evaluation from a Spanish teacher many years ago gives the answer: "I have become a human being in my classes!"

 **New Words**

sequence ['si:kwəns] *n.* 序列；顺序	involvement [ɪn'vɒlvmənt] *n.* 参与；牵连；包含
hurdle ['hɜ:dl] *n.* 障碍；跨栏	
evaluate [ɪ'væljueɪt] *v.* 评价；估价	administer [əd'mɪnɪstə] *v.* 管理；执行
consciousness ['kɒnʃəsnəs] *n.* 意识；知觉	move [mu:v] *n.* 举措；步骤；策略

negotiation [nɪˌgəʊʃɪ'eɪʃn] *n.* 协商，谈判

feature ['fi:tʃə] *n.* 特色，特征

logbook ['lɒgbʊk] *n.* 日志

poster ['pəʊstə] *n.* 海报；张贴

consultant [kən'sʌltənt] *n.* 顾问；咨询者

markedly ['mɑːkɪdli] *adv.* 明显地；显著地

superfluous [suː'pɜːfluəs] *adj.* 多余的；不必要的

presuppose [ˌpriːsə'pəʊz] *v.* 假定；以……为先决条件

transparent [træns'pærənt] *adj.* 易懂的；透明的；显然的

reflection [rɪ'flekʃn] *n.* 反思；沉思

pivot ['pɪvət] *n.* 枢轴；中心点

detract [dɪ'trækt] *n.* 减损，降低

flaw [flɔː] *v.* 有裂纹；有缺陷

prerequisite [ˌpriː'rekwəzɪt] *n.* 先决条件

troublesome ['trʌblsəm] *adj.* 使人苦恼的；麻烦的

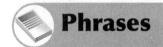

be subject to 受制于，使服从

apart from 除了，除……之外

take hold 掌控，抓住

nursery rhyme 童谣；儿歌

in that connection 在这方面

in its own right 凭借自身能力，独立地

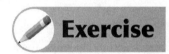

Decide whether the following statements are true (T) or false (F) according to Text B. Give your reasons for the false ones.

(　　) (1) A school should provide its pupils with all the knowledge and the skills they will need in their adult lives.

(　　) (2) Autonomous learning aims at a move from an exclusively teacher-directed teaching environment with a focus on teaching to a possible learner-directed learning environment with a focus on learning.

(　　) (3) In the foreign language teaching and learning classroom, then as now, learners are placed in groups.

(　　) (4) It's best not to reduce teacher dependence and increase student independence in an autonomous classroom.

(　　) (5) Getting the learners actively involved in their own learning is primarily the teacher's responsibility.

(   ) (6) Many language teachers are able to describe the structure of their lessons.

(   ) (7) Evaluation is the pivot of the whole process in an autonomous classroom.

(   ) (8) Evaluation detracts time from the "real" teaching and learning because it is too time-consuming.

(   ) (9) A prerequisite for active learner interaction is that the teacher stops talking for a long period of time and makes space for the learners to talk among themselves.

(   ) (10) The situation now is favorable for the teacher who decides to develop learner autonomy in her class.

 # Supplementary Reading

Text	Notes
Autonomous Learner Model	

1. Where Did the Autonomous Learner Model Begin

The Autonomous Learner Model (ALM) was developed years ago at Arvada West High School in Arvada, Colorado, by Professor George Betts and Jolene Kercher. The goal was to give students the opportunity to become independent, self-directed learners. What is exciting is that this model of education was not developed by teachers but by students. These students came from two different groups—those who were not achieving[1] and those who were achieving in high school. They were two different groups but both had the same need—to make school meaningful and to be more involved in the development of what they were going to learn. The teachers were there not to direct students but to assist them in the process of becoming lifelong learners. ALM for the gifted[2] and talented was developed specifically to meet the diversified[3] cognitive, emotional, and social needs of learners. The model is currently implemented[4] at all grade levels with the gifted and talented as well as all learners in the regular classroom. Emphasis is placed on meeting the individualized[5] needs of learners through the use of activities in the five major Dimensions[6] of the Model.

2. What Is the Autonomous Learner Model

ALM has more advantages over the gifted and talented students in terms of promoting self-directed learning. The

Notes:

[1] achieving *adj.* 成绩优良的

[2] gifted *adj.* 有天赋的；有才华的

[3] diversified *adj.* 多样化的；各种的

[4] implement *v.* 实施，执行

[5] individualized *adj.* 个性化的；有个性的

[6] dimension *n.* 维度，方面

major goal of the model is to facilitate[7] the growth of students as independent, self-directed learners, with the development of skills, concepts and positive attitudes within the cognitive, emotional and social domains.

The model is designed to move students toward the role of learners, controlling the learning process, with teachers adopting the role of facilitator. With a flexible approach the model can be used in the regular classroom (with all learners and across all phases of development), in small group settings, as an individual course, or in specific or cross curricula[8] learning areas.

The ALM advocates the development of student's "passion"[9] learning—where the child engages in in-depth learning rather than merely covering breadth of a topic. A key focus of the program is lifelong learning, with emphasis placed on meeting the individualized needs of learners through the use of activities in the following five major dimensions of the model.

3. What Are the Dimensions of the ALM

As Figure 6-3 indicates, the five dimensions of the Autonomous Learner Model progress a student to the role of an independent learner. Each component has a list of activities that facilitate the growth of students to become self-directed learners.

Dimension one: Orientation[10]

The Orientation dimension is the foundation for independent learning. Students have the opportunity to build a basic understanding of giftedness, and their own interests and abilities.

Dimension two: Individual Development

The Individual Development dimension helps students improve their learning skills, consider future career possibilities, and develop a positive attitude for lifelong learning.

Dimension three: Enrichment[11]

Enrichment activities emphasize awareness of what is outside the classroom to be studied, how to pursue these topics, and how to synthesize[12] the information into a meaningful product.

[7] facilitate *v.* 促进；帮助

[8] curricula *n.* 课程（curriculum 的复数形式）

[9] passion *n.* 激情，热情

[10] orientation *n.* 定位，方向

[11] enrichment *n.* 拓展；丰富；改进

[12] synthesize *v.* 合成；综合

Dimension four: Seminars[13]

The fourth dimension, Seminar, provides opportunities for students to design, implement, and evaluate a structured learning experience that is shared with other interested people in the school and community.

Dimension five: In-depth[14] Study

The final dimension, In-depth Study, provides an opportunity for learners to select an area of interest that will be studied in-depth over a long period of time.

[13] seminar n. 讨论会

[14] in-depth adj. 深入的，彻底的

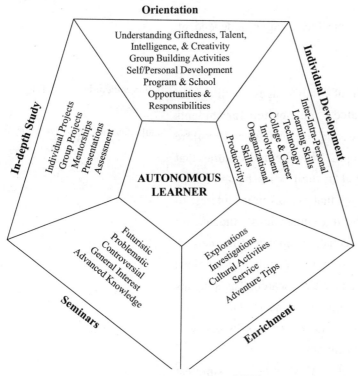

Figure 6-3   Five Dimensions of ALM

4. What Are the Standards of the ALM

The ALM standards are different from those standards in the curriculum areas used in most schools. These standards are not related to skills within a content area, but to the "total" individual. These standards are applied to provide opportunities for students to become lifelong learners:

- Develop more positive self-concept and self-esteem[15].
- Comprehend[16] own abilities in relationship to self and society.

[15] self-esteem n. 自尊；自负

[16] comprehend v. 理解，领悟

- Develop skills to interact effectively with peers, siblings[17], parents and other adults.
  - Increase knowledge in a variety of areas.
  - Develop critical and creative thinking skills.
  - Develop decision-making and problem-solving skills.
  - Integrate[18] activities that facilitate the cognitive, emotional, social, and physical development of the individual.
  - Develop an individual's passion for learning.
  - Demonstrate responsibility for own learning, in and out of the school setting.
  - Ultimately become responsible, creative, independent, life-long learners.

5. Suggestions for the ALM

The ALM has a multitude of[19] advantages for the gifted learner. It offers a differentiated[20] curriculum for students by challenging them to go beyond the surface and explore areas of interest in greater depth. This method ensures that students will be fully engaged in their work because they are learning concepts and topics that are of direct interest to them. Additionally, through the five dimensions, students are encouraged to become self-directed, independent learners as they seek out information on their topics of study and solutions to the problems they encounter in their research. The students are not only learning about a particular concept, but they are also developing critical thinking and research skills that will serve them well in their future vocations.

Despite these advantages, the ALM is not the simplest model to implement in the classroom. In order to effectively accomplish the ALM in the classroom, teachers and administrators[21] should adhere to the following suggestions for a smooth implementation:

First, Professional development. Teachers must receive the necessary training to progress students through the five dimensions of the model. Educators should be comfortable instructing on the model and administering its various components in the classroom and outside its walls.

Second, Programming search. A programming search provides the students a wealth of resources to use in performing

[17] sibling *n.* 兄弟姊妹

[18] integrate *v.* 整合；使……成整体

[19] a multitude of 大批的，众多的

[20] differentiated *adj.* 差异化的

[21] administrator *n.* 管理者

their research. Teachers can assist students by helping them develop contact information on content specialists, who could serve on the student's support team. Additionally, teachers can assist students in developing specific research skills that will aid them in their in-depth studies. Finally, teachers should communicate about any relevant school and community events and competitions that will further the research and learning on their students. The programming search is necessary to develop the Advanced Learning Plan (ALP), which serves as the outline for the student's individualized curriculum.

Third, advanced[22] learning plan. Before students can perform research on a topic of interest, they must have developed an ALP with the cooperation of their support team (educators, parents, and administrators). Teachers must remind themselves that the students should develop, implement, and evaluate their own ALPs, i.e., educators are doing this process "with" the students and not "to" the students. Before the students start developing their ALP, teachers must instruct on what an ALP is, why it is necessary, what outcomes[23] are expected, and how the plan will be assessed. Students will develop their own ALP plan under the guidance of the teachers. Once the students have a better grasp of the entire process, they will become more responsible for the ALPs.

Fourth, pacing.[24] For many students who have never completed an in-depth study, the overall task can be very overwhelming[25]. A step-by-step procedure should be followed for completing this monumental task. Teachers should assist students adhering to[26] their ALPs and the suggested procedures so that the students do not fall behind in their projects. It would be helpful to conference with the students on a regular basis to ensure that they are meeting their research goals and completing their in-depth studies in a timely fashion.

The end result of the Autonomous Learner Model is for students to develop into lifelong, independent learners. As part of the learning experience, teachers can use the above suggestions to help students successfully complete their seminars and in-depth studies. When implemented properly, the teacher's guidance and the dimensions in this model will help

[22] advanced *adj.* 高级的，先进的

[23] outcome *n.* 结果，结局

[24] pacing *n.* 把握节奏

[25] overwhelming *adj.* 令人难以应对的；压倒性的

[26] adhere to 坚持；拥护，追随

students cultivate those necessary skills needed in their current studies and future endeavors[27].	[27] endeavor *n.* 努力，尽力

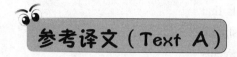

教育目标之自主学习

1. 自主学习定义

亨利·霍勒克将自主学习定义为"掌管自己学习的能力"。这意味着学习者应自己负责决定有关学习的方方面面，即：

- 确定学习目标；
- 确定内容和进度；
- 选择使用的方法和技巧；
- 监控学习过程（节奏、时间、地点等）；
- 评估自己的所学。

传统而言，教师通常代表一些更高机构，如学校、教育主管部门、考试委员会和政府部门来管理学生的学习。所以，课程设置是从外部强加给学习者的，而且没有具体考虑他们的个人经历、需求、兴趣和愿望。把学习的责任从教师转移到学习者身上，不仅对教育的组织方式有深远的影响，而且对社会结构中至关重要的权利关系也有深远的影响。学习者应制定自己的学习目标，为了完成这些目标，他们不仅应决定学习的内容，还要决定学习的方式。此外，他们应负责学习的成功程度，包括学习过程和目标的实现。换句话说，课程设置应源于学习者，基于他们过去的经验和对现在、未来的需求。当然，霍勒克并不认为自主学习能力是与生俱来的。相反，他坚持认为必须在专家的帮助下才能培养出学习能力。不可避免地，对这种帮助的需求成为重新定义教师角色的一个核心因素。

2. 自主学习和学校教育

对传统教育结构最有力的攻击之一是：学校将价值观制度化，使得学生将过程与主旨相混淆。"学校教育"使学生混淆了教与学、升学与教育、文凭与能力、滔滔不绝与表达新观点的能力。传统的学校"摒弃了日常生活中的知识并将其标注为教育工具"。这意味着，即使它为学习者提供了新的信息和体验，学校也在学生和他们想要学习的内容和过程之间设置了障碍。传统的学校教育基于这样一种错觉，即"学"大多都是"教"的结果。事实上，大多数学习都是在无意间发生的，即使是有意识的学习也不是程序化教学的结果。例如，孩子是在无意识的情况下学会的母语。

学习应是积极主动的，是为了满足个人需要而进行的。培养自主学习的益处可以总结如下：

- 因为学习者自己设定日程，所以学习会更专心、更有目的性，因而从短期和长期来看效果都更好；

- 由于学习的责任在于学习者，传统教师主导的教育模式中经常出现的学习与生活之间的障碍应该不会出现；

- 如果学习和生活之间没有障碍，学习者将自主行为的能力转移到生活的其他领域应该不会有困难，这可使他们成为对社会更有用的成员和更有效的参与者。

各级正规教育通常声称，它推崇的学习会改善个人生活，从而丰富社会。正如我们所看到的，促进自主学习的一个主要原因是希望消除学习和生活之间的障碍。

3. 对自主学习的误解

和其他任何强有力的观点一样，自主学习的概念在某些方面引起了强烈的敌意。然而，这种敌意往往是建立在对自主学习是什么以及自主学习要求什么，以及这样或那样错误认识的基础上的。也许最普遍的误解是将自主学习等同于"自学"，自学实际上是在没有老师的情况下学习。当然，部分自学者获得了高度的自主性，但多数人不会。自主学习根本而言并非一个如何组织学习的问题。

误解还包括，在课堂环境中，自主学习要求教师放弃所有的主动性和控制力。这个误解有两个主要来源。第一个认为自主学习使得教师显得多余，这与第一个误解密切相关；第二种观点认为，教师的任何干预都可能会破坏学习者所追求的"自主"。

另一个与课堂学习有关的误解是，自主是教师施加于学生的。换句话说，它是一种新的教学方法。这也并非完全错误，因为没有教师的积极鼓励，学生是不可能成为自主学习者的，但自主学习的培养绝不是通过一系列的教案来规划的。

第四个误解认为自主学习是单一的、容易描述的行为。诚然，我们通过学生的行为来识别自主学习者，但自主学习可以呈现多种不同的形式，这取决于学生的年龄、他们在学习上的进步程度、他们认为自己当前的学习需要是什么，等等。也就是说，自主学习可以以许多不同的方式表现出来。

第五，与第四个误解密切相关的是，有时人们错误地认为自主学习是某些学生所达到的一种稳定状态。某些教师可能会自夸，他/她的学生都是自主学习的，这显得他们与普通学习者不同。事实是，自主学习往往来之不易，它的持久性也很难保障。在一个领域呈现高度自主学习的学生，在另一个领域并不一定能做到自主学习。

4. 自主学习的培养

自主学习可定义为掌控自己学习的能力，即学生要对自己的学习负责。这种学习模式就是所谓的以学生为中心的学习，学习的重心在于学生，而非教师。这一思想改变了传统的教学范式，使教学过程由侧重"教"转变到侧重"学"。自主学习者不只依赖于教师在课堂上的角色，学生必须设定自己的目标、策略和风格，做出决定并解决问题。教师的角色转变为引导者。同样，自主学习者通过将发散性及收敛性思维和特定求知领域的最小外部指导相结合来解决问题或发展新思想。也就是说，为了促进自主学习，课堂中"教"的功能应该被最小化。

在自主学习的课堂，老师不再是唯一拥有知识并解答问题的人。学生也有可能获得信息并给出满意的答案。通过应用这种学习方式，学习活动不必总是在学校进行，也可以在家里或室外的某个地方进行。然而，这并不意味着教师的角色不再重要。教师成为学习活动的组织者和引导者。他 / 她的角色不仅仅在于传授知识，更在于提高学生的自主学习意识。

培养自主学习能力，就是要转变并逐步将责任释放给学习者。在下面的学习模型（图6-1）中，道格拉斯·费雪和南希·弗雷深入探讨了逐步释放责任的教学框架的方法和原因。逐步释放责任是让学生具备他们所需要的积极参与和自我主导的学习能力。在日常教学中，它意味着有计划地融合四个基本且相互关联的教学阶段：

- 焦点教学：通过确立课程目标、建立策略和技能模型、有声思维和学生反应，为学生的学习做好准备。
- 引导教学：策略性地使用提示、线索和问题，引导学生提出新见解。
- 协作学习：让学生和同伴通过探索、解决问题、讨论和思考来巩固他们的理解。
- 自主学习：要求学生运用所学的技能和知识创造出真实的产品，并提出新的问题。

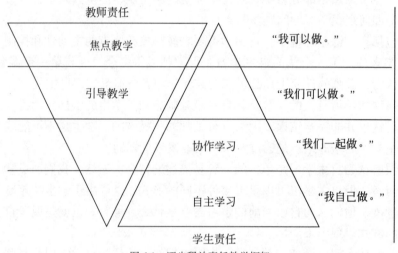

图 6-1　逐步释放责任教学框架

自主学习并非直接让教师免于掌管，而是让教师扮演指导者的角色。逐步形成自己学习策略的学生被称为反应性自主学习者。这是初始阶段，不久之后，当学生意识到要互相合作时，他们实际上已经表现出了他们的责任感。最终，教师可以轻松一点，学生会变得积极主动，有能力决定目标，计划学习策略，体验学习活动，并评估自己的进步。

Unit

7

Transfer of Learning

1. Introduction

Transfer of learning is the application of skills and knowledge learned in one context being applied in another context. The notion was originally introduced as transfer of practice by Edward Thorndike and Robert S. Woodworth. They explored how individuals would transfer learning in one context to another similar context—or how "improvement in one mental function" could influence a related one. Today, transfer of learning is usually described as the process and the effective extent to which past experiences (the transfer source) affect learning and performance in a new situation (the transfer target). Transfer of learning is one of the most important ideas in teaching and learning. As a teacher, we want our students to learn to make effective future use of what we are teaching. Every student can benefit by learning in a manner that supports integrating their new knowledge and skills into their current knowledge and skills. We want to help prepare student to make effective use of this expanded and integrated capability in dealing with problems, tasks, and decision-making they will encounter in the future.

2. Type 1 and Type 2 Transfer

Type 1 Transfer, i.e., Traditional Transfer, is the process of a person making use of his or her learned knowledge and skills in new environments and in new problem-solving and task-accomplishing situations. It is widely accepted that Type 1 Transfer of learning is one of the most fundamental and important ideas in learning. Through both informal and formal learning, people gain increased levels of expertise in a very wide range of areas. Some of the knowledge and skills that people gain are later reused—or, modified and reused—in dealing with both old and new problems, tasks, and other types of challenges that people encounter in the future.

Type 2 Transfer, i.e., Constructivism and Metacognition Transfer, is a process of building on and integrating new knowledge into previous knowledge. Physically, learning is a chemical and neuron growth process going on at the cellular level in the brain. In recent years, research in brain science has provided us with a substantial amount of new information about how a brain actually learns and uses its knowledge. We have learned about metacognition—Thinking about one's thinking. When learners become conscious of their thinking, they become aware of their strengths and the strategies that are useful to their own learning. That is, people can learn from their mistakes if they receive and appropriately understand feedback on their mistakes.

3. Near and Far Transfer

The Near Transfer of Learning Theory postulates that some problems and tasks are so nearly alike that transfer of learning occurs easily and naturally. A particular problem or task is studied and practiced to a high level of automaticity. When a nearly similar problem or task is encountered, it is automatically solved or accomplished with little or no conscious thought. Near Transfer is the direct application level of learning that involves a higher level of cognitive processing. That is, overlap exists between situations; original and transfer contexts are similar.

For example, a major goal in learning to read is to develop a high level of decoding automaticity. That is, one goal in reading instruction is to have students become very good at Near Transfer of the decoding component of reading. We want students to be able to do this with both fiction and non-fiction, texts in different subject areas, different fonts, different font sizes, different qualities of paper, and so on. This automaticity allows the conscious mind of a reader to focus on the meaning and implications of the material being read. A significant percentage of children are able to achieve this at a personally useful level by the end of the third grade.

However, many potential transfer of learning situations do not lend themselves to the automaticity approach of Near Transfer. There is little overlap between situations, that is, original and transfer target settings are dissimilar. These are Far Transfer situations. Far Transfer presents challenges for students due to the decrease in the degree of similarity and pragmatic relevance between the forms of original knowledge and target knowledge. The unfamiliarity of the target context, or a higher number of variables are involved. Far Transfer also requires more modification of the original knowledge than Near Transfer to adapt to the target transfer condition.

Take a simple example: suppose that a boy knows how to tie a bow knot in a pair of shoes he is wearing. The mother tells the boy to put on an apron and tie the strings in a bow knot behind his back. Many children have trouble with this transfer of learning, but some can do it easily. Thus, it can be a Far Transfer for some and a Near Transfer for others. People vary considerably in their abilities to see, feel, or sense similarities between different problem situations. In any particular problem-solving situation, some people seem to be innately much more able to do Far Transfer than others.

4. Low Road and High Road Transfer

The Low Road and High Road Transfer of Learning Theory was developed by David

Perkins and Gavriel Salomon. Low Road Transfer happens when stimulus conditions in the transfer context are sufficiently similar to those in a prior context of learning to trigger well-developed semi-automatic responses. These responses need not be mediated by external or mental representations. Low Road Transfer figures most often in Near Transfer. For example, when a person moving a household rents a small truck for the first time, the person finds that the familiar steering wheel, shift, and other features evoke useful car-driving responses. Driving the truck is almost automatic, although in small ways a different task.

High Road Transfer, in contrast, depends on mindful abstraction from the context of learning or application and a deliberate search for connections: What is the general pattern? What is needed? What principles might apply? What is known that might help? Such transfer is not in general reflexive. It demands time for exploration and the investment of mental effort. However, High Road Transfer can be accomplished easily, for instance, by bridging between contexts as remote as arteries and electrical networks or strategies of chess play.

5. Learning and Transfer

Bransford, Brown and Cocking identified four key characteristics of learning as applied to transfer. They are:

- The necessity of initial learning;
- The importance of abstract and contextual knowledge;
- The conception of learning as an active and dynamic process;
- The notion that all learning is transfer.

First, the necessity of initial learning for transfer specifies that mere exposure or memorization is not learning; there must be understanding. Learning as understanding takes time, such that expertise with deep, organized knowledge improves transfer. Teaching that emphasizes how to use knowledge or that improves motivation should enhance transfer.

Second, while knowledge anchored in context is important for initial learning, it is also inflexible without some level of abstraction that goes beyond the context. Practices to improve transfer include having students specify connections across multiple contexts or having them develop general solutions and strategies that would apply beyond a single-context case.

Third, learning should be considered an active and dynamic process, not a static product. Instead of one-shot tests that follow learning tasks, students can improve transfer by engaging in assessments that extend beyond current abilities. Improving transfer in this way requires instructor prompts to assist students—such as dynamic assessments—or student development of metacognitive skills without prompting.

Finally, the fourth characteristic defines all learning as transfer. New learning builds on previous learning, which implies that teachers can facilitate transfer by activating what students know and by making their thinking visible. This includes addressing student misconceptions and recognizing cultural behaviors that students bring to learning situations.

A student-learning centered view of transfer embodies these four characteristics. With this conception, teachers can help students transfer learning not just between contexts in academics, but also to common home, work, or community environments.

6. Enhancing Transfer Between School and Everyday Life

The ultimate goal of transfer is for students to generalize the knowledge they have learned in school to practical environments such as home, community, and workplace. The following guidelines can be followed to promote transfer to non-school environments.

Collaboration: Various studies have proven that much work outside of school is done in groups. Students need exposure to this type of collaborative work in order to better transfer knowledge to non-classroom environments.

Use of tools: Many school tasks require the use of the student mind whereas many non-classroom tasks allow and require the use of relevant tools. Increased student exposure to functional and relevant tools, such as technology, will only enhance transfer in the non-classroom setting.

Contextualized reasoning: Abstract reasoning is primarily reinforced in school, like the use of mathematical formulas. In settings outside of school, such as the grocery store, people often use contextualized reasoning to solve various problems. Many adults are able to choose either context-based or abstract-based reasoning to cater to their specific need. The implementation of strategies for both types of reasoning will provide students with the opportunity to develop equally and use interchangeably outside of the school environment.

New Words

notion ['nəʊʃən] n. 概念，观念

originally [ə'rɪdʒənəli] adv. 最初，起初；本来

capability [ˌkeɪpə'bɪləti] n. 才能，能力

encounter [ɪn'kaʊntə] v. 遭遇，邂逅；遇到

fundamental [ˌfʌndə'mentəl] adj. 基本的，根本的

expertise [ˌekspɜ:'ti:z] n. 专门知识；专门技术

modified ['mɒdɪfaɪd] adj. 改进的，修改的；改良的

neuron ['njʊərɒn] n. 神经元，神经单位

cellular ['seljʊlə] adj. 细胞的；由细胞组成的

substantial [səb'stænʃəl] a. 大量的；实质的

appropriately [ə'prəʊpriətli] adv. 适当地；合适地

postulate ['pɒstjuleɪt] v. 假定；认为

automaticity ['ɒtəmə'tɪsɪti] n. 自动，自动性

decode [ˌdi:'kəʊd] v. 解码

fiction ['fɪkʃən] n. 小说；虚构

font [fɒnt] n. 字体；字形

pragmatic [præg'mætɪk] adj. 实际的；实用主义的

relevance ['reləvəns] n. 关联；相关性

variable ['veərɪəbl] n. 变量；可变因素

apron ['eɪprən] *n.* 围裙

innately [ɪ'neɪtli] *adv.* 天赋地；与生俱来地

trigger ['trɪgə] *v.* 引发，引起；触发

deliberate [dɪ'lɪbərət] *adj.* 有意识的；深思熟虑的

reflexive [rɪ'fleksɪv] *adj.* 自发的

artery ['ɑ:təri] *n.* 动脉；干道

contextual [kən'tekstʃuəl] *adj.* 有情境的，有上下文的

inflexible [ɪn'fleksəbl] *adj.* 顽固的；不能转变的

specify ['spesɪfaɪ] *v.* 详细说明；指定

static ['stætɪk] *adj.* 静态的；静电的

one-shot ['wʌn-ʃɒt] *adj.* 只有一次的

embody [ɪm'bɒdi] *v.* 体现，使具体化

academics [ækə'demɪks] *n.* 学术，学术知识

collaboration [kə,læbə'reɪʃən] *n.* 合作；勾结

reinforce [,ri:ɪn'fɔ:s] *v.* 加强，强调

formula ['fɔ:mjələ] *n.* 公式；配方

interchangeably [ɪntə'tʃeɪndʒəbli] *adv.* 可交换地，可互换地

Phrases

transfer of learning 学习迁移

in a manner 在某种程度上；以这样的方式

build on 建立，以……为基础

Near Transfer 近迁移，相似性转移

Far Transfer 远迁移，差别性转移

bow knot 蝴蝶结

Low Road Transfer 低阶迁移，低径迁移

High Road Transfer 高阶迁移，高径迁移

steering wheel 方向盘

cater to 迎合；为……服务

font size 字体大小，字号

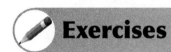

Exercises

Ex. 1 Give the English equivalents of the following Chinese expressions.

(1) 概念，观念　　　　_____

(2) 专门知识；专门技术　_____

(3) 反馈；回复　　　　_____

(4) 假定；认为　　　　_____

(5) 关联；相关性　　　_____

(6) 变量；可变因素　　_____

(7) 抽象；抽象概念　　_____

(8) 学习迁移　＿＿＿＿＿＿＿＿＿＿＿＿＿＿＿＿＿＿＿＿＿
(9) 近迁移，相似性转移　＿＿＿＿＿＿＿＿＿＿＿＿＿＿＿＿＿
(10) 高阶迁移，高径迁移　＿＿＿＿＿＿＿＿＿＿＿＿＿＿＿＿＿

Ex. 2　Explain the following terminologies in English.

(1) Type 1 Transfer　＿＿＿＿＿＿＿＿＿＿＿＿＿＿＿＿＿＿＿
(2) Type 2 Transfer　＿＿＿＿＿＿＿＿＿＿＿＿＿＿＿＿＿＿＿
(3) Near Transfer　＿＿＿＿＿＿＿＿＿＿＿＿＿＿＿＿＿＿＿＿
(4) Far Transfer　＿＿＿＿＿＿＿＿＿＿＿＿＿＿＿＿＿＿＿＿＿
(5) Low Road Transfer　＿＿＿＿＿＿＿＿＿＿＿＿＿＿＿＿＿＿
(6) High Road Transfer　＿＿＿＿＿＿＿＿＿＿＿＿＿＿＿＿＿

Ex. 3　Decide whether the following statements are true (T) or false (F) according to Text A. Give your reasons for the false ones.

(　　) (1) Transfer of learning is the process that past experiences affect learning and performance in a new situation.

(　　) (2) Type 1 Transfer, namely Traditional transfer, is not important in terms of learning.

(　　) (3) Type 2 Transfer, also called Constructivism Transfer, is a process of building on and integrating new knowledge into previous knowledge.

(　　) (4) Learning is a mental process without involvement of physical activities or chemical reactions.

(　　) (5) When Near Transfer happens, similarities exist between situations, that is, original and transfer contexts are similar.

(　　) (6) If there is little overlap between situations, transfer could not happen.

(　　) (7) High Road Transfer is almost the automatic transfer of knowledge from prior context to the new context.

(　　) (8) Exposure to or memorization of knowledge is a kind of learning.

(　　) (9) Having students specify connections across multiple contexts could help transfer of learning.

(　　) (10) The ultimate goal of transfer is for students to generalize the knowledge they have learned in school to practical environments such as home, community, and workplace.

Ex. 4　Fill in the blanks with the words given below.

within	positive	function	belief	educate
memorize	competencies	between	transfer	contexts

Processes of learning and the transfer of learning are central to understanding how people develop important (1)_____ learning is important because no one is born with the ability to (2)_____ competently as an adult in society. It is especially important to understand the kinds of learning experiences that lead to (3)_____, defined as the ability to extend what has been learned in one context to new (4)_____. Educators hope that students will transfer learning from one problem to another (5)_____ a course, from one year in school to another, (6)_____ school and home, and from school to workplace. Assumptions about transfer accompany the (7)_____ that it is better to broadly (8)"_____" people than simply "train" them to perform particular tasks. Some kinds of learning experiences result in effective memory but poor transfer; others produce effective memory plus (9)_____ transfer. Transfer is affected by the degree to which people learn with understanding rather than merely (10)_____ sets of facts or follow a fixed set of procedures.

Text B

Lessons for Life: Learning and Transfer

When students go out into the world and encounter new experiences, rarely will they have a manual telling them exactly what to do. They will need to draw on what they have learned before to solve new challenges. How do we teach them to transfer what they have learned from one situation to another? How can we teach them to use their knowledge in new ways? How can students use what they have learned by applying it to solve new problems? That is the challenge of transfer. Given the vast array of knowledge needed in life, the teacher's challenge is to determine what is the least amount of material that he or she can teach really well that will allow students to use the knowledge in the widest possible range of situations.

Transfer is the ability to extend what one has learned in one context to new contexts. In some sense, the whole point of school learning is to be able to transfer what is learned to a wide variety of contexts outside of school. Yet the ability to transfer information or ideas is not a given. Quite often, information learned in a specific way, or in a particular context, does not transfer to another. For example, students may memorize words for a quiz, but they cannot use the words in their writing. Students may learn mathematical facts, but they do not know how to apply these concepts when they are confronted with a different kind of problem outside of school. Students may conjugate verbs in a second language, but they cannot remember how to use them correctly in conversation.

If the ultimate goal of schooling is to help students transfer what they have learned in school to the everyday settings of home, community and work, we have much to learn from the non-school environments where people work. Studies conducted in places like U.S. ships, hospital emergency rooms, and dairy farms have found at least three contrasts between schools and everyday settings:

- School environments place more emphasis on individual work than most other environments, which tend to emphasize collaboration.

- School work tends to involve more "mental work", whereas everyday settings invest more in tools and technologies to solve problems.

- Abstract reasoning is emphasized in school, whereas contextualized reasoning is used more often in everyday settings.

The overall implication is that for effective transfer to take place, learning should be organized around the kinds of authentic problems and projects that are more often encountered in non-school settings. However, as we discuss below, overly contextualized reasoning can limit an individual's ability to transfer. It is thus important to provide opportunities for students to use knowledge in multiple contexts so that they can see how skills or problem-solving strategies can be generalized.

All new learning involves transfer to some extent; learning can be transferred from one problem to another, from one class to another, between home and school, and between school and the workplace. Specific transfer (also called Near Transfer) refers to the application of knowledge to a specific, very similar situation. For example, a student can add a string of numbers on a worksheet in the classroom and can also add a similar string of numbers in the grocery store. General transfer (also called Far Transfer) refers to the application of knowledge or general principles to a more complex, novel situation. An example of general transfer is a student who understands the principles of the scientific method applies them to design and conduct an experiment, to critique other experiments, and to test competing hypotheses in an area where he or she has developed content knowledge. General transfer is more broadly useful, and it is also more challenging to develop.

Researchers have found that a number of factors influence a learner's ability to understand or apply new knowledge:

First, the nature of the initial learning experience.

One factor that influences initial learning is whether students have learned something so that they understand it or whether they have simply memorized facts or procedures. For example, a student may memorize the properties of veins and arteries, but don't understand why these features are important. It makes difference between knowing that arteries are elastic in order to recognize the fact on a test and understanding that arteries are elastic and are thicker than veins because they must withstand the force of blood pumping in surges. Students who possess this deeper understanding of the original material—how and why arteries work as they do—are better equipped to transfer this initial knowledge to a new situation and grapple with this more complex problem.

The way in which teachers organize ideas and learning experiences is another factor that makes a difference in how deeply students understand. Understanding requires drawing connections and seeing how new ideas are related to those already learned—how they are alike and different. One way to facilitate learning with understanding is to offer "contrasting cases". Appropriately arranged contrasts can help people notice new features that previously escaped their attention and learn which features are relevant or irrelevant to a particular concept. For example, the concept of linear function becomes clearer when contrasted with nonlinear.

Second, the contexts for both the initial learning and the new situation.

Although students can transfer a great deal of knowledge into a learning situation, one of the primary goals of school is to help students transfer knowledge out to new situations. One kind of transfer occurs when people learn the parts of a task and then use those parts to do something much more complicated, just as football players do when they practice specific skills and then put them together into a new play. Another kind of transfer occurs when learners have to take what they have learned in one situation and apply it to a new situation at roughly the same level of complexity. For instance, if a student has learned about the notion of a revolution while studying U.S. history, he or she can transfer or apply the notion of revolution to the study of French history. Learners can transfer within a subject matter, as with the concept of revolution, as well as across subject matter areas.

Encouraging the transfer of knowledge out to new, more complex situations might involve asking students to study a particular problem in the classroom and then assigning a project that requires applying these understandings outside the classroom. For instance, students might take what they learn in the classroom about calculation and graphing and go to a nearby intersection to do a traffic flow study to determine whether an extra stop sign or stoplight is needed.

Third, the ability of learners to see similarities and differences across situations.

Part of the challenge of transfer is knowing when two situations share a fundamental structure and thus should trigger the use of a previously learned concept or principle. Teachers can help students use their knowledge across dissimilar situations in at least three ways:

- Provide a context for the subject matter;
- Capitalize on general principles;
- Encourage the understanding of structures that tie subject matter knowledge together.

These three instructional principles have all been found to influence learning and transfer.

In school settings, the ways in which teachers present ideas and engage students in working on them have a great deal to do with whether transfer of learning will later occur. Learning discrete, unconnected facts outside of a broader context reduces the likelihood that students will be able to remember and apply their knowledge later. Learning information that is never applied or put into practice also reduces the likelihood of later transfer. For instance, students will be less likely to remember the formula for volume if they memorize it than if they derive the formula themselves through the exploration and manipulation of substances encapsulated in different shaped containers.

It is also important to understand the central principles that apply across cases. Researchers have discovered that learners can be taught how to recognize when problems may share certain elements or similarities. Analogies are particularly powerful forms of representation that are instances of transfer in and of themselves since they require applying what one knows about one thing to another.

Fourth, learners' metacognitive abilities to reflect on and monitor their own learning.

Engaging learners in metacognitive activities—helping them become more aware of how to focus on critical ideas or features of problems, generate themes or procedures, and evaluate their own progress—can improve transfer and reduce the need for explicit prompting. Two general metacognitive questions learners can ask themselves to facilitate transfer are: "How is this problem like others I have solved before?" and "Does anything here remind me of anything I have learned earlier?"

Research on teaching in reading, writing, and mathematics has demonstrated how teaching self-monitoring strategies and helping students practice expert strategies can positively influence their ability to transfer to new situations. Students can be taught to ask themselves "How is this example or problem similar to or different from others I have encountered?" They can also be taught to apply certain thinking and performance strategies in multiple situations.

To conclude, learning is a process that takes place over time; it is influenced by learners' past experiences and current dispositions; it can be shaped by feedback and active self-monitoring of understanding, and it depends on access to resources for continued learning. In other words, transfer in its most powerful general form is the ability to apply a wide range of learning strategies to new learning situations.

New Words

manual ['mænjuəl] *n.* 手册，指南

challenge ['tʃæləndʒ] *n.* 挑战；质疑

conjugate ['kɒndʒugeɪt] *v.* 变形，变位

schooling ['skuːlɪŋ] *n.* 学校教育

setting ['setɪŋ] *n.* 环境，背景

abstract ['æbstrækt] *adj.* 抽象的；深奥的

contextualize [kən'tekstʃuəlaɪz] *vt.* 情景化，使……溶入背景

authentic [ɔː'θentɪk] *adj.* 真正的，真实的

generalize ['dʒenərəlaɪz] *v.* 推广；使……一般化

novel ['nɒvəl] *adj.* 新颖的，新奇的

critique [krɪ'tiːk] *v.* 批判；评论

hypotheses [haɪ'pɒθəsiːz] *n.* 假设；假定（hypothesis的复数）

property ['prɒpəti] *n.* 性质，性能

vein [veɪn] *n.* 血管

elastic [ɪ'læstɪk] *adj.* 有弹性的；易伸缩的

pump [pʌmp] *v.* 抽吸；泵送；抽运

surge [sɜːdʒ] *n.*（大量液体）汹涌；突然涌动

graphing [græfɪŋ] *n.* 绘制图形

intersection [ˌɪntə'sekʃən] *n.* 交叉；十字路口

discrete [dɪ'skriːt] *adj.* 离散的，不连续的

derive [dɪ'raɪv] *v.* 源于；得自；推导

manipulation [məˌnɪpju'leɪʃən] *n.* 操纵；操作；处理

encapsulate [ɪn'kæpsjuleɪt] *v.* 将……装入胶囊；将……封进内部

disposition [ˌdɪspə'zɪʃən] *n.* 性情，倾向，气质

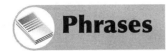 **Phrases**

draw on 利用；吸收

the vast array of 大量的

in some sense 在某种意义上，在某种程度上

be confronted with 面临，面对

emergency room 急诊室

to some extent 在一定程度上，在某种程度上

grapple with 努力克服；扭打

irrelevant to 与……不相关

linear function 线性函数，一次函数

capitalize on 利用

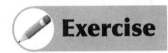 **Exercise**

Decide whether the following statements are true (T) or false (F) according to Text B. Give your reasons for the false ones.

(　　) (1) The challenge of transfer lies in how students can use what they have learned to solve new problems.

(　　) (2) The point of schooling is to teach students facts and theory.

(　　) (3) The skill to transfer information or ideas is a gifted ability.

(　　) (4) School environments place more emphasis on collaboration than most other environments, which tend to emphasize individual work.

(　　) (5) Abstract reasoning is emphasized in school, whereas contextualized reasoning is used more often in everyday settings.

(　　) (6) For effective transfer to take place, learning should be organized around the kinds of authentic problems and projects.

(　　) (7) Some learning involves transfer; some does not.

(　　) (8) Understanding knowledge usually requires drawing connections and seeing how new ideas are related to those already learned.

(　　) (9) Teaching students self-monitoring strategies can positively influence their ability to transfer to new situations.

(　　) (10) Learning transfer in its most powerful general form is the ability to apply a wide range of learning strategies to familiar learning situations.

Supplementary Reading

Text	Notes
Ten Ways to Improve Transfer of Learning	

Ten Ways to Improve Transfer of Learning

Whether you're a student or working professionally looking to keep your skills current, the importance of being able to transfer what you learn in one context to an entirely new one cannot be overstated[1]. Of course, the goal of any learning or training is to eventually be able to apply it in real-world situations, but a recent survey finds that 60% of employers don't believe recent graduates are well-prepared for their jobs.

[1] overstate *v.* 夸张，夸大

One possible reason for this is that memory is context dependent, so transferring or recalling something that was learned in a classroom setting to a fast-paced[2] work environment isn't always easy. Once you understand how to do about transferring your knowledge to new contexts, however, you could change jobs or even careers and still find ways to apply your prior knowledge to the situations and problems you might face in a new role.

[2] fast-paced *adj.* 快节奏的；快速的

With this in mind, here are some tips for taking what you learn in educational settings and applying it in the workplace and other areas of your life.

1. Focus on the Relevance[3] of What You're Learning

[3] relevance *n.* 关联；相关性

Research shows that when learning is relevant, students are able to connect what they're learning to what they have already known and build new neural connections and long-term memory storage. So if you want your learning to be engaging and be remembered in other contexts, it's important to establish relevance early on. Think about how you might apply what you're learning today in your future job or everyday life and then try to tie it to some of your short- or long-term goals.

For instance, if one of your long-term goals is to land a job in IT, focusing on how your course will help you reach that goal can make even the most tedious study material seem more engaging[4], because you understand that it's important to your future goals.

[4] engaging *adj.* 吸引人的；有趣的

2. Take Time to Reflect and Self-explain

Before you can transfer knowledge to new contexts, you need to understand the concept inside and out[5], which is why it's important to take time for reflection and self-explanation. Research shows that self-explanation can help you to identify any incorrect assumptions, lead to a deeper understanding of the material, and ultimately promote knowledge transfer. So when you're learning about something that's completely new to you, take a moment to think about how you would explain it in your own words, whether this means using simpler words that are easier for you to remember or finding a way to connect the new information to something you have already known by using real-world examples.

3. Use a Variety of Learning Media

Another way to facilitate the transfer of learning to new contexts is to use as many different learning media as possible, from text and imagery to video and audio. Research shows that using pictures, narration, and text can help prevent your cognitive resources from becoming overloaded[6] and improve learning transfer. One study found that learners who used relevant visuals were able to retain more information and scored higher on transfer tests than those who used only text. The researchers also perceived the content as easier to learn when visuals were used. Even if your course doesn't have visuals or narration built into it, you can try to find ways to supplement[7] what you're learning by using a variety of educational resources such as YouTube and TED Talks or iTunes U, EdX, and Coursera.

4. Change Things Up as Often as Possible

It's easy to get stuck in a rut[8] with your learning by studying around the same time, in the same location, and using the same study strategies every day. However, when you get used to constantly studying in the same way, it can be difficult to transfer the knowledge you acquire to new environments and situations. Research shows that organizing your learning in a more random way improves retention[9] and transfer after (but not during) the training. Therefore, although studying in different environments and conditions may initially make it

[5] inside and out 从内到外地；彻底地

[6] overload v. 超载，超过负荷

[7] supplement v. 增补，补充

[8] get stuck in a rut 墨守成规

[9] retention n. 保留；记忆力

harder to remember what you're learning, in the long run it will help you retain the information more effectively. This concept is known as desirable difficulties, because although introducing certain difficulties into the learning process will initially feel uncomfortable, it also encourages a deeper processing of materials.

5. Identify Any Gaps[10] in Your Knowledge

Without a complete understanding of the concept or information you're learning, transferring it to new contexts will be more difficult. With this in mind, it's important to identify any gaps in your knowledge and then work on strengthening your weaker areas. One excellent way to do this is through practice testing, as you'll be able to see exactly what types of questions you're getting wrong and what topics you have to master. Similarly, practice tests will also show you which topics you have already mastered, which allows you to focus on the areas that need the most work.

[10] **gap** *n.* 缺口；差距

6. Establish Clear Learning Goals

Establishing clear learning goals will give you a better understanding of what you're trying to get out of your learning and how you might later transfer that knowledge and apply it in your work or personal life. If you know what the expected learning outcomes are, you'll also be able to focus on the right material. When setting learning goals, it's better to be specific rather than general, so you'll be able to measure your progress as you go along, but make sure your goals are realistic. For example, if you're learning a new language, making it your goal to be fluent within one month is not very realistic. Making it your goal to learn the vocabulary and phrases necessary to go shopping or eat out at a restaurant is more doable, however.

7. Practice Generalizing

Generalizing is the ability to transfer the knowledge or skills you gain in one setting to a new one. It's all about seeing the bigger picture and looking for more widely applicable rules, ideas, or principles. For example, a child that learns to stack wooden blocks could generalize that skill and later use it to build more elaborate creations using Lego bricks[11]. So when studying a new topic or concept, think about your past

[11] **Lego bricks** 乐高积木

lessons or experiences and look for patterns and relationships. You can then determine whether these generalizations can be supported by other evidence you know.

8. Make Your Learning Social

If much of your learning happens when you're alone, it can help to have a chance to discuss it with others. This gives you the opportunity to explain what you're learning in your own words and apply your knowledge to new situations. Research shows that collaborative learning promotes engagement and benefits long-term retention. Even if you're not learning on the job or in a group setting, you can try online learning tools like Twitter, Blackboard, Edmodo, Quora, and others.

9. Use Analogies[12] and Metaphors[13]

Analogies and metaphors are great for drawing on your prior knowledge or experience and making associations between seemingly unrelated ideas. Therefore, when learning something new and trying to connect it to something you already know, it can help to think of appropriate analogies or metaphors. Analogies compare two things and show how they are similar, such as "It was as light as a feather" or "He was solid as a rock." A metaphor is a figure of speech[14] that describes something in a way that isn't literally true but helps to explain an idea or make a stronger impact, such as "Love is a battlefield.".

10. Find Daily Opportunities to Apply What You've Learned

Applying what you've learned at school to real-world problems takes a lot of practice, so it's important to look for opportunities to apply what you're learning in your everyday life. For example, if you have been studying a new language, make a conscious effort to remember the foreign names of different objects around the house when you get up in the morning. If you just attended a customer service training course, try to employ one of the new strategies you learned when dealing with customers on your first day back at work.

Not sure how to start applying what you have learned in your job or everyday life? You need go back and check your learning goals to remind yourself of what you set out to learn.

[12] analogy *n.* 类比；比喻

[13] metaphor *n.* 暗喻，隐喻

[14] figure of speech 修辞手法

参考译文（Text A）

学 习 迁 移

1. 引言

学习迁移是指将在一个情境中学习到的技能和知识应用到另一个情境中。这个概念最初是由爱德华·桑代克和罗伯特·伍德沃斯作为"实践迁移"而提出的。他们探索了个体如何将在一种情境下的所学转移到另一种类似的情境中，或"一种心理功能的改善"如何影响另一种相关的心理功能。如今，学习迁移通常被描述为过去的经验（迁移源）在新情况下（迁移目标）影响学习和绩效的过程和有效程度。学习迁移是教与学的重要思想之一。作为一名教师，我们希望学生在将来能够有效地利用我们所教的知识。每个学生都可以通过将新知识和技能融入已有的知识和技能而受益。我们希望帮助学生有效地利用这种拓展的、综合的能力来处理将来遇到的问题、任务和决策。

2. 一类迁移和二类迁移

第一类转移，即传统的迁移，是指一个人在新的环境中，在解决新问题和完成新任务时，利用所学的知识和技能的过程。一类迁移是学习过程中最基本、最重要的思想之一，这一点已被广泛接受。通过正式和非正式的学习，人们在非常广泛的领域获得了更高水平的专业知识。人们获得的一些知识和技能以后会再次用到，或者说，将来在应对遇到的新老问题、任务和其他挑战时——会被改良并再次使用。

第二类迁移，即建构主义和元认知迁移，是在原有知识的基础上构建和整合新知识的过程。从物理层面讲，学习是大脑细胞层面的化学和神经元生长过程。近年来，脑科学的研究为我们提供了大量关于大脑如何学习和使用知识的新信息。我们了解了元认知——即对自己思维的思考。当学习者领悟到自己的思维时，他们就能意识到自己的优势和对自己学习有用的策略。也就是说，如果人们接受并恰当地理解其错误的教训，他们便可以从错误中获取经验。

3. 近迁移和远迁移

近迁移学习理论认为，由于一些问题和任务非常相似，学习迁移会很容易、很自然地发生，即一个特定的问题或任务被学习和练习到高度的自动性。当遇到相似的问题或任务时，会自动地解决或完成这个问题，而不需要有意识的思考。近迁移是涉及更高层次认知加工学习的直接应用。也就是说，情景之间存在重叠，原情景与迁移情景是相似的。

例如，阅读的一个重要目标是发展高水平的自动解码能力。也就是说，阅读教学的一个目标就是让学生在阅读中变得非常擅长解码成分的近迁移。对于小说和非小说，不同学科领域的文本、不同的字体、不同的字号、不同的纸张等，我们希望学生都能自动解码。这种自动性使读者的意识集中在阅读材料的意义和内涵上。绝大多数儿童能够在三年级结束时达到这个对他们本人有用的水平。

然而，许多潜在的学习情境的迁移并不适用近迁移的自动性方式。场景之间几乎没有重叠，即原始情景和迁移的目标情景并不相似，这就是远迁移的情形。由于原有知识与目标知识之间的相似度和实用相关性降低，远迁移给学生带来了挑战。因为对目标情景不熟悉，或涉及更多的变量，为了适应目标迁移条件，和近迁移相比，远迁移需要对原有知识进行更多的改进。

举个简单的例子，假设一个男孩已经知道如何在鞋子上打蝴蝶结。妈妈会让男孩穿上围裙，在背后打一个蝴蝶结。许多孩子在这个学习迁移上有困难，但有些孩子可以很容易地做到。因此，对一些人来说，这可能是一个远转移，而对另一些人来说，这可能是一个近转移。在不同的问题情境中，人们在观察、触摸或感觉的能力上有很大的差异。在特定的解决问题的场景中，有些人似乎天生就比其他人更有能力做到远迁移。

4. 低通路迁移和高通路迁移

学习理论的低通路迁移和高通路迁移是由大卫·帕金斯和加夫列尔·所罗门发展起来的。当迁移情境中的刺激条件与先前学习情境中的刺激条件足够相似时，就会发生低通路迁移，从而触发良好的半自动反应。这些反应不需要由外部或心理表征来调节。低通路迁移往往出现于近迁移情形下。例如，当一个人搬家时要第一次租用一辆小卡车，熟悉的方向盘、挡位和其他功能会唤起有用的驾车反应。驾驶卡车几乎是自动的，尽管在某些小方面是一个不同的任务。

相反，高通路迁移需要对学习或应用的情景进行有意识的抽象，并仔细寻求其关联：通用模式是什么？需要什么？哪些原则可能适用？哪些已知信息可能会有帮助？这种迁移一般不是自发的，它需要时间去探索并且投入脑力。然而，通过将一些貌似遥远的情景关联起来，如动脉与电网或棋艺，高通路迁移也可以轻易地完成。

5. 学习和迁移

布兰斯福德、布朗和科金确定了关于学习迁移的四个关键特征，分别为：

- 初始学习的必要性；
- 抽象和语境知识的重要性；
- 学习是一个主动的、动态的过程观念；
- 所有学习都是迁移的观念。

首先，就迁移而言，初始学习的必要性强调，仅仅接触或记忆不是学习，必须要理解。理解性的学习需要时间，所以有深度的、有组织的专业知识能够促进迁移。注重如何应用知识或提高动机的教学会增强迁移。

其次，基于某个情景的知识对于初始学习很重要，但如果没有更高层次的抽象来超越那个情景，知识是没有灵活性的。增强迁移的练习包括让学生指出多个情景之间的关联，或者让他们设计出通用的、不仅限于某一个情景的解决方案和策略。

再次，学习应是一个积极和动态的过程，而不是静态的。学生可以通过参与超出现有能力的评估来提高迁移能力，而不是在学习任务之后进行一次性测试。以这种方式促进迁移需要教师的鼓励来帮助学生——比如动态评估——或者让学生在没有提示的情况下发展元认知技能。

最后，第四个特征将所有学习定义为迁移。新学习建立在以前的学习基础上，这意味着教师可以通过激活学生已有的知识并使他们的思维具体化来促进迁移。这包括纠正学生的误解并认可学生带到学习情境中的文化行为。

以学生学习为中心的迁移观体现了这四个特点。有了这个观念，教师不仅可以帮助学生在不同的学术环境中学习，还可以帮助他们在普通家庭、工作或社区环境中学习。

6. 加强学校与日常生活之间的迁移

迁移的最终目的是让学生把学校学到的知识延伸到实际的环境中，如家庭、社区和工作场所。以下措施可以促进学习迁移到非学校环境。

合作。各种研究证明，很多校外工作都是以小组的形式完成的。学生需要接触这种合作性工作，以便更好地将知识迁移到非课堂环境。

使用工具。许多的学校任务要求学生使用思维，而许多非课堂任务允许并要求学生使用相关工具。增加学生对功能性相关工具（如技术）的接触，会增强非课堂环境中知识的迁移。

情境推理。抽象推理是学校教育的重点，如数学公式的使用。在校外的环境，比如杂货店中，人们经常使用情境推理来解决各种问题。许多成年人能够选择情景推理或抽象推理来满足他们的特定需求。这两种推理策略的实施可为学生提供在校外环境中均衡发展和交替使用这两种推理的机会。

Unit

8

Text A

How the Internet Changes How We Learn

In this century, online learning will constitute 50% of all education. The rapid rise of learning on the Internet will occur not because it is more convenient, cheaper, or faster, but because cognitive learning on the Internet is better than learning in person. Interactive, online learning will revolutionize education. The education revolution will have as profound and as far-reaching an effect upon the world as the invention of printing. Not only will it affect where we learn, it will also influence how we learn and what we learn. Recent research shows that online learning is equally as effective as learning in person. When online learning is combined with a more interactive and facilitative in-person learning, it will easily outperform today's outmoded one-size-fits-all traditional lecture delivery system.

1. How We Learn Today

For most of history the standard educational setting has been an instructor standing in front of a group of people. This is the most common learning design in society, whether it be for college credit classes, non-credit courses, training in business and industry, high school instruction, or even a Sunday school class.

Basically, 90% of all education has been "information transfer", the process of transferring information and knowledge from the teacher's head into the heads of the learners. To do that, teachers have had to talk most of the time. Right up until today, that mode of delivery has been the most effective, most efficient, most desirable way to learn.

However, as educators we know that the traditional lecture is not the only way to learn. Learners learn in many different ways, at different times, and from a variety of sources. We also know that learning is not purely a cognitive process, but that it also involves the emotions and even the spirit.

The Internet is destroying the traditional educational delivery system of an instructor speaking, lecturing or teaching in front of one or more learners. What the Internet is doing is to explode the traditional method of teaching into two parts—cognitive learning, which can be accomplished better with online learning, and affective learning, which can be accomplished better in a small group discussion setting.

2. Why Cognitive Learning Can Be Done Better on the Internet

Cognitive learning includes facts, data, knowledge, and mental skills, which can be achieved faster, cheaper and better online. Online learning has advantages over classroom learning in the following aspects.

A learner can learn during his or her peak learning time. The peak learning time of learner A is from 10 am to noon, but learner B's peak time may be between midnight and 3 am. With traditional in-person classes, only some learners will be involved during their peak learning time. The rest will not fully benefit.

A learner can learn at his or her own speed. With traditional classes, a learner has one chance to hear a concept, technique or piece of knowledge. With online learning, a learner can replay a portion of audio, reread a unit, review a video, and retest him or herself.

A learner can focus on specific content areas. With traditional classes, each content area is covered and given the relative amount of emphasis and time that the teacher deems appropriate. However, in a ten-unit course, a given learner will not need to focus on each unit equally. For each of us, there will be some units we know already, and somewhere we have little knowledge. With online learning, we as learners can focus more time, attention and energy on those units, modules or sections of the course where we need the most help and learning.

A learner can test him or herself daily. With online learning, a learner can take quizzes and tests easily, instantly receiving the results and finding out how well he or she is doing in a course.

A learner can interact more with the teacher. Contrary to common opinion today, online learning is more personal and more interactive than traditional classroom courses. In an online course, the instructor only has to create the information transfer once, i.e., lectures, graphics, texts, videos. Once the course units or modules have been developed, there is need only for revisions later on. The instructor is then free to interact with participants in the course.

A learner can acquire the data and facts faster using the Internet. Officials at University Online Publishing, which has been involved in online learning more than most organizations, say that a typical 16-week college course, for example, can be cut to 8 weeks because students learn more quickly online.

Finally, technology has consistently been proven to drive down costs. Recent reports indicate that education costs are growing at over 5% each year, well above the 3% average for all other sectors of the economy. With education costs in the traditional system soaring, technological innovations promise the ability to deliver an education more cheaply.

3. More Interaction Occurs with Online Learning

The heart and soul of an online course will not be the lecture, the delivery, the audio or video. Rather, it will be the interaction between the participants and the teacher, as well as the interaction among the participants themselves. This daily interaction among participants, for example, will form a "Virtual Community".

Because of the instructor's need to convey information, the time able to be devoted to questions is very short. In an online course, everyone can ask questions, as many questions as each learner wants or needs. In an online course, there is more discussion. Every person can make comments at the same time. A transcript of a typical online discussion would take hours to give verbally. Online, we can participate in discussions easily, absorbing more information in a much shorter time and engaging in more interaction.

4. How the Internet Changes In-person Learning

Because the Internet can deliver information more quickly, at a lower cost, whenever a learner wants, as often as a learner wants, and with more interaction and dialogue, the Internet will replace the traditional in-person classroom delivery system as the dominant mode of delivery for education and delivery. However, the Internet will not replace in-person learning.

While we will spend 50% of our time learning online, we will spend the other 50% of our time learning in person. However, in-person learning will also be radically different from what is most common today. There will be almost no need for the traditional lecture. Instead, there will be a tremendous need for teachers to become facilitators of learning, understanding how we learn, and working with learners as individuals. The sage on the stage will become the guide on the side.

Though part of learning is centered around content, we as educators know that more of learning is dependent on the learner as an individual, a person. Learning is not just cognitive; it also involves the emotions and the spirit. It involves "unlearning". It involves "grieving the loss of old ideas".

The likely format for this kind of learning will be chairs in a circle, with a facilitator leading discussions, dialogues, role plays and more. This kind of learning has been around for a long time and its value well-established. Its use will grow exponentially because the Internet allows the cognitive information to be delivered faster, cheaper, better, thus allowing more time and resources to be devoted to facilitative in-person learning.

As online courses grow and change how we learn, some courses will involve almost all in-person learning and teaching. Meanwhile some courses will involve almost all online learning. Probably the majority of courses will involve both online learning and in-person learning.

5. What an Online Course Looks Like

A typical online course or the online portion of course, looks like this:
- There will be hundreds of thousands of topics from which to choose.
- Your online teacher will probably be the foremost authority in the subject in the world.

- There will be learners from all around the world.
- There will be an average of 1,000 learners in a course.

6. Conclusion

Online learning is rapidly becoming recognized as a valid learning delivery system. The number of part-time students in higher education now outnumbers full-time students. Each college or university is offering online courses. Online graduate programs and certificate programs have doubled over the last years. Online learning has grown exponentially in the business sector.

Online learning will do for society what the tractor did for food. A century ago food was expensive, in limited supply, and with very little variety. Today food is relatively cheap, in great supply in our society, and with tremendous variety. The Internet will do the same for education. More people will be able to learn more, for much less cost, and with a tremendous variety in choice of topics and subjects. It is something that societies of the past could only dream about. It will come true for us in a very short time.

 **New Words**

interactive [ˌɪntər'æktɪv] *adj.* 交互式的；互动的

revolutionize [ˌrevə'luːʃənaɪz] *v.* 发动革命；彻底改革

profound [prə'faʊnd] *adj.* 深厚的；意义深远的

far-reaching [fɑː-'riːtʃɪŋ] *adj.* 深远的；影响深远的

facilitative [fə'sɪlɪˌteɪtɪv] *adj.* 使便利的；促进的

outperform [ˌaʊtpə'fɔːm] *v.* 胜过；做得比……好

outmoded [ˌaʊt'məʊdɪd] *adj.* 过时的，不流行的

delivery [dɪ'lɪvəri] *n.* 讲课；演讲

peak [piːk] *adj.* 峰值的，高峰的

deem [diːm] *v.* 认为，视作

module ['mɒdjuːl] *n.* 课程模块

revision [rɪ'vɪʒən] *n.* 修正；修订

soar [sɔː] *v.* 高飞，猛增

facilitator [fə'sɪlɪteɪtə] *n.* 引导者；导师；促进者

sage [seɪdʒ] *n.* 圣人；贤人

exponentially [ˌekspə'nenʃəli] *adv.* 以指数方式

outnumber [ˌaʊt'nʌmbə] *v.* 比……多；数字上超过

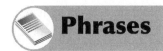 **Phrases**

---

one-size-fits-all 一刀切的，通用的
contrary to 与……相反，背道而驰

heart and soul 灵魂，全心全意
virtual community 虚拟社区

 Exercises

Ex. 1 Give the English equivalents of the following Chinese expressions.

(1) 交互式的；互动的 _____

(2) 胜过；做得比……好 _____

(3) 课程模块 _____

(4) 高飞，猛增 _____

(5) 引导者；导师 _____

(6) 圣人；贤人 _____

(7) 一刀切的，通用的 _____

(8) 与……相反，背道而驰 _____

(9) 灵魂，全心全意 _____

(10) 虚拟社区 _____

Ex. 2 Decide whether the following statements are true (T) or false (F) according to Text A. Give your reasons for the false ones.

( ) (1) The chief reason of rapid rise of online learning is that it is more convenient, cheaper, and faster.

( ) (2) Online learning is not as effective as learning in person.

( ) (3) When online learning is combined with interactive and facilitative in-person learning, it will easily outperform the traditional lecture delivery system.

( ) (4) Learning is not purely a cognitive process; it also involves the emotions and the spirit.

( ) (5) Cognitive learning can be accomplished better with online learning, while affective learning can be accomplished better in a small group discussion setting.

( ) (6) Early morning is the peak learning time for all learners.

( ) (7) The heart and soul of an online course is the lecture, the delivery, the audio or video.

( ) (8) Online learning will replace in-person learning some day.

( ) (9) The teachers should transform from the sage on the stage to the guide on the side.

(   ) (10) Online learning is rapidly becoming recognized as a valid learning delivery system.

Ex. 3 **Answer the following questions according to Text A.**

(1) Why is online learning becoming increasingly popular?

(2) Which mode is more important, online learning or in-person learning?

(3) How is Internet changing the way of our learning?

(4) Why could cognitive learning be done better on the Internet?

(5) Will more interactions occur with online learning? Why?

(6) Will online learning replace in-person learning? Why or why not?

(7) What does an online course look like?

(8) What is the trend of online learning in the higher education sector?

Ex. 4 **Fill in the blanks with the words given below.**

offered	schedule	degrees	dissimilarities	full-time
present	nontraditional	alternative	delivered	liberates

Online education is a type of educational instruction that is (1)_____ via the internet to students using their home computers. During the last decade, online courses and (2)_____ have become popular alternative for a wide range of (3)_____ students, including those who want to continue working (4)_____ or raising families. Most of the time, online degree programs and courses are (5)_____ via the host school's online learning platform, although some are delivered using (6)_____ technologies. Although there are subtle (7)_____, the main difference between online and traditional learning is the fact that online education (8)_____ the student from the usual trappings of on-campus degree programs—including driving to school, planning their (9)_____ around classes, and being physically (10)_____ for each sequence of their coursework.

Text B

Pitfalls of Online Learning

While online programs have significant strengths and offer unprecedented accessibility to quality education, there are weaknesses inherent in the use of this medium that can pose potential threats to the success of any online program. These problems fall into six main categories.

1. Technology

- Equity and accessibility to technology

Before any online program hopes to succeed, it must have students who are able to access the online learning environment. Lack of access whether it be for economical or logistics reasons will exclude otherwise eligible students from the course. This is a significant issue in rural and lower socioeconomic neighborhoods. Furthermore, speaking from an administrative point of view, if students cannot afford the technology the institution employs, they are lost as customers. As far as internet accessibility is concerned, it is not universal, and in some areas, internet access poses a significant cost to the user. If the participants' time online is limited by the amount of internet access they can afford, then instruction and participation in the online program will not be equitable for all students in the course.

- Computer literacy

Both students and facilitators must possess a minimum level of computer knowledge in order to function successfully in an online environment. For example, they must be able to use a variety of search engines and be comfortable navigating on the World Wide Web, as well as be familiar with Newsgroups, FTP procedures and email. If they do not possess these technology tools, they will not succeed in an online program; a student or faculty member who cannot function on the system will drag the entire program down.

- Limitations of technology

User friendly and reliable technology is critical to a successful online program. However, even the most sophisticated technology is not 100% reliable. Breakdowns can occur at any point along the system. For example, the server which hosts the program could crash and cut all participants off from the class; a participant may access the class through a networked computer which could go down; individual PCs can have numerous problems which could limit students' access; finally, the Internet connection could fail, or the institution hosting the connection could become bogged down with users and either slow down, or fail all together. In situations like these, the technology is neither seamless nor reliable and it can detract from the learning experience.

2. The Students

While an online method of education can be a highly effective alternative medium of education for the mature, self-disciplined students, it is an inappropriate learning environment for more dependent learners. Online asynchronous education gives students control over their learning experience, and allows for flexibility of study schedules for non-traditional students. However, this places a greater responsibility on the student. In order to successfully participate in an online program, students must be well organized, self-motivated, and possess a high degree of time management skills in order to keep up with the pace of the course. For these reasons, online education is not appropriate for younger students (i.e., elementary or secondary school age), and other students who are dependent learners and have difficulty assuming responsibilities required by the online paradigm.

3. The Facilitator

Successful on-ground instruction does not always translate to successful online instruction. If facilitators are not properly trained in online delivery and methodologies, the success of the online program will be compromised. An instructor must be able to communicate well in writing and in the language in which the course is offered. An online program will be weakened if its facilitators are not adequately prepared to function in the Virtual Classroom.

An online instructor must be able to compensate for the lack of physical presence by creating a supportive environment in the Virtual Classroom where all students feel comfortable participating and especially where students know that their instructor is accessible. Failure to do this can alienate the class both from each other and from the instructor. However, even if a virtual professor is competent enough to create a comfortable virtual environment in which the class can operate, still the lack of physical presence at an institution can be a limitation for an online program. For the faculty as well as the participants, such things as being left out of meetings and other events that require on-site interaction could present a limiting factor in an online program.

4. The Administration and Faculty

Some environments are disruptive to the successful implementation of an online program. Administrators and/or faculty members who are uncomfortable with change and working with technology or feel that online programs cannot offer quality education often inhibit the process of implementation. These people represent a considerable weakness in an online program because they can inhibit its success.

Sometimes administration cannot see beyond the bottom line and look at online programs only as ways to increase revenues and are thus not committed to seeing online programs as a means of providing quality education to people who would otherwise not be able to access it. In such a case, an institution that is not aware of the importance of proper facilitator training, essential facilitator characteristics, and limitations of class size would not understand the impact that these elements can have on the success of an online program.

5. The Online Environment

- Levels of synergy

Online learning has its most promising potential in the high synergy represented by active dialog among the participants, one of the most important sources of learning in a Virtual Classroom. However, in larger classes (20 or more students), the synergy level starts to shift on the learning continuum until it eventually becomes independent study to accommodate the large class. At this point, dialog is limited as well as interaction among participants and the facilitator. The medium is not being used to its greatest potential.

- What should not be taught online

In the excitement and enthusiasm for online programs that has been generated recently, it is important to recognize that some subjects should not be taught online because the electronic medium in its current state of development does not permit the best method on instruction. Examples are hands-on subjects such as public speaking, surgery, dental hygiene, and sports where physical movement and practice contribute to the achievement of the learning objectives. These subjects are probably best taught in a face-to-face traditional learning environment. Hybrid courses may represent a temporary solution to this problem thus making that portion of the course more accessible to a greater number of people who would otherwise have difficulty getting to campus. However, solutions of that sort still underline the fact that online teaching cannot satisfy all educational needs and goals. Just because it may be technologically possible to simulate a physical learning experience, this does not necessarily mean that it is the best way to teach it.

6. The Curriculum

The curriculum of any online program must be carefully considered and developed in order to be successful. Many times, in an institution's haste to develop distance education programs, the importance of the curriculum and the need for qualified professionals to develop it is overlooked. Curriculum and teaching methodology that are successful in on-ground instruction will not always translate to a successful online program where learning and instructional paradigms are quite different. Online curriculum must reflect the use of dialog among students, and group interaction and participation. Traditional classroom lectures have no place in a successful online program. Education of the highest quality can and will occur in an online program provided that the curriculum has been developed or converted to meet the needs of the online medium.

Today is a very exciting time for technology and education. Online programs offer technology-based instructional environments that expand learning opportunities and can provide top quality education through a variety of formats and modalities. With the special needs of adult learners who need or want to continue their education, online programs offer a convenient solution to conflicts with work, family and study schedules. Institutions of higher education have found that online programs are essential in providing access to education for the populations they wish to serve. In order for an online program to be successful, the curriculum, the facilitator, the technology and the students must be carefully considered and balanced in order to take full advantage of the strengths of this format and at the same time, avoid pitfalls that could result from its weaknesses.

 **New Words**

pitfall ['pɪtfɔ:l] n. 陷阱；误区，易犯的错误	eligible ['elɪdʒəbl] adj. 合格的；符合条件的
unprecedented [ʌn'presɪdentɪd] adj. 空前的；无前例的	administrative [əd'mɪnɪstrətɪv] adj. 管理的，行政的
accessibility [əkˌsesə'bɪləti] n. 易接近；可访问性	equitable ['ekwɪtəbl] adj. 公平的，公正的
logistics [lə'dʒɪstɪks] n. 后勤；物流	navigate ['nævɪgeɪt] v. 导航；航海；浏览
otherwise ['ʌðəwaɪz] adv. 原本，本来	breakdown ['breɪkdaʊn] n. 故障；崩溃
	server ['sɜ:və] n. 服务器

self-disciplined [self -'dɪsəplɪnd] *adj.* 有自我约束力的；自律的

asynchronous [eɪ'sɪŋkrənəs] *adj.* 异步的；不同时的

flexibility [ˌfleksə'bɪləti] *n.* 灵活性；弹性

on-ground [ɒn-graʊnd] *adj.* 面对面的

methodology [ˌmeθə'dɒlədʒi] *n.* 方法，方法论

compromise ['kɒmprəmaɪz] *v.* 妥协；危害

accessible [ək'sesəbl] *adj.* 易接近的；可访问的

alienate ['eɪliəneɪt] *v.* 使疏远，离间

administration [əd,mɪnɪ'streɪʃən] *n.* 管理，行政；行政管理机关

disruptive [dɪs'rʌptɪv] *adj.* 破坏的；制造混乱的

implementation [ˌɪmplɪmen'teɪʃən] *n.* 实现；履行

inhibit [ɪn'hɪbɪt] *v.* 抑制；禁止

revenue ['revənju:] *n.* 税收收入；财政收入；收益

synergy ['sɪnədʒi] *n.* 协同，协同作用；协作

hybrid ['haɪbrɪd] *adj.* 混合的；杂种的

simulate ['sɪmjuleɪt] *v.* 模拟；模仿；假装

curriculum [kə'rɪkjuləm] *n.* 课程；课程体系

haste [heɪst] *n.* 匆忙；急忙；轻率

convert [kən'vɜ:t] *v.* 转变；转换

modality [məʊ'dæləti] *n.* 形式，形态；模态

Phrases

computer literacy 计算机素养；电脑知识

search engine 搜索引擎

at any point 在任何时候

go down（电脑）出故障

bog down 停顿；陷入困境

Virtual Classroom 虚拟教室；虚拟课堂

compensate for 赔偿，补偿

be committed to 致力于；委身于；以……为己任

dental hygiene 牙齿卫生；口腔卫生学

provided that 如果；条件是；倘若

result from 起因于；由……造成

Exercise

Answer the following questions according to Text B.

(1) What are the pitfalls of online learning in terms of technology?

(2) What kinds of students is online education not appropriate for?

(3) What quality should an online instructor possess?

(4) What are the pitfalls of online learning in terms of administration and faculty?

(5) Under what conditions could online learning have its most promising potential?

(6) What subjects are not appropriate for online education?

(7) Could the curriculum and pedagogy of on-ground instruction be easily converted to online program? Why or why not?

(8) In order for an online program to be successful, what factors should educators take into consideration?

 Supplementary Reading

Text	Notes
Ten Things to Know About MOOCs A massive open online course (MOOC) is an online course aimed at unlimited participation and open access via the web. In addition to traditional course materials such as filmed[1] lectures, readings, and problem sets, many MOOCs provide interactive courses with user forums[2] to support community interactions among students, professors, and teaching assistants as well as immediate feedback to quick quizzes and assignments. MOOCs, as a recent and widely researched development in distance education, were first introduced in 2006 and emerged as a popular mode of learning in 2012. Anybody with internet can audit[3] university classes through MOOCs. These courses are often partnerships between universities and providers such as edX or Coursera, though others exist. MOOCs have evolved in the past few years. Here are 10 things to know about these courses. 1. MOOCs Can Be Accessed for Free. When MOOCs gained momentum[4] in 2011, their creators were "more motivated by providing opportunities for learning to individuals who could not otherwise access that learning", says Ray Schroeder, vice chancellor[5] for online learning at the University of Illinois—Springfield[6]. That remains a function of MOOCs, he says, but not the only function. Still, in most cases, anybody can audit a MOOC at no charge.	[1] film *v.* 录制；摄制电影 [2] forum *n.* 论坛，讨论会 [3] audit *v.* 旁听；审计 [4] momentum *n.* 势头；动力 [5] chancellor *n.* 校长；总理 [6] University of Illinois—Springfield 伊利诺伊大学春田分校

2. Many Are Launched with Universities.

Because edX and Coursera partner with top universities to develop MOOCs, students learn from distinguished[7] professors, adding to MOOCs' legitimacy. "These are faculty members who have taught online, who have taught in many cases for quite a few years," Schroeder says.

[7] distinguished *adj.* 著名的；卓著的

3. A Lot of MOOCs Now Offer Paid Credentials[8].

Though MOOCs can be free, Coursera and edX offer paid "verified certificates" for successful completion. Students must pass assessments and prove their identities. Employers can confirm certificates online. "We see a larger and larger number of our learners, especially in courses that confer[9] direct benefits—for instance, to one's career—opting[10] to pay for the certificate," Daphne Koller, president and co-founder of Coursera, told U.S. News.

[8] credential *n.* 证书；文凭

[9] confer *v.* 授予；给予
[10] opt *v.* 选择

4. Paying for a MOOC Provides Extra Features[11].

Along with a credential, students who pay for MOOCs often gain access to extra features. "In many of Coursera's career-related MOOCs, for example, students might receive additional feedback from instructors, and sometimes access to supplemental readings and assessments," a company spokeswoman told U.S. News.

[11] feature *n.* 特色，特征，功能

5. College Credit Is Sometimes an Option.

Some MOOCs also offer college credit, such as in edX's Global Freshman Academy with Arizona State University. For-credit MOOCs are open to incoming and returning freshmen at a cost. Many experts say schools sometimes provide credit through MOOCs, though pinpointing[12] the extent that it happens is difficult.

[12] pinpoint *v.* 明确指出，准确解释

6. MOOC-based Degrees Are Emerging.

EdX has partnered with 14 universities to launch MicroMasters degrees. Students complete a portion of a master's through several MOOCs and a capstone[13], and then apply to finish it on campus. Coursera also has two MOOC-based options at the University of Illinois—Urbana-Champaign[14]: an iMBA and Master of Computer Science in data science.

[13] capstone *n.* 顶点课程

[14] University of Illinois—Urbana-Champaign 伊利诺伊大学香槟分校

7. Completion Rates for Free MOOCs Are Low.

For auditors[15], edX MOOC average completion rates are less than 10%—but are generally much higher when students pay. "It did add a level of commitment[16], because otherwise you can kind of walk away at any point," Kelly Walsh, a chief information officer at the College of Westchester who completed a Coursera MOOC last year, told U.S. News.

8. Some Initial Concerns About MOOCs Have Dwindled[17].

MOOCs have long sparked[18] debate among experts. Advocates viewed them as free professional development tools, including in developing countries, while critics pointed to low completion rates and a lack of student-faculty interaction. However, with the new paid models, some of the negative perceptions[19] are diminishing.

9. They Allow High Schoolers to Explore College.

MOOCs also enable high schoolers to gauge interest in college majors and sample actual university classes. "It gives me a realistic understanding of what it means to be an economics major, and what it means to be a statistics major, what it means to be a computer science major," 18-year-old Mahir Jethanandani, who enrolled in MOOCs during high school, told U.S. News.

10. MOOCs Are Used Around the World.

Providers outside the U.S. also develop MOOCs. Agarwal, the edX CEO, wrote that in countries such as Saudi Arabia, MOOCs are used to combat skills gaps in labor markets. "While the potential for large-scale change is certainly impressive, the role that MOOCs can play in individual lives cannot be understated[20] as well," Agarwal wrote.

As indicated earlier, despite their potential to support learning and education, MOOCs have a major concern related to attrition rates[21] and course drop out. Even though the number of learners who enroll in the courses tends to be in the thousands range, only a very small portion of the enrolled learners complete the course. It is reported that the average completion rate for such MOOCs is approximately 15%. The data from Coursera suggest a completion rate of 7%–9%. One

[15] auditor n. 选课者；旁听生

[16] commitment n. 承诺，保证

[17] dwindle v. 减少；变小

[18] spark v. 发动；鼓舞

[19] perception n. 认知，观念，看法

[20] understate v. 低估；少报；保守地说

[21] attrition rate 退学率；损耗率

example is the course Bioelectricity, in the Fall of 2012 at Duke University[22], where 12,725 students enrolled, but only 7,761 ever watched a video, 3,658 attempted a quiz, 345 attempted the final exam, and 313 passed, earning a certificate. However, students paying $50 for a feature have completion rates of about 70%.

Before analyzing the factors related to attrition rates and course drop out, one important thing that should be kept in mind is that average completion rate for MOOCs is not a good indicator[23]. Completion rate cannot reflect the overall view of every student because different students have diverse purposes. For example, some students take part in the MOOCs just for interest or finding extrinsic[24] value of course. They drop the course if the course cannot satisfy their purpose. Research indicates that completion rates is not the right metric[25] to measure success of MOOCs. Alternate metrics are proposed to measure effectiveness of MOOCs and online learning.

[22] **Duke University** 杜克大学

[23] **indicator** *n.* 指标，指示剂

[24] **extrinsic** *adj.* 外在的；非固有的

[25] **metric** *n.* 度量标准

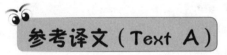

互联网如何改变我们的学习方式

在 21 世纪，在线学习将占所有教育的 50%。网络学习的迅速崛起并不仅仅是因为它更方便、更便宜、更快捷，而是因为网上的认知学习比面对面学习更好。互动式在线学习将使教育发生革命性的变化。此次教育革命对世界的影响将和印刷术的发明一样深远。它不仅会影响我们的学习场所，还会影响我们的学习方法和学习内容。最近的研究表明，在线学习和面对面学习一样有效。当在线学习与更具互动性和促进性的面对面学习相结合时，它将很容易胜过如今过时的、一刀切的传统授课系统。

1. 传统的教学模式

在历史的大部分时间里，标准的教育模式一直是教师站在一群人前面讲课。这是社会上最常见的教学设计，无论是大学的学分课程、非学分课程，职业培训、高中教学，还是主日学校课程。

基本上 90% 的教育都是"信息传递"，即把信息和知识从教师的头脑转移到学生的头脑的过程。为了做到这一点，教师不得不使用大部分时间来讲课。直到今天，这种授课方式一直被认为是最有效、最高效、最理想的教学方式。

然而，作为教育者，我们知道传统的讲课并不是唯一的学习方法。学习者以不同的方式，在不同的时间，从不同的来源学习。我们也知道学习不仅仅是一个认知过程，它还牵涉情感甚至精神。

互联网正在瓦解那种老师面对一个或多个学生讲课的传统教育模式。它正在把传统的教学模式分解为两个部分——认知学习和情感学习。前者可以通过在线学习更好地完成，后者可以通过小组讨论更好地实现。

2. 为什么认知学习可以在网上做得更好

认知学习包括事实、数据、知识和心理技能，这些都可以在网上更快捷、更便宜、更好地实现。在线学习在以下几个方面比课堂学习更有优势。

学习者能够在他的学习效率高峰期学习。学习者 A 的学习效率高峰期可能是从上午 10 点到中午，而学习者 B 的学习效率高峰期可能在午夜到凌晨 3 点之间。在传统的面对面授课中，只有一部分学习者能在他们的学习效率高峰期参与学习，其余的则不能充分受益。

学习者可以按照自己的速度学习。在传统课堂上，学习者只有一次机会听老师讲解概念、技巧或知识。通过在线学习，学习者可以重播部分音频，重读一个单元，回顾一个视频，并再次测试自己。

学习者可以专注于特定的内容领域。在传统课堂上，为了把每个内容都讲到，老师会以自认为相对合适的方式讲解重点，分配时间。然而，在一节有十个单元的课程中，一个特定的学习者并不需要平均地关注每一个单元。对于个人而言，有些单元的知识他已经了解，而某些单元又知之甚少。通过在线学习，学习者可以把更多的时间、注意力和精力放在最需要学习的单元、模块或部分上。

学习者可以每天测试自己。通过在线学习，学习者可以很方便地参加测验和测试，即时收到结果，并可了解自己这门课程学得如何。

学习者可以与老师进行更多的互动。与当今的普遍观点相反，在线学习比传统课堂更个性化，互动性更强。在线上课程中，教师只需要创建一次信息传递，如讲座、图表、文本、视频等。课程单元或模块一旦设计出来，以后只需要修改即可。这样老师就有更多的时间与课程参与者互动。

学习者可以通过互联网更快地获取数据和事实。"大学在线出版"比其他组织更热衷于在线学习，其管理人员举例说，一个典型的 16 周的大学课程可以被削减到 8 周，因为学生在网上学习的速度更快。

最后，技术一直被证明能够降低成本。最近的报告显示，教育成本每年以超过 5% 的速度增长，远远高于其他所有经济部门 3% 的平均水平。随着传统教育体系中教育成本的飙升，技术创新有望以更低的成本提供教育。

3. 网上学习互动更多

在线课程的核心和灵魂不是讲座、授课、音频或视频，而是参与者和老师之间的互动，以及参与者之间的互动。例如，参与者之间的日常互动将形成一个"虚拟社区"。

由于教师需要传达信息，所以能够专注于解答问题的时间就非常短了。而在在线课程中，每个人都可以提问，想问多少都可以。在网络课程中，有更多的讨论，每个人都可以同时发表意见。一份典型的在线讨论的文字记录如果通过口头来表达的话，需要花费数小时的时间。在网上，学习者可以很方便地参与讨论，在较短的时间内吸收更多的信息，进行更多的互动。

4. 互联网如何改变面对面学习

由于互联网传递信息的方式更快，成本更低，不限时间，不厌其烦，且互动与对话更多，互联网将取代传统的课堂授课模式，成为教育和授课的主导方式。然而，互联网并不会完全取代面对面学习。

当学习者把 50% 的时间花在网上学习时，他们会把另外 50% 的时间花在面对面学习上。然而，面对面的学习也将与今天最常见的学习方式截然不同。几乎不需要传统的讲座，教师将非常有必要成为学习的推动者，懂得学生如何学习，并作为个体与学生合作。讲台上的圣人将变为学生身边的指导者。

虽然部分学习是以内容为中心的，但作为教育者，我们知道，更多的学习取决于学习者本身，即一个个体。学习不仅仅是认知，它还包括情感和精神。它包括"舍却所学"，也包括"抛却旧观点"。

这种学习的形式可能是大家坐成一个圆圈，由主持人引导讨论、对话、角色扮演等。这种学习方式已经存在很长时间了，其价值也得到了公认。它的使用将以指数级增长，因为互联网可以更快捷、更便宜、更好地传递认知信息，从而允许更多的时间和资源用于引导性的面对面学习。

随着在线课程的发展并改变我们的学习方式，部分课程基本上还是面对面教学，但同时部分课程将几乎都是在线学习，大部分课程可能既有在线学习也有面对面学习。

5. 在线课程是怎样的

一个典型的在线课程，或课程的线上部分，是这样的：
- 有数十万个主题可供选择；
- 在线课程的老师可能是该学科的世界权威；
- 有来自世界各地的学习者；
- 每门课程平均有 1 000 名学习者。

6. 结语

在线学习正迅速得到认可并成为一种有效的教学系统。高等教育的兼职学生人数现在已超过了全职学生。每个学院或大学都提供在线课程。在线研究生课程和证书课程在过去几年翻了一番。在线学习在商业领域呈指数级增长。

在线学习对社会的贡献，正如拖拉机对食物的贡献。一个世纪以前，食品价格昂贵，供应有限，品种也很少。今天，食物相对便宜，供应充足，种类繁多。互联网对教育也会有同样的作用。更多的人将能够以更低的成本学习更多的知识，并且主题和学科的选择有极大的多样性。这在以前只能是梦想，在很短的时间内，这将梦想成真。

Unit

9

Text A

Big Data in the Classroom

1. Introduction

Big data is the data sets that are so big and complex that traditional data-processing software is inadequate to deal with. Big data challenges include data capture, data storage, data analysis, search, sharing, transfer, visualization, querying, updating, information privacy and data source. Lately, the term big data tends to refer to the use of predictive analytics, user behavior analytics, or certain other advanced data analytics methods to extract value from data.

Big data is improving teaching and learning in an unprecedented way. The inclusion of the computer in K-12 classes is nothing new. In more recent times, however, pupils are not turning to their screens to learn a little BASIC or play a round of *Oregon Trail*—they are increasingly experiencing data-driven teaching as a fully integrated part of a post-textbook, personalized academic process.

If you think about the impact of technology on our lives today, algorithms are analyzing our behaviors—both online and offline—all the time. They shape what we do in the moment, and they often steer us toward what we do next. At many online stores— Amazon, for example—the ideas, suggestions and products in front of you are frequently placed there based on data gleaned from your order history, browsing habits and numerous other factors.

Education has entered this ecosystem, too. In the data-driven classroom, the concept of digitally collecting and analyzing students' work—at the district level and above—is already deeply a part of how school systems track and report performance. On the level of the individual classroom, digital curricula and data are changing the way teachers teach—and, in turn, students learn.

2. Big Data Improves the Speed and Accuracy of Feedback

In the past, it has taken days and weeks for students to get feedback on assignments. This is extremely detrimental to the learning process. Slow feedback means that students are often underprepared for tests and lack the necessary comprehension of a subject to really excel. As schools continue to adopt the use of computers and other devices, a whole data stream of information becomes available both to the teacher and student that can give feedback on a student's performance. This feedback would go far beyond establishing a grade for the student and provide insights into why a student selected the answer and identify patterns that the teacher can use to adjust lessons to better meet the needs of the students. This kind of individual assessment would take a significant amount of a teacher's time to perform with each student, but big data technology provides means whereby feedback on students can be almost instantaneous.

3. Big Data Improves Teaching

Quick feedback increases both student learning and teacher preparation. With access to the students' results in a comprehensive and quick way, teachers are better able to tailor their lessons to the needs of the students. Instead of waiting for test time to find out areas of low comprehension, teachers can figure it out before they teach their next lesson. Better teaching results in better learning. Big data also gives administrators better tools with which they can analyze teaching effectiveness.

For example, at Roosevelt Elementary School near San Francisco, teachers use software called DIBELS with reading assignments to better determine which students need help and what areas they need help in. Teachers at the school need to study the analytics, and from there they can help the students who need it. We have seen time and again that simply measuring students by standardized test scores is an ineffective method. It most often leads to decreased student learning because of the sole focus of excelling on the test and nothing else. With a variety of different tools to measure teaching excellence, school officials can better evaluate teachers and, if needed, make necessary changes.

4. Big Data Improves Learning

As mentioned above, quicker feedback improves student outcomes. The pupils can immediately see where they excelled and where they struggled and then take necessary actions. That data may even be used to keep college students from dropping out.

For instance, at Rio Salado College, administrators started a big data early intervention program that tracked students' progress and alerted them when students were at risk of dropping out. Eventually, the college saw a 40% dip in dropout rates, giving students a better chance at succeeding. Over time, big data will also give instructors insights into recurring student struggles, which can help the instructor provide unique, personalized teaching for students. Because of the teaching improvements as well, students will benefit from lessons tailored more to their specific needs. That information can also be important for teachers in succeeding years.

More than just streamlining assignments and the grading process, data-driven classrooms open up the experience of what students learn, when they learn and at what level. Big-data-fueled predictive analytics could pinpoint what a student is mastering (or not mastering), and what modules of a lesson plan best suit them under those circumstances. It improves personalized, adaptive learning.

5. Scoring and Problem Management

In simple ways, applications such as BubbleScore allow teachers to either deliver multiple-choice tests via mobile devices or scan and score paper exams via mobile-device cameras. Tools like these typically allow instructors to export results to grade books and track progress along defined parameters—helpful for reporting under Common Core and state standards, for example.

When it comes to issues that can arise in the classroom—a student handing in writing that might not be his own, for example—data is also at teachers' disposal. One company, iParadigms, leverages big data to cross-reference written work with public databases and other online resources. Its apps verify that all material submitted is original to the student writer.

Big data can change the way teachers teach and students learn. Finding ways to provide tailored instruction to individual students has been very difficult in the past, and many students have failed to reach anywhere near their potential as a result. However, big data can provide the tools necessary for teachers to better understand students' needs, which in turn can give students better opportunities for success.

6. Privacy

A major concern schools will face as they implement this kind of technology will be how they protect the privacy of students. People are becoming increasingly concerned about their online privacy. It is especially important to address privacy in school settings where we are seeing an increase in bullying. Imagine the harm that could be done to a student if poor performance were leaked to another student. In addition, how could negative performance information potentially affect a students' ability to attend college or succeed in a career if the data fell into the wrong hands? It is more important than ever that schools implement the necessary means to keep students information safe under all circumstances.

Some would argue that the measure of a school's success in education is not how many students graduate, but rather how much students learn and what they are able to do with that knowledge. Graduation rates are still very important and generally provide a clear picture of the students who did, in fact, learn while at school. They can be given too much importance, though, if the focus is on graduation rather than learning. With the plethora of managed services now offered by big data in the cloud, most districts and schools can afford to implement big data without getting involved in the technical aspects of big data implementation. This will increase both learning rates and graduation rates.

The adoption of big data technology in the school system will take time as many schools face limited resources, and privacy concerns will need to be addressed thoroughly. However, when the right balance is found, big data may prove to be an invaluable resource both for teachers and students throughout the learning process.

New Words

visualization [ˌvɪʒʊəlaɪ'zeɪʃən] *n.* 形象化；可视化

querying ['kwɪərɪŋ] *n.* 数据查询

analytics [ˌænə'lɪtɪks] *n.* 分析学；分析方法

extract ['ekstrækt] *v.* 提取；取出

glean [gli:n] *v.* 收集（资料）

detrimental [ˌdetrɪ'mentəl] *adj.* 不利的；有害的

pattern ['pætən] *n.* 模式；图案

sole [səʊl] *adj.* 唯一的；仅有的

excel [ɪk'sel] *v.* 精通；擅长；超过

alert [ə'lɜ:t] *v.* 警告；警示

dip [dɪp] *n.* 下沉，下降

insight ['ɪnsaɪt] *n.* 洞察力；深刻理解

recurring [rɪ'kɜ:rɪŋ] *adj.* 循环的；再发的

streamline ['stri:mlaɪn] *v.* 使现代化；使合理化；使简单化

adaptive [ə'dæptɪv] *adj.* 适应的，自适应的

multiple-choice ['mʌltəpl-tʃɔɪs] *adj.* 多项选择的

parameter [pə'ræmɪtə] *n.* 参数；系数

leverage ['li:vərɪdʒ] *v.* 利用

cross-reference [krɔ:s-'refərəns] *v.* 相互对照；查重

original [ə'rɪdʒənəl] *adj.* 原始的；原创的

implement ['ɪmplɪment] *v.* 实施，执行

address [ə'dres] *v.* 处理，应对

bully ['bʊli] *v.* 欺负；欺凌

Phrases

data capture 数据采集，数据捕获
K-12 从幼儿园到 12 年级
Oregon Trail《俄勒冈之路》（一款冒险游戏）
in the moment 当下，此刻
to really excel 出类拔萃，表现超群

Common Core 共同核心课程
at one's disposal 由某人做主；任某人处理；供某人使用
plethora of 过多的

Exercises

Ex. 1 Give the English equivalents of the following Chinese expressions.

(1) 大数据　　　　＿＿＿＿＿＿＿＿＿＿＿＿＿＿＿＿
(2) 分析学；分析方法　＿＿＿＿＿＿＿＿＿＿＿＿＿＿
(3) 模式；图案　　　＿＿＿＿＿＿＿＿＿＿＿＿＿＿＿

(4) 干预；介入　　　　＿＿＿＿＿＿＿＿＿＿＿＿＿＿＿＿＿＿

(5) 洞察力；深刻理解　＿＿＿＿＿＿＿＿＿＿＿＿＿＿＿＿＿＿

(6) 多项选择的　　　　＿＿＿＿＿＿＿＿＿＿＿＿＿＿＿＿＿＿

(7) 原始的；原创的　　＿＿＿＿＿＿＿＿＿＿＿＿＿＿＿＿＿＿

(8) 数据采集，数据捕获　＿＿＿＿＿＿＿＿＿＿＿＿＿＿＿＿＿

(9) 当下，此刻　　　　＿＿＿＿＿＿＿＿＿＿＿＿＿＿＿＿＿＿

(10) 由某人做主；任某人处理　＿＿＿＿＿＿＿＿＿＿＿＿＿＿＿

Ex. 2　Decide whether the following statements are true (T) or false (F) according to Text A. Give your reasons for the false ones.

(　　) (1) Big data has very limited potential in improving teaching and learning.

(　　) (2) Algorithms are analyzing our behaviors all the time, both online and offline.

(　　) (3) Big data improves the speed and accuracy of school feedback, comparing with the traditional way.

(　　) (4) Big data does not necessarily enable teachers to learn students' learning results in a more comprehensive and quicker way.

(　　) (5) Big data gives administrators better tools with which they can analyze teaching effectiveness.

(　　) (6) Big-data-fueled predictive analytics could pinpoint what a student is mastering or not mastering.

(　　) (7) Big data could help to find out plagiarism in assignments.

(　　) (8) Privacy is not an issue to worry about in terms of big data.

(　　) (9) Big data is not necessarily a good resource for teachers and students.

(　　) (10) Big data could improve teaching, but not learning.

Ex. 3　Answer the following questions according to Text A.

(1) What is the recent definition for big data?

(2) What are the challenges of big data?

(3) How do the online stores recommend ads to their users?

(4) What are the advantages of giving student's performance feedback by means of big data?

(5) Why is simply measuring teachers by standardized test scores an ineffective method?

(6) By what means could big data prevent college students from dropping out?

(7) Why are educators becoming increasingly concerned about online privacy?

(8) What factors should we take into consideration when measuring a school's success in education?

Ex. 4 Fill in the blanks with the words given below.

reframing	determining	customized	insights	solution
internal	records	transformed	attract	before

Education industry is flooding with a huge amount of data related to students, faculties, courses, results and whatnot. It was not long (1)_____ we realized that the proper study and analysis of this data can provide (2)_____ that can be used to improve the operational effectiveness and working of educational institutes. Following are some of the fields in education industry that have been (3)_____ by big data motivated changes.

" (4)_____ programs and schemes" for each individual can be created using the data collected on the basis of a student's learning history to benefit all students. This improves the overall student results.

" (5)_____ the course material" according to the data that is collected on the basis of what student learns and to what extent by real-time monitoring of what components of a course are easier to understand.

New (6)_____ in "grading systems" have been introduced as a result of proper analysis of student data.

Proper analysis and study of every student's (7)_____ will help in understanding the student's progress, strengths, weaknesses, interests and more. It will help in "(8)_____ which career would be most appropriate" for the student in the future.

The applications of big data have provided a (9)_____ to one of the biggest pitfalls in the education system, that is, the one-size-fits-all fashion of academic set up, by (10)_____ in eLearning solutions.

Text B

Big Data in eLearning

One of the most amazing aspects of eLearning in today's world is that it is constantly evolving. Thanks to emerging technologies and improved instructional design models, the possibilities are endless for the future of eLearning. A concept that has been a hot topic among the eLearning community recently is "big data". However, what, exactly, is big data, and how does it benefit the eLearning industry?

1. What Is Big Data?

You have probably heard the term "big data", and maybe you have wondered what it is. Big data refers to the large amount of data that is flowing through many sources every second, along with brand-new types of data. It is data that is too large, complex and dynamic for any conventional data tools to capture, store, manage and analyze. Thanks to advancements in technology, this data can now be analyzed, which is helpful for health care, government, retail and manufacturing, and of course, eLearning.

Big data, in terms of the eLearning industry, is the data that are created by learners while they are taking an eLearning course or training module. We are now able to collect and track the data through learning management systems, social networks and other media that track how learners interact with aspects of the eLearning course. For example, if an employee is interacting with a training module centered around company policies, his or her progress, assessment results, social sharing, and any other data being produced during the eLearning course are "big data". The learning management system that has been set by the organization or the eLearning professionals collects the data.

The term "big data" does not only apply to the volume of data itself, but the individual pieces of data that are being collected. These pieces of data can be analyzed to offer organizations or eLearning professionals the opportunity to determine how a learner is acquiring information, at what pace, and to pinpoint any problems that may exist within the eLearning strategy itself.

2. Benefits That Big Data Offers to eLearning Professionals

Big data can help us understand the real patterns of our learners more effectively because it allows us to track a learner's experience in an eLearning course. By examining the digital breadcrumbs or digital footprints, we are able to track the learner's journey throughout the entire learning experience.

By tracking big data in eLearning, we can see which parts are too easy and which parts are so difficult that they get stuck. Some other parts of the journey we can track and analyze are the pages they revisit often, the sections they recommend to peers, the learning styles they prefer and the time of day they learn the best.

There are a variety of benefits that big data can offer to eLearning professionals, all of which have the power to impact the future of eLearning and revolutionize the way we analyze and assess the eLearning experience. Here are just a few of the most significant advantages associated with big data.

First, it allows eLearning professionals to understand how the learners are digesting the information and which learning needs appeal the most to them. For instance, big data allows eLearning professionals to determine if a reality-based scenario is more effective than a text-based problem solving activity.

Second, it enables eLearning professionals to pinpoint areas that may need to be fine-tuned within the eLearning course or module. For example, if multiple learners are taking an excessive amount of time to finish a particular module, this probably means that the module needs to be improved in order to make it more manageable for the learners.

Third, it provides an analysis of which eLearning modules are visited the most and in the case of social learning which eLearning modules or links are shared with other learners. For example, you can determine which link is shared via Facebook the most.

Fourth, data is received almost immediately, rather than having to wait for long periods of time to receive assessments. This means that eLearning professionals can begin implementing changes or utilizing the data to fine-tune their eLearning strategy right away.

Last, based upon patterns, eLearning professionals have the power to predict where learners may struggle or excel. This way, they can develop their eLearning courses so that learners get the chance to achieve the best possible results.

3. How Big Data will Impact the Future of eLearning

There are a number of reasons why big data may, very well, revolutionize the eLearning industry. First and foremost, it will allow eLearning professionals to customize the eLearning experience to provide learners with more effective, engaging, and informative eLearning courses and modules. Big data also have the potential to impact the future of eLearning by:

- Offering invaluable feedback

While online surveys and discussions may offer feedback regarding the effectiveness of eLearning courses and modules, big data gives eLearning professionals the chance to receive invaluable feedback that can be used to pinpoint where the learner, and the eLearning course itself, may need to be improved. For instance, if a learner is able to look at an analysis of where he or she falls short while taking the eLearning course, he or she can then figure out how to correct the issue moving forward. At the same time, if the online facilitator observes that the majority of the learners struggle with a particular module or assignment, he or she can make proper adjustments to improve learners' performance.

- Allowing eLearning professionals to design more personalized eLearning courses

If eLearning professionals are given the opportunity to know how their learners are acquiring information and what works best for them, in terms of content and delivery, this will result in more personalized and engaging eLearning courses. As such, modules can be custom-tailored to meet the individual needs of the learner, which will offer a high quality and meaningful learning experience.

- Targeting effective eLearning strategies and eLearning goals

Big data in eLearning gives us an inside look at which eLearning strategies are working and which ones are not necessarily helpful in terms of eLearning goal achievement. For example, you can determine which eLearning courses are contributing to skill development and which eLearning modules or elements may be irrelevant. As such, you can then devote resources to the aspects that are working, so that the learners can realize the preparation they need to fulfill their career goals.

- Tracking learner patterns

With big data, eLearning professionals gain the rare ability to track a learner throughout the entire process, from start to finish. In other words, you can see how well they perform on a test, or how quickly they finish a challenging eLearning module. This helps you to pinpoint the patterns that will not only enable you to learn more about the learning behaviors of the individual learner, but your learners' group as a whole.

- Expanding our understanding of the eLearning process

As eLearning professionals, it is essential that we learn as much as possible about how learners acquire and digest knowledge. Big data gives us the chance to gain an in-depth understanding of the eLearning process and how the learners are responding to the eLearning courses we are delivering to them. We can even figure out which time of day they learn most effectively or which delivery methods allow them to retain information most efficiently. This information can then be used to take our eLearning strategies to the next level.

To make a long story short, embracing big data reshapes eLearning and it is a win-win situation for both the eLearning professionals and the learners.

 **New Words**

brand-new [ˌbrænd-'njuː] *adj.* 崭新的；最近获得的	appeal [ə'piːl] *v.* 有吸引力，迎合爱好
conventional [kən'venʃənəl] *adj.* 传统的；普通的；惯例的	fine-tune [faɪn-tjuːn] *v.* 调整；对…进行微调
	customize ['kʌstəmaɪz] *v.* 定制，按客户具体要求制造
breadcrumb ['bredkrʌm] *n.* 面包碎屑；痕迹	irrelevant [ɪ'reləvənt] *adj.* 不相干的；不切题的
digest [daɪ'dʒest] *v.* 消化；吸收；融会贯通	win-win [wɪn-wɪn] *adj.* 双赢的；互利互惠的

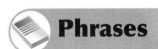 **Phrases**

retail and manufacturing 零售和制造业	fall short 功亏一篑；不符合标准
get stuck 陷入僵局；遇到困难	as such 就其本身而言；同样地
first and foremost 首先；首要的是	in-depth 深入地；全面地

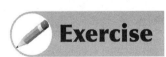 **Exercise**

Decide whether the following statements are true (T) or false (F) according to Text B. Give your reasons for the false ones.

(   ) (1) Big data is usually too large, complex and dynamic for any conventional tools to capture, store, manage and analyze.

(　　) (2) Big data, in terms of the eLearning industry, is the data that are created by learners while they are taking an eLearning course or training module.

(　　) (3) Big data analytics could help to understand how the learners are acquiring information and their learning pace, but could not pinpoint the problems that exist within the eLearning strategy itself.

(　　) (4) Tracking big data in eLearning could help us to understand which parts are too easy and which parts are too difficult for learners.

(　　) (5) It is difficult for eLearning professionals to predict where learners may struggle or excel.

(　　) (6) It is not likely that the eLearning professionals could custom-tailor their course to meet the individual needs of learners.

(　　) (7) Big data in eLearning gives us an inside look at which eLearning strategies are working and which ones are not.

(　　) (8) Big data analytics could help us to find out which time of day the students learn most effectively or which delivery methods allow them to retain information most efficiently.

 # Supplementary Reading

Text	Notes

Big Data: How Analytics Benefits Higher Education
 	
    For the past few years, big data has been making waves[1] across nearly every industry. However, nowhere is this more true than the educational sector. Higher education institutions are typically some of the first adopters of new technology, and colleges and universities across the world have been shaping their educational, recruitment[2] and retention[3] programs thanks to insights gleaned from big data analytics.
 	
    What's more, with more employment opportunities for data scientists and analysts than ever before, many schools are offering new courses to ensure students are ready for their future careers. Big data analytics has much to offer when it comes to higher education. Let us take a look at a few ways by which colleges, universities and other schools can leverage these processes to their full advantage.
 	
1. Pulling from an Array of Internal Sources
    While nearly every organization in any industry has a
	[1] **making waves** 兴风作浪，掀起波澜
	
	[2] **recruitment** *n.* 招生；招聘
	[3] **retention** *n.* 留级；扣留，滞留；记忆力

wealth of informational assets at its disposal, this is particularly true for educational institutions. Schools obtain a treasure trove[4] of information from current and prospective students—and this is only a single big data source. Educational organizations are also turning to older systems to gather details and analyze them for valuable insights, opening up new possibilities.

"Colleges and universities, inundated[5] with data from legacy systems[6] and incentivized by renewed accountability[7] pressures, have begun to link disparate[8] information from across the campus," Bridget Burns, University Innovation Alliance's executive director, wrote for Forbes. "Historically limited to transactional data from registrars[9] and student information systems, the application of data-driven decision-making has begun to permeate[10] all aspects of campus life and operations—as enterprising[11] leaders harness predictive analytics to tackle bottleneck[12] courses, power advising initiatives[13] and share best practices with their peers."

In this way, schools are not just leveraging all of their available resources. Administrators are also seeking out innovative ways to apply analytics findings to processes all across the institution.

2. Setting Sights on[14] Social Media

Schools are looking beyond their own big data for further insights as well. Leveraging social media information has now become a more common trend. In this way, schools' recruitment teams and administrators can learn as much about a particular student or group of pupils as possible.

A recent Kaplan Test Prep survey found that 40% of admission officers currently engage social media resources to get additional information about applicants. This process is also becoming more popular with scholarship funds as organizations seek to award monies to the most promising student candidates.

3. Geographical Targeting: Hitting Students Where They Live

Recruitment efforts have been especially impacted by big data, where analytics can help reveal where schools should focus their efforts and what kind of return on investment they can expect.

[4] treasure trove　无主珍宝；宝藏；宝物

[5] inundate *v.* 淹没；泛滥；（洪水般的）扑来

[6] legacy system　遗留系统；旧系统

[7] accountability *n.* 义务；责任

[8] disparate *adj.* 不同的；不相干的

[9] registrar *n.* 登记员；注册主任

[10] permeate *v.* 渗透；弥漫

[11] enterprising *adj.* 有事业心的；有进取心的；有魄力的

[12] bottleneck *n.* 瓶颈；障碍物

[13] initiative *n.* 方案；倡议

[14] set sights on　把目光投向；着眼于

Similar to the retail industry, higher education institutions can reduce their marketing spending by creating more targeted campaigns that appeal to audiences in a specific area. For example, if big data insights show that not only students in certain cities apply regularly to a college, but are most often accepted, the organization can adjust its marketing efforts accordingly.

"If the admission office of the university has a firm understanding of which geographical locations include the most applicants who enroll, it can cut marketing costs and produce enhanced results," Lauren Willison, Florida Polytechnic[15] University director of admissions wrote in a guest post for IBM. "Rather than investing in unfocused campaigns that target a wide audience, money can be invested in specific markets that are more likely to boost the university's yield rate."

4. Post-application: Selecting Students to Accept

Big data analytics does not end after a student has submitted his/her application. *Fast Company*[16] contributor[17] Neal Ungerleider reported that more institutions are also leveraging big data to help make decisions about which students will be accepted. Analysis of certain datasets can show which candidates are the most likely to succeed at the college or university, and which might be more prone to[18] drop out or fail.

This type of predictive analytics is currently being used by Wichita State University, where it is helping administrators make better-informed decisions. Research shows that the school's recruitment approach results in 96% accuracy in pinpointing which applicants are "high-yield" or will likely do well at the institution.

5. Identifying Educational Troubles

Analytics can also be used by schools to pinpoint which pupils might be struggling in their educational pursuits. One of the best ways this strategy has been applied is to identify troubles earlier in a student's academic career. For instance, if a student is underperforming[19] in prerequisite[20] classes, advisors can help guide them before they fall behind, fail a course or drop out of school.

[15] polytechnic *n.* 理工院校

[16] *Fast Company* 《快公司》（美国最具影响力的商业杂志之一）

[17] contributor *n.* 投稿人；贡献者

[18] be prone to 易于……；有……的倾向

[19] underperform *v.* 表现不佳；学习不如预期

[20] prerequisite *n.* 先修课程；先决条件

"Instead of falling through the cracks[21], students receive an early intervention with solutions such as rearranging course loads or exploring other paths to a degree," Willison pointed out.

[21] crack *n.* 裂缝；裂痕

6. From Big Data to Big Dollars

With so many industries buzzing about the advantages that big data analytics can offer, more individuals are seeking to pursue careers in this field. As a result, institutions are putting more big data, data science and analytics courses and programs into place. TechRepublic[22] recently published a list of the top 20 schools offering such education, with Carnegie Mellon, Stanford and Santa Clara University topping the list.

[22] TechRepublic *n.* 一个美国科技网站

7. Requirements and Considerations

Big data analytics can offer nearly endless opportunities to improve campus processes and enhance education. However, there are a few challenges and requirements that administrators should be aware of, not the least of which is data security.

Institutions must have a secure environment in which to gather and work with their data, particularly if information includes students' sensitive personal details. What's more, with so many likely disparate data sources, it is essential to consider the work involved in integrating and organizing these datasets. It is best to have experts to help address and support the issues of big data.

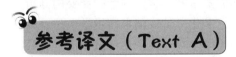

参考译文（Text A）

课堂中的大数据

1. 引言

大数据是指太大、太复杂，以至于传统的数据处理软件无法处理的数据集。大数据的挑战包括数据获取、存储、分析、搜索、共享、传输、可视化、查询、更新、信息隐私和数据源。近来，大数据一词倾向于指使用预测分析、用户行为分析或其他某些高级的数据分析方法从数据中提取价值。

大数据正以前所未有的方式改善教学。将计算机纳入 K-12 教育并不是什么新鲜事。然而，近年来，学生不再仅仅通过屏幕来学习一些 BASIC 编程或玩《俄勒冈之旅》这款游戏——他们越来越多地体验到数据驱动的教学，并将其作为后教科书时代不可分割的一部分和个性化学习的过程。

想一下科技对当今生活的影响，算法一直在分析我们的行为——无论是线上还是线下——每时每刻。它们塑造了我们当下的行为，并常常引导我们的下一个举动。在许多在线商店——如亚马逊——你面前的观点、建议和产品往往是根据你的订单历史、浏览习惯和其他诸多因素分析得来的。

教育也进入了这个生态系统。在数据驱动的课堂中，数字化收集和分析学生学习的概念——不管是在本地区之内或之外——已经成为学校系统追踪和报告成绩的重要组成部分。在课堂层面，数字化的课程和数据正在改变教师的教学方式，进而改变学生的学习方式。

2. 大数据提高了反馈的速度和准确性

在过去，学生需要几天甚至几周的时间才能得到作业的反馈，这对学习极为不利。反馈慢意味着学生对考试准备不足，对科目缺乏必要的理解，导致不能做到出类拔萃。学校使用计算机和其他设备，教师和学生可以获得完整的数据流信息，以便对学生的表现做出反馈。这种反馈将远不止是给学生一个评分，还可以分析学生为什么选择这个答案，并找到教师可以用来调整教学的方法以便更好地满足学生需求。这种个性化的评价以往需要教师花费大量的时间来对每个学生进行评估，但大数据技术提供的方法对学生的反馈几乎是即时的。

3. 大数据改善教学

快速反馈可以改善学生的学习和教师的备课。通过全面、快速地获取学生的学习情况，教师能够更好地根据学生的需要来调整教学内容。教师不必等到考试时才发现学生理解较差的部分，而是在下次上课之前就发现问题。教得更好，学得也更好。大数据也为管理者提供了更好的工具，让他们能够分析教学效果。

例如，在旧金山附近的罗斯福小学，教师们使用名为 DIBELS 的软件批改阅读作业，以更好地确定哪些学生需要帮助，以及他们在哪些方面需要帮助。学校的老师需要用分析学帮助有需要的学生。我们已经多次观察到，仅仅通过标准化考试成绩来衡量学生是一种效果不佳的方法。这通常会导致学生学习能力下降，因为学生只专注于在考试中拔得头筹而不求其他。有了各种不同的工具来衡量教学水平，学校领导可以更好地评估教师，如果需要，还可以做出必要的改变。

4. 大数据促进学习

如上所述，更快的反馈可以提高学生的学习成绩。学生可以立即看到他们在哪里做得好，在哪里做得不好，然后采取必要的行动。这些数据甚至可能被用来防止大学生辍学。

例如，在里约热内卢萨拉多学院，管理人员启动了一个大数据早期干预项目，追踪学生的学习进度，并在学生有辍学风险时警示他们。最终，这所大学的辍学率下降了 40%，这使学生有更好的成功机会。随着时间的推移，大数据还会让教师了解学生多次出现的困难之处，帮助教师为学生提供独特的、个性化的教学。教学也会随之改进，学生将从更适合他们具体需要的课程中受益。这些信息在未来几年对教师来说也很重要。

数据驱动的课堂不仅革新了作业和评分过程，还为学生开启了学习内容、学习时间和学习层次的新体验。大数据驱动的预测分析可以精确地指出学生掌握了什么（或没有掌握什么），以及在这些情况下，课程计划的哪些模块最适合他们，提高了个性化和适应性学习。

5. 评分和问题管理

简单来讲，通过 BubbleScore 等应用程序，教师可以通过移动设备进行多项选择题考试，也可以通过移动设备摄像头扫描试卷并评分。诸如此类的工具可以让教师将结果导出到成绩册中，并根据所定义的参数追踪进度。例如，这对于按照共同核心课程标准和州标准进行报告很有帮助。

当涉及课堂上可能出现的问题时——例如，学生交的作业可能不是自己的原创——教师也可以将此交给大数据处理。一家名为 iParadigms 的公司利用大数据将书面作业和公共数据库及其他在线资源进行比对，由其应用程序验证学生提交的所有材料是否属于学生原创。

大数据可以改变教师教学和学生学习的方式。在过去，想要为每个学生提供量身定制的教学是非常困难的，许多学生因此未能发挥出自己的潜能。然而，大数据可以为教师提供必要的工具来更好地了解学生的需求，从而使学生有更好的成功获得机会。

6. 隐私

在实施这种技术时，学校将面临的一个重要问题是如何保护学生的隐私。人们越来越关心他们的在线隐私。解决校园环境中的隐私问题尤其重要，因为我们发现校园欺凌现象呈上涨趋势。想象一下，如果一个学生的不良表现被泄露给另一个学生，会对他造成什么样的伤害。此外，如果数据落入不良之人之手，这些负面信息可能会潜在地影响这个学生上大学的机会或在事业上取得成功的机会。比以往任何时候都更重要的是，学校要采取必要的措施，在任何情况下确保学生信息的安全。

有些人认为，衡量一所学校在教育方面的成功与否，不是看有多少学生毕业，而是看学生学了多少知识，以及他们能用这些知识做什么。毕业率仍然是非常重要的，它通常能清楚地反映出那些在学校里认真学习的学生的情况。然而，如果把重点放在毕业而不是学习上，便过于偏颇了。由于云中的大数据提供了很多的托管服务，大多数地区的学校都能在不参与大数据实施技术的情况下应用大数据。学习率和毕业率都会得到提高。

在学校系统中采用大数据技术需要时间，因为很多学校资源有限，隐私问题也需要彻底解决。然而，当找到合适的平衡点时，大数据会成为教师和学生在整个学习过程中的宝贵资源。

Unit 10

Text A

When VR Meets Education

Since the 1950s, Virtual Reality (VR) has been hovering on the periphery of technology without achieving accepted mainstream application or commercial adoption. Since 2012, VR startups have raised more than $1.46 billion in venture capital, including more than $100 million in funding during the last four consecutive quarters.

According to Citi analyst Kota Ezawa, 2016 is the year when VR took off in earnest, with the VR market grew to a $15.9 billion industry in 2019. Citi also said the market for hardware, networks, software and content reached $200 billion by 2020.

The content share of this market is of particular interest, as this segment of the tech industry has historically been dedicated to gaming—but the world is changing. We are shifting from the now relatively benign universe in Aldous Huxley's *Brave New World* to Ernest Cline's VR paradigm as described in *Ready Player One*. Like Huxley, Cline has written of a dystopian environment wherein technology has overtaken humanity.

For our purpose, let us consider VR as a useful tool, and perhaps even a productive enhancement to human interaction, bringing together people from around the world to engage and interact—regardless of social, economic or geographic disparities. In the abstract as well as the applied, modern education is poised to take advantage of this latest tech innovation.

Over the last several years, VR has moved from being the purview of the military and aviation to the mainstream of professional development, as managers, instructors, coaches and therapists have claimed increasing benefit from immersive experiences.

While statistics on VR use in K-12 schools and colleges have yet to be gathered, the steady growth of the market is reflected in the surge of companies (including zSpace, Alchemy VR and Immersive VR) solely dedicated to providing schools with packaged educational curriculum and content, teacher training and technological tools to support VR-based instruction in the classroom. Myriad articles, studies and conference presentations attest to the great success of 3D immersion and VR technology in hundreds of classrooms in educationally progressive schools and learning labs in the U.S. and Europe.

Much of this early foray into VR-based learning has centered on the hard sciences—biology, anatomy, geology and astronomy—as the curricular focus and learning opportunities are notably enriched through interaction with dimensional objects, animals and environments. The *World of Comenius*, a software in a biology lesson at a school in the Czech Republic that employed a Leap Motion controller and specially adapted Oculus Rift DK2 headsets, stands as an exemplary model of innovative scientific learning.

In other areas of education, many classes have used VR tools to collaboratively construct architectural models, recreations of historic or natural sites and other spatial renderings. Instructors also have used VR technology to engage students in topics related to literature, history and economics by offering a deeply immersive sense of place and time, whether historic or evolving.

In what may turn out to be an immersive education game changer, Google launched its Pioneer Expeditions in September 2015. Under this program, thousands of schools around the world are getting—for one day—a kit containing everything a teacher needs to take their class on a virtual trip: Asus smartphones, a tablet for the teacher to direct the tour, a router that allows Expeditions to run without an Internet connection, a library of 100+ virtual trips (from the Great Wall of China to Mars) and Google Cardboard viewers or Mattel ViewMasters that turn smartphones into VR headsets.

This global distribution of VR content and access will undoubtedly influence a pedagogical shift as these new technologies allow a literature teacher in Chicago to "take" her students to Verona to look at the setting for Shakespeare's *Romeo and Juliet*, or a teacher in the Bronx to "bring" her Ancient Civilizations class to the ancient Mayan ruins at Chichen Itza.

And with VR platforms like AltspaceVR and LectureVR (an initiative of Immersive VR Education) emerge, entirely new possibilities are available for teachers of all kinds, as the technology of making avatars and supporting "multi-player" sessions allows for an exponentially scaled level of socialization and outreach.

Potentially, a collaboration between these innovative VR platform offerings could result in a curator or artist guiding a group of thousands around a museum exhibition or cultural site, or an actor or professor leading a virtual master class in real time with students from all over the world.

Perhaps the most utopian application of this technology will be seen in terms of bridging cultures and fostering understanding among young students, as it will soon be possible for a third-grade class in the U.S. to participate in a virtual trip with a third-grade class in India or Mexico.

Despite the fact that VR is still developing, real progress has been seen in the economic scaling of the technology. The cost to the consumer of VR hardware (headsets, in particular) has steadily declined, as noted in the head-mounted displays (HMDs) commercially available today: Google Cardboard for \$20 and Samsung Gear VR for \$99. Oculus Rift, a desktop VR device, is available for pre-order for \$599.

The fact that the *New York Times* recently supplied more than one million subscribers with Google Cardboard headsets to access its newly launched VR experiences has further advanced accessibility and mainstreaming of the device, as well as this innovative means of media consumption.

Overall, access to some type of mobile VR device is affordable for many more individual users and, in turn, many more schools. Some forward-thinking instructors are even using 3D printers to print their own customized HMDs with their technology students, a solution that dovetails with the popular maker-trend philosophy.

So maybe we are ready for the futuristic world of *Ready Player One*. However, perhaps the utopian rather than dystopian construct is not only more appealing, but also more relevant in this global community.

Educators and students alike are seeking an ever-expanding immersive landscape, where students engage with teachers and each other in transformative experiences through a wide spectrum of interactive resources. In this educational reality, VR has a definitive place of value.

New Words

hover ['hɒvə] v. 徘徊；盘旋

periphery [pə'rɪfəri] n. 外围，边缘

startup ['stɑ:tʌp] n. 创业公司，初创企业

consecutive [kən'sekjətɪv] adj. 连贯的；连续的

quarter ['kwɔ:tə] n. 季度；四分之一

benign [bɪ'naɪn] adj. 温和的；和蔼的

dystopian [dɪs'təupiən] adj. 反乌托邦的；反假想国的

disparity [dɪ'spærəti] n. 差异，不同

poised [pɔɪzd] adj. 泰然自若的，镇定的

purview ['pɜ:vju:] n. 范围，权限

aviation [ˌeɪvi'eɪʃən] n. 航空；飞机制造业

immersive [ɪ'mɜ:sɪv] adj. 拟真的；沉浸式的

myriad ['mɪriəd] adj. 无数的；种种的

foray ['fɒreɪ] n. 涉足，初次尝试

anatomy [ə'nætəmi] n. 解剖；解剖学

astronomy [ə'strɒnəmi] n. 天文学

recreation [ˌrekrɪ'eɪʃən] n. 娱乐；消遣

rendering ['rendərɪŋ] n. 表演；（建筑物等）透视图

router ['ru:tə] n. 路由器

avatar ['ævətɑ:] n. 头像；角色；化身

outreach ['autri:tʃ] n. 延伸，拓广

curator [kjuə'reɪtə] n. 馆长；监护人；管理者

utopian [ju:'təupiən] adj. 乌托邦的；理想化的

subscriber [səb'skraɪbə] n. 订阅者；认购人

dovetail ['dʌvteɪl] vt. 与……吻合

spectrum ['spektrəm] n. 范围；光谱；频谱

Phrases

venture capital 风险投资；创业投资；风险基金	Czech Republic 捷克共和国
	Leap Motion 体感控制器；体感控制
Brave New World《美丽新世界》（小说）	Oculus Rift DK2 一款头戴式虚拟现实设备
Ready Player One《头号玩家》（小说）	Google Cardboard 一款智能手机头戴式显示器
in the abstract 抽象地；理论上	Mattel ViewMasters 美泰公司开发的一款虚拟现实眼镜
attest to 证明；证实	
World of Comenius《夸美纽斯世界》（一款基于 VR 的教育软件）	Mayan ruins 玛雅遗址
	Samsung Gear 三星的一款智能手表

 Abbreviation

Virtual Reality (VR) 虚拟现实

 Exercises

Ex. 1 Give the English equivalents of the following Chinese expressions.

(1) 乌托邦的；理想化的 _____

(2) 头像；角色；化身 _____

(3) 教育学的；教学法的 _____

(4) 涉足，初次尝试 _____

(5) 拟真的；沉浸式的 _____

(6) 差异；不同 _____

(7) 创业公司，初创企业 _____

(8) 外围，边缘 _____

(9) 风险投资；风险基金 _____

(10) 证明；证实 _____

Ex. 2 Decide whether the following statements are true (T) or false (F) according to Text A. Give your reasons for the false ones.

( ) (1) VR has achieved accepted mainstream application since the day it was born.

(   ) (2) The VR industry has historically been dedicated to gaming.

(   ) (3) VR isolates people rather than brings people together.

(   ) (4) The education industry now is still reluctant to apply VR technology to teaching and learning.

(   ) (5) Many companies are dedicated to providing schools with packaged educational curriculum and content, teacher training and technological tools to support VR-based instruction in the classroom.

(   ) (6) Much of the early foray into VR-based learning has centered on the hard sciences, such as biology, anatomy, geology and astronomy.

(   ) (7) VR technology is not able to engage students in topics related to literature, history and economics.

(   ) (8) The adoption of VR technology in education will undoubtedly cause a pedagogical shift.

(   ) (9) The most ideal application of VR technology will be seen in terms of bridging cultures and fostering understanding among young students.

(   ) (10) Students may engage less with their teachers and peers if VR devices are used.

Ex. 3 **Answer the following questions according to Text A.**

(1) How much have VR startups raised in venture capital since 2012?

(2) When did VR industry take off in earnest according to Citi analyst Kota Ezawa?

(3) Why is VR considered as a useful tool to human interaction?

(4) Are 3D immersion and VR technology successful in the classrooms and learning labs? How do you know?

(5) Why has much of the early foray into VR-based learning centered on the hard sciences, such as biology, anatomy, geology and astronomy?

(6) Will the VR educational platforms limit the students' interaction? Why or why not?

(7) What is the most utopian application of VR technology in education?

(8) Will the cost of VR device be a big problem for individual users? Why or why not?

Ex. 4 **Fill in the blanks with the words given below.**

displayed	realistic	artificial	therein	interactive
create	sensory	simulate	movement	dimensional

VR typically refers to computer technologies that use software to generate (1)_____ images, sounds and other sensations that replicate a real environment or (2)_____ an imaginary setting, and (3)_____ a user's physical presence in this environment, by enabling the user to interact with this space and any objects depicted (4) using specialized display screens or projectors and other devices. VR has been defined as "a realistic and immersive simulation of a three (5)_____ environment, created using (6)_____ software and hardware, and experienced or controlled by (7)_____ of the body" or as an "immersive, interactive experience generated by a computer". A person using VR equipment is typically able to "look around" the (8)_____ world, move about in it and interact with features or items that are depicted on a screen or in goggles. VR artificially create (9)_____ experiences, which can include sight, touch, hearing, and, less commonly, smell. Most VR are (10)_____ either on a computer monitor, a projector screen, or with a VR headset.

Text B

Five VR Trends to Watch in Education

Virtual Reality (VR) is taking off in higher education. VR devices increased 85% in 2020, with gaming and educational applications driving most of that growth. However, what areas of VR should educators specifically focus on and what tech can they look out for?

"We can expect to see certain trends in VR to move forward, while others will disappear. As devices continue to shrink we will see the development of augmented and mixed reality experiences that will power compelling visualizations, immersive storytelling, gamified simulations and learning experiences," said Maya Georgieva, an education tech strategist, author and speaker with more than 15 years of experience in higher education and global education.

Her partner, Emory Craig, is an educator, speaker and researcher of VR and wearable technologies in the learning environment. He is currently the director of eLearning at the College of New Rochelle, where he leads instructional technology initiatives. "Education is on the cusp of a profound change in the way we use VR technology," Craig said. "People are starting to use it in higher education even though the tech is very fluid at the moment."

Craig and Georgieva both agree that the VR market is rapidly changing, and there are various technologies in hardware, distribution platforms and content creation software that are ready to use. Here are five areas with promising developments for educators.

1. More Affordable Headsets

While headsets like the Microsoft HoloLens, which Microsoft refers to as a mixed reality device, are sought after for being highly advanced in terms of applications and content. These run on the pricier side. "Most schools have just one or two, while many have zero," Georgieva said.

"Right now, if you want the Oculus Rift or HTC Vive, which I really like, you're talking a thing close to $2,000 per setup," noted Craig.

As VR achieves more mainstream application or commercial adoption, however, educators can expect to see more high quality headsets at lower price points. Georgieva recently gave an industry talk at the 2017 SXSW education conference, where she shared with educators what to expect in headsets and options that will enable them to experiment with VR without breaking the bank.

Microsoft has been collaborating with its partners, such as HP, Acer, Dell and Lenovo, to develop VR headsets that will work with lower-end desktops. Later this year, the companies will debut headsets for $299, "which is much more affordable compared to HoloLens," commented Georgieva. "These headsets, while tethered to PCs, will provide a somewhat immersive experience and we expect that they will quickly find their way to campus labs and makerspaces."

In addition, many Kickstarter crowdfunding efforts are bound to make high-end headsets more accessible for teaching. "That'll be a way for schools to get more innovative and get to experiment with these devices at lower price points," Craig said, citing the NOLO project as an example, which will be releasing its product in June. The NOLO system is meant for mobile VR headsets and gives users that "6 degrees of freedom" motion tracking that is currently only found in high-end headsets.

2. Hand Controllers That Will Bring Increased Interactivity

Craig and Georgieva both agree that hand controllers add a whole new level of engagement for users. "I've been using Google Daydream and I love it because adding a hand controller to mobile VR, I think, makes a world of difference," said Craig, pointing out that Samsung has also implemented its own hand controller for Gear VR.

"Microsoft just announced their new motion controllers at Microsoft Build, which together with the headset will bring the price to $399. While we still have to test the quality of these devices, this no doubt will open new options for experimentation," Georgieva said.

Both HTC Vive and Oculus have hand controllers that enable full-motion interactive experiences that can power experiential learning. "We already see interesting applications for STEM education. It will be also interesting to see how platforms like zSpace, with their stylus and AR glasses, continue to develop their immersive applications," said Georgieva.

3. Easy-to-Use Content Creation Platforms

There is a great deal of experimentation going on with VR content at the moment. Most of the content development is happening in the fields of entertainment, games and sports, but surprisingly "a lot of interest and energy is being pulled toward the development of medical content and we see the visual fidelity and interactive options maturing rapidly in virtual medical simulations," according to Georgieva.

Craig sees a parallel between the emergence of mobile phones and VR and how most students have their own mobile devices now. "I have my students using cell phones in the classroom as I think they're an incredibly powerful tool. Many apps are coming from developers, and we're making very powerful use of them in the classroom. I think the same thing will happen with VR, where the hardware will be produced by outside vendors and the platforms will be developed by content makers or others in the VR community. Both K-12 and higher education communities are going to adopt those platforms for our learning needs."

Game engines like Unity and Unreal are often a starting point for creating simulations. However, these platforms can be somewhat complex for non-technical users. Digital Bodies says other platforms that should make it even easier for educators to get started creating and using virtual experiences may emerge.

"Very specifically targeted platforms—things like Labster, which creates virtual chemistry labs—will become important in specialized subjects," Craig said. "To be able to put together molecules virtually, as opposed to in real life, they make us enter into this world of simulation where we're free to play around and make mistakes—and that will be powerful for the learning environment."

In addition to platforms, there are many apps in the works that enable users to tag content, add layers and otherwise manipulate VR content. "We are witnessing a variety of mobile apps maturing and likely to see more development over this summer," Georgieva said.

ThingLink, for example, recently introduced a school-specific editor for creating 360-degree and VR content. Lifeliqe, Aurasma and Adobe are also working on more interactive tools.

4. 360-Degree Cameras

Newer 360-degree cameras have introduced more user-friendly features, like video stitching and live streaming, which educators can utilize to introduce more video content in course materials.

"I've talked to faculty and students and they've said VR video content is much easier to produce. At the same time, they get to create real stories from that—not just a field trip but more for a storytelling type of experience or project," Craig said.

He has been using 360-degree video in several of his classes at the College of New Rochelle and has helped a few faculty members experiment with VR content. "It's interesting for students to begin to explore this area and think about how they might use this as, for example, future nurses or artists who might transition their work to a 360-degree environment down the road."

Georgieva also sees more products coming up in this category, such as the Samsung Gear 360 camera that was released last March. It can capture video in 4K resolution, live-stream in 2K resolution and allows users to edit and share content in real time.

5. Social VR Spaces

Aside from steep setup costs and technological barriers, another challenge in using VR in a classroom or lab is that the student is isolated within the experience.

"Education works best when you're talking with each other. Eye contact is extremely important for the learning environment," Craig said. "That collaboration, communication and connection has to get into our VR platforms and it will. I think within the year, you'll see a number of social VR platforms."

AltspaceVR has tremendous potential, he noted, since it uses avatars and supports multiplayer sessions that allow for socialization and user interaction. "With the front row feature, you can go and be part of an event or audience. You can be part of a small group with your friends, or go alone. No matter which option you choose, you feel like you're in direct contact with the performer," Craig said.

Facebook has been continuing to develop its own VR platform, Facebook Spaces, which is in beta. LectureVR is a similar platform on the horizon.

"Facebook Spaces may offer a compelling example of how we can leverage the social aspect of VR, from inspiring virtual clubs and tutoring options to experiential learning that can greatly enhance both the onsite and online student experiences," Georgieva said.

 **New Words**

specifically [spə'sɪfɪkli] *adv.* 特别地；明确地；具体地

shrink [ʃrɪŋk] *v.* 缩小，收缩

augmented [ɔ:g'mentɪd] *adj.* 增广的；增音的；增强的

compelling [kəm'pelɪŋ] *adj.* 引人注目的；激发兴趣的

gamified ['geɪmɪfaɪd] *adj.* 游戏化的

cusp [kʌsp] *n.* 尖头；尖端；风口浪尖

hololens ['hɒləʊlenz] *n.* [激光]全息透镜

pricey ['praɪsi] *adj.* 高价的，过分昂贵的

debut ['deɪbju:] *v.* 初次登台；登场

tether ['teðə] *v.* 用绳或链拴住；连接

crowdfunding ['kraʊd'fʌndɪŋ] *n.* 众筹；群众募资

high-end [haɪ-'end] *adj.* 高端的，高档的

full-motion [fʊl-'məʊʃən] *adj.* 全动态；全动感

stylus ['staɪləs] *n.* 触笔（在电脑屏幕上书写、画画等用）

fidelity [fɪ'deləti] *n.* 保真度；精确

molecule ['mɒlɪkju:l] *n.* 分子；微粒

resolution [ˌrezə'lu:ʃən] *n.* 分辨率；决议

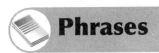 **Phrases**

look out for 留心；设法得到
HTC Vive 一款头戴式虚拟现实显示器
motion controller 运动控制器；动作控制器；体感控制器
video stitching 视频拼接
live streaming 实时流媒体；现场直播

down the road 将来的某个时候；一段时间之后
in real time 实时的；即时的
aside from 除……之外
in beta 在测试中
on the horizon 在地平线上；即将来临的

 **Abbreviations**

South by Southwest (SXSW) 一家美国的教育公司
Science, Technology, Engineering, Mathematics (STEM) 源于美国的一种教育模式
Augmented Reality (AR) 增强现实技术

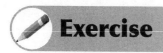 **Exercise**

Decide whether the following statements are true (T) or false (F) according to Text B. Give your reasons for the false ones.

(　) (1) VR technology does not gain any acceptance in higher education.

(　) (2) Pedagogy will not change with the application of VR technology in the classroom.

(　) (3) We can expect to see more high quality VR headsets at lower price.

(　) (4) The Kickstarter crowdfunding efforts will make high-end VR headsets more accessible for teaching.

(　) (5) According to Craig, both K-12 and higher education communities are going to adopt the VR content platforms for learning needs.

(　) (6) Future nurses or artists might transition their work to a 360-degree environment.

(　) (7) The educators do not find any challenges in applying VR in the classroom.

(　) (8) It is unlikely that collaboration, communication and connection can get into the educational VR platforms.

(　) (9) Some VR technology allows users to make avatars and supports multiplayer sessions so that socialization and user interaction could be achieved.

(　) (10) By leveraging the social aspect of VR, we can greatly enhance both the onsite and online student experiences.

 Supplementary Reading

Text	Notes
How VR Can Close Learning Gaps in Your Classroom	
Virtual Reality (VR) may be the type of educational	

breakthrough that comes along once in a generation, heralding[1] a tectonic[2] shift toward immersive content for teaching and instruction.

By presenting a complete view of the world in which it is situated, VR offers a new opportunity to close some of the pedagogical gaps that have appeared in 21st century classroom learning. These gaps stem from[3] the fact that curriculum and content in education have not caught up with rapid technology advancements.

Below I introduce three of these gaps and how they might be addressed by VR content soon to be produced and distributed commercially. Put aside[4], if you will, considerations of budget and adoption that accompany any new technology entering the education world.

1. The Attention Gap

Much has been written about social media's impact on our diminishing attention span[5], which may now be even shorter than that of a goldfish.

There are exceptions. Many of us are able to engage for extended periods of time when gaming or using simulations. Research has shown that we remember 20% of what we hear, 30% of what we see, and up to 90% of what we do or simulate. VR yields the latter scenario impeccably[6]. Singularity Hub's[7] Alison Berman describes, for example, how VR might allow a student to simulate flying through the bloodstream while learning about different cells he encounters.

2. The Time-effective Use Gap

While classrooms conceptually teach life skills, actual opportunities to apply them are more rare. VR can help make students' time in the classroom more effective preparing for the job market.

Use of VR is already returning positive results on the athletic field. Photorealism[8], the attempt to reproduce an image as realistic as possible in another medium, has had such success that the NFL[9] and the Dallas Cowboys are beginning to use it to train football players. Wearing a VR headset, a player sees practice film as the backdrop[10] and experiences of the reality

[1] herald *v.* 预示……的来临
[2] tectonic *adj.* 构造的；建筑的

[3] stem from 源于，来自

[4] put aside 撇开；暂不考虑

[5] attention span 注意力的持续时间

[6] impeccably *adv.* 无可挑剔地；完美地
[7] Singularity Hub 奇点中心，一个专注于报道尖端科技的新闻网站

[8] photorealism *n.* 照相现实主义

[9] NFL（National Football League）美国国家橄榄球联盟

[10] backdrop *n.* 背景；背景幕

being on the field. More significantly (to some), photorealism might someday allow students to perform surgery in science class.

3. The Pedagogy Gap

If you want to be fluent in German, you do not learn Swedish. In a similar way, if you want students to learn information and skills about economy, you do not teach them in text. You teach them in video and in immersive content they can "touch"—thus bridging the gap between what the world looks and acts like and what modern pedagogy actually teaches students to do.

Teachers are already striving to integrate YouTube and Netflix into curriculum to offer individualized instruction, but there are limitations on what even the best video resources can do. UN senior advisor and filmmaker Gabo Arora says in a recent *Wired*[11] article:

"A YouTube video or a talk can give you information but not necessarily the ability to immerse yourself in the world of another, and also interact with people. There's something about how VR is being made—there's a spontaneity[12] and naturalness that's not necessarily coming out in other means."

Virtual Reality is anything but rote memorization. It offers a new type of discovery and organic exploration to encourage lifelong learning.

4. Learning the Language

I believe this is the future of virtual blended learning, a virtual environment that offers real-life application through photorealism. Premium[13] VR systems might not be ready for mass educational consumption for another couple of years. However, by naming this emerging discipline, I hope we can begin to create and define its applications and the creative power it has to influence and instruct.

Below are other important VR terms, as well as a list of companies forging ahead[14] with virtual blended learning applications.

- VR is everything that is not real. It allows you to experience a world that does not have a physical form.

[11] Wired《连线》，一家美国杂志

[12] spontaneity *n.* 自发性；自然发生

[13] premium *adj.* 高价的；优质的

[14] forge ahead 锐意进取；取得进展

● Head Mounted Display (HMD) is the current form of hardware delivering VR experiences to users, and one of the most common VR terms you will hear about today. An HMD is typically a pair of goggles[15] or a helmet[16] of some type, with which you are viewing the VR experience. 2016 saw the commercial releases of VR headsets from Oculus Rift, HTC Vive, Sony Morpheus, Microsoft Hololens, in addition to those already available from Google Cardboard and Samsung Gear VR.

● Augmented Reality (AR) is the virtual world augmented with real life notions. A simple example would be using a gyroscope[17] to play games on your Android phone. For more sophisticated applications in the marketplace, look to Boeing's experiments or the Marines, who are using it for field training. Then there is Microsoft Hololens, which will be one of the first commercial HMDs of its kind offering high-definition holograms[18] seamlessly integrated into physical places. Note also that Magic Leap's augmented reality development platform garnered[19] $542 million in investments from Google and others last year.

VR is arriving—but as with any new technology, it will take time to develop best practices. This year is a great time to dive in and ask questions, before consumer adoption takes off in the next. You will be glad you did!

[15] goggles *n.* 护目镜；眼罩；风镜
[16] helmet *n.* 钢盔，头盔

[17] gyroscope *n.* 陀螺仪；回转仪

[18] hologram *n.* 全息图；全息摄影
[19] garner *v.* 获得；把……储入谷仓

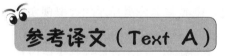

参考译文（Text A）

当虚拟现实邂逅教育

自 20 世纪 50 年代以来，虚拟现实（VR）一直徘徊在主流技术的边缘，在主流应用或商业应用方面没有得到公认。但在 2012 年，虚拟现实初创公司已经筹集了超过 14.6 亿美元的风险投资，其中包括过去连续四个季度超过 1 亿美元的资金。

根据花旗银行的分析师绘泽浩太的说法，2016 年是虚拟现实真正腾飞的一年。2019 年，虚拟现实市场增长到 159 亿美元。花旗还称，2020 年，硬件、网络、软件和内容市场的规模达到 2,000 亿美元。

这一市场的内容份额尤其令人感兴趣，因为这部分科技产业历来专注于游戏——但世界正在发生变化。我们正从奥尔德斯·赫胥黎《美丽新世界》中目前相对温和的宇宙，转

向《头号玩家》中欧内斯特·克莱恩描述的虚拟现实范式。和赫胥黎一样，克莱恩也描述了一个反乌托邦的环境，在这个环境中，科技已经超越了人类。

为了我们的目的，让我们把虚拟现实看作一种有用的工具，甚至可以看作是对人类互动的一种富有成效的推进，把来自世界各地的人们聚集在一起，让其参与并互动——不管社会、经济或地理差异如何。无论在理论上还是在应用上，现代教育都准备利用这一最新的技术创新。

在过去的几年里，虚拟现实已经不局限于军事和航空领域，成为职业发展的主流。因为经理、讲师、教练和治疗师都声称，这种沉浸式体验带来了越来越多的好处。

尽管在 K-12 学校和大学中使用虚拟现实的数据尚待统计，但相关公司（包括 zSpace、Alchemy VR 和 Immersive VR）的大量涌现反映了这个市场的稳步增长，这些公司完全致力于为学校提供打包的教育课程和内容、教师培训，以及技术工具来支持基于虚拟现实教学在课堂的应用。无数的文章、研究和会议展示都证明了 3D 浸入和虚拟现实技术在欧美数百个教育创新学校的课堂和实验室取得了巨大成功。

这种基于虚拟现实的学习早期大多集中在自然科学领域——生物学、解剖学、地质学和天文学——因为这些课程的重点和学习机会通过与立体物体、动物和环境的互动得到明显地充实。《夸美纽斯世界》是捷克一所学校的生物课软件，它采用了"厉动"体感控制器和特别改装的 Oculus Rift DK2 头戴设备，堪称创新科学学习的典范。

在其他教育领域，许多班级使用虚拟现实工具合作构建建筑模型，再建历史或自然景观和其他空间效果图。教师们还利用虚拟现实技术，让学生们沉浸在与文学、历史和经济学相关的话题中，无论是历史上的还是正在演变的，都能给他们在时间和地点上带来一种身临其境的感觉。

谷歌在 2015 年 9 月推出了先锋探险项目，这可能会成为沉浸式教育游戏的变革。在这个框架下，世界各地成千上万的学校可以得到一个组件一天的使用权，这个组件包含老师带领他们班级学生进行虚拟之旅的所有工具：华硕智能手机、供老师指挥旅程的平板电脑、一个让探险项目在没有互联网时也可运行的路由器、一个拥有 100 多个虚拟旅程的图书馆（从中国的长城到火星），以及谷歌公司的纸板盒眼镜或美泰公司开发的虚拟现实眼镜，其能把智能手机变成虚拟现实头戴式显示器。

虚拟现实内容和访问的全球分布无疑将影响教学方法的转变，因为这些新技术可以让位于芝加哥的文学老师将学生"带到"维罗纳去看莎士比亚的戏剧《罗密欧与朱丽叶》的故事场景，或让位于纽约布朗克斯"古代文明"课程的老师把学生"带到"奇琴伊察的古玛雅遗址。

新近出现的沉浸式虚拟现实教育平台，如 AltspaceVR 和 LectureVR，给各类教师提供了全新的可能性。因为创建虚拟角色和支持"多玩家"远程信息连接的技术可以实现指数级规模的社交和拓展。

这些创新的虚拟现实平台产品之间的合作可能会使一名策展人或艺术家带领数千人参观博物馆展览或文化遗址，或一名演员或教授实时地主导一个来自世界各地学生的虚拟大师班。

也许这项技术最理想的应用将是搭建文化桥梁和增进年轻学生之间的理解，因为不久的将来，美国的三年级学生就可以和印度或墨西哥的三年级学生一起参加虚拟旅行。

尽管虚拟现实仍在发展中，但此技术在经济方面已经取得了真正的进步。对消费者而言，虚拟现实硬件（尤其是头戴设备）的价格一直在稳步下降。例如，如今市面上的头戴式显示器（HMDs）：谷歌的纸板盒眼镜售价 20 美元，三星 Gear VR 售价 99 美元，桌面虚拟现实设备 Oculus Rift 的预购价格为 599 美元。

《纽约时报》最近向 100 多万用户提供了谷歌硬纸板头戴式设备，让用户可以访问其新推出的虚拟现实体验，这进一步推动了该设备的可访问性和主流化，以及这种创新的媒体消费方式。

总的来说，越来越多的个人用户甚至学校能够负担得起使用某种类型的移动虚拟现实设备。一些有远见的教师甚至使用 3D 打印机和他们技术专业的学生一起打印他们自己个性化的头戴式显示器，这一方案也与现在流行的创客趋势相吻合。

所以也许我们已经为《头号玩家》中的未来世界做好了准备。然而，也许乌托邦式与反乌托邦式的构想相比，不仅更有吸引力，而且在这个全球社会中更有意义。

教育工作者和学生都在寻求一种不断扩展的沉浸式环境，在这种环境中，学生通过广泛的互动资源与老师和同学以变革性体验的方式进行互动。在这种教育现实中，虚拟现实具有明确的价值定位。

Unit 11

Artificial Intelligence in Education

For decades, science fiction authors, futurists, and moviemakers alike have been predicting the amazing (and sometimes catastrophic) changes that will arise with the advent of widespread artificial intelligence. So far, Artificial Intelligence (AI) has not made any such crazy waves, and in many ways has quietly become ubiquitous in numerous aspects of our daily lives. From the intelligent sensors that help us take perfect pictures, to the automatic parking features in cars, to the sometimes frustrating personal assistants in smartphones, AI of one kind or another is all around us, all the time.

While we've yet to create self-aware robots like those in the popular movies like *2001: A Space Odyssey* and *Star Wars*, we have made smart and often significant use of AI technology in a wide range of applications that, while not as mind-blowing as androids, still change our day-to-day lives. One place where artificial intelligence is poised to make big changes (and in some cases already is) is in education.

While we may not see humanoid robots acting as teachers within the next decade, there are many projects already in the works that use computer intelligence to help students and teachers get more out of the educational experience. Here are just a few of the ways and tools that will shape and define the educational experience of the future.

1. AI Can Automate Basic Activities in Education, Like Grading.

In college, grading homework and tests for large lecture courses can be tedious work, even when teaching assistants split it between them. Even in lower grades, teachers often find that grading takes up a significant amount of time, which could be used to interact with students, prepare for class, or work on professional development.

While AI may not ever be able to truly replace human grading, it is getting pretty close. It is now possible for teachers to automate grading for nearly all kinds of multiple choices, and fill-in-the-blank testing and automated grading of student writing may not be far behind. Today, essay-grading software is still in its infancy and not quite up to par, yet it can (and will) improve over the coming years, allowing teachers to focus more on in-class activities and student interaction than grading.

2. Educational Software Can Be Adapted to Student Needs.

From kindergarten to graduate school, one of the key ways AI will impact education is through the application of greater levels of individualized learning. Some of this has already been happening through growing numbers of adaptive learning programs, games, and software. These systems respond to the needs of the student, putting greater emphasis on certain topics, repeating things that students haven't mastered, and generally helping students to work at their own pace, whatever that may be.

This kind of custom-tailored education could be a machine-assisted solution to help students at different levels work together in one classroom, with teachers facilitating the learning and offering help and support when needed. Adaptive learning has already had a huge impact on education across the nation (especially through programs like Khan Academy), and as AI advances in the coming decades, adaptive programs like these will be likely to improve and expand.

3. It Can Point Out Places Where Courses Need to Improve.

Teachers may not always be aware of gaps in their lectures and educational materials that can leave students confused about certain concepts. AI offers a way to solve this problem. Coursera, a massive open online course provider, has already been putting this into practice. When a large number of students are found to submit the wrong answer to a homework assignment, the system alerts the teacher and gives future students a customized message that offers hints to the correct answer.

This type of system helps to fill in the gaps in explanation that can occur in courses, and helps to ensure that all students are building the same conceptual foundation. Rather than waiting to hear back from the professor, students get immediate feedback that helps them to understand a concept and remember how to do it correctly the next time around.

4. Students Could Get Additional Support from AI Tutors.

While there are obviously things that human tutors can offer but machines cannot, at least not yet, the future could see more students being tutored by tutors that only exist in zeros and ones. Some tutoring programs based on AI already exist and can help students through basic mathematics, writing, and other subjects.

These programs can teach students fundamentals, but so far aren't ideal for helping students learn high-order thinking and creativity, something that real-world teachers are still required to facilitate. Yet it shouldn't rule out the possibility of AI tutors being able to do these things in the future. With the rapid pace of technological advancement that has marked the past few decades, advanced tutoring systems may not be a pipe dream.

5. AI-driven Programs Can Give Students and Educators Helpful Feedback.

AI can not only help teachers and students to craft courses that are customized to their needs, but it can also provide feedback to both about the success of the course as a whole. Some schools, especially those with online offerings, are using AI systems to monitor student progress and to alert professors when there might be an issue with student performance.

These kinds of AI systems allow students to get the support they need and allow professors to find areas where they can improve instruction for students who may struggle with the subject matter. AI programs at these schools aren't just offering advice on individual courses, however. Some are working to develop systems that can help students to choose majors based on areas where they succeed and struggle. While students don't have to take the advice, it could mark a brave new world of college major selection for future students.

6. It Is Altering How We Find and Interact with Information.

We rarely even notice the AI systems that affect the information we see and find on a daily basis. Google adapts results to users based on location; Amazon makes recommendations based on previous purchases; Siri adapts to our needs and commands; and nearly all web ads are geared toward our interests and shopping preferences.

These kinds of intelligent systems play a big role in how we interact with information in our personal and professional lives, and could just change how we find and use information in schools and academia as well. Over the past few decades, AI-based systems have already radically changed how we interact with information and with newer, more integrated technology, students in the future may have vastly different experiences doing research and looking up facts than the students of today.

7. It Could Change the Role of Teachers.

There will always be a role for teachers in education, but what that role is and what it entails may change due to new technology in the form of intelligent computing systems. As we have already discussed, AI can take over tasks like grading, help students improve learning, and may even be a substitute for real-world tutoring. Yet AI could be adapted to many other aspects of teaching as well. AI systems could be programmed to provide expertise, serving as a place for students to ask questions and find information or could even potentially take the place of teachers for very basic course materials. In most cases, however, AI will shift the role of the teacher to that of facilitator.

Teachers will supplement AI lessons, assist students who are struggling, and provide human interaction and hands-on experiences for students. In many ways, technology has already been driving some of these changes in the classroom, especially in schools that are online or embrace the flipped classroom model.

8. AI Can Make Trial-and-error Learning Less Intimidating.

Trial and error is a critical part of learning, but for many students, the idea of failing, or even not knowing the answer, is paralyzing. Some simply do not like being put on the spot in front of their peers or authority figures like a teacher. An intelligent computer system, designed to help students to learn, is a much less daunting way to deal with trial and error. AI could offer students a way to experiment and learn in a relatively judgment-free environment, especially when AI tutors can offer solutions for improvement. In fact, AI is the perfect format for supporting this kind of learning, as AI systems themselves often learn by a trial-and-error method.

9. Data Powered by AI Can Change How Schools Find, Teach, and Support Students.

Smart data gathering, powered by intelligent computer systems, has already been making changes to how colleges interact with prospective and current students. From recruiting to helping students choose the best courses, intelligent computer systems are helping make every part of the college experience more closely tailored to student needs and goals.

Data mining systems have already been playing an integral role in today's higher-education landscape, but AI could further alter higher education. Initiatives are already underway at some schools to offer students AI-guided training that can ease the transition between college and high school. We don't know whether the college selection process may end up a lot like Amazon or Netflix, with a system that recommends the best schools and programs for student interests.

10. AI May Change Where Students Learn, Who Teaches Them, and How They Acquire Basic Skills.

While major changes may happen a few decades in the future, the reality is that artificial intelligence has the potential to radically change just about everything we take for granted about education.

Using AI systems, software, and support, students can learn from anywhere in the world at any time, and with these kinds of programs taking the place of certain types of classroom instruction, AI may just replace teachers in some instances (for better or worse). Educational programs powered by AI have already been helping students to learn basic skills, but as these programs grow and as developers learn more, they are likely to offer students a much wider range of services.

 **New Words**

catastrophic [ˌkætə'strɒfɪk] *adj.* 灾难的；悲惨的	self-aware [ˌself-ə'weə] *adj.* 有自我意识的；能自我感知的

mind-blowing ['maɪnd-bləʊɪŋ] *adj.* 使兴奋的；引起幻觉的

android ['ændrɔɪd] *n.* 机器人；安卓系统

humanoid ['hju:mənɔɪd] *adj.* 像人的；仿生的

automate ['ɔ:təmeɪt] *v.* 使自动化，使自动操作

grading ['greɪdɪŋ] *n.* 批改；打分；阅卷

hint [hɪnt] *n.* 暗示，提示

craft [krɑ:ft] *v.* 精巧地制作

Siri ['siri] *n.* 苹果公司产品中的智能语音助手

academia [ˌækə'di:miə] *n.* 学术界；学术生涯

intimidating [ɪn'tɪmɪdeɪtɪŋ] *adj.* 吓人的，令人生畏的

paralyzing ['pærəˌlaɪzɪŋ] *adj.* 使人瘫痪的；使人麻痹的

daunting ['dɔ:ntɪŋ] *adj.* 使人气馁的，令人却步的

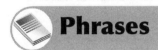

Phrases

science fiction 科幻小说，科幻文学

with the advent of 随着……出现，随着……的到来

in its infancy 在初始阶段，处于发展初期

up to par 达到标准，合乎标准

graduate school 研究生院

Khan Academy 可汗学院（一个免费的网上教育平台）

pipe dream 白日梦，空想

gear toward 改变调整某事物；专门朝向某事发展

data mining 数据挖掘（指从资料中发掘资讯或知识）

who knows but that 多半；亦未可知

Abbreviation

Artificial Intelligence (AI) 人工智能

✎ Exercises

Ex. 1 Give the English equivalents of the following Chinese expressions.

(1) 有自我意识的；能自我感知的 _____

(2) 机器人；安卓系统 _____

(3) 批改；打分；阅卷 _____

(4) 专门知识；专门技术 _____

(5) 使人气馁的，令人怯步的 _____

(6) 随着……出现，随着……的到来 _____

(7) 在初始阶段，处于发展初期 _____

(8) 数据挖掘 _____

(9) 多半；亦未可知 _____

(10) 人工智能 _____

Ex. 2 Decide whether the following statements are true (T) or false (F) according to Text A. Give your reasons for the false ones.

(   ) (1) There is still a long way to go for AI to be used in our daily life.

(   ) (2) AI won't make any waves in education.

(   ) (3) AI technology has already been used in automatic grading, such as multiple choices and blank filling.

(   ) (4) The essay-grading software is very mature now.

(   ) (5) Adaptive learning has already had a huge impact on education, especially through programs like Khan Academy.

(   ) (6) Teachers sometimes could not realize the gaps in their lectures and educational materials that can leave students confused about certain concepts.

(   ) (7) The future could see more students being tutored by tutoring programs based on AI.

(   ) (8) Currently the tutoring programs can teach students fundamentals, as well as high-order thinking and creativity.

(   ) (9) AI will shift the role of the teacher to that of facilitator.

(   ) (10) AI-guided training cannot ease the transition between high school and college.

Ex. 3 Answer the following questions according to Text A.

(1) Could you give some examples of AI's application in daily life?

(2) Could AI help with teacher's grading work? Could you elaborate?

(3) Could you explain "adaptive learning"?

(4) By what means can AI point out places where courses need to improve?

(5) What kind of knowledge can AI tutors teach students at present?

(6) In what way might the AI system change the role of a teacher?

(7) Why is the AI system a much less daunting way to deal with trial and error in learning?

(8) What can AI-guided training do for the newly admitted college students?

Ex. 4 Fill in the blanks with the words given below.

accessible	disciplines	possibilities	cooperated	accuracy
hands-on	trend	key	approaches	aims

China's action plan on AI education calls for the integration of AI with mathematics, statistics, physics, biology, psychology, and sociology, among other (1)_____. It promoted the "AI + X" interdisciplinary approach in universities and (2)_____ to set up 100 majors that combine AI and other subjects in 2020.

The (3)_____ is how to use AI in various disciplines, said Weng Kai, a teacher in Zhejiang University's AI Research Institute. "We hope AI technology is (4)_____ to every student so that they may combine AI as a tool with their own research, which may lead to new (5)_____," Weng said.

Researchers from both the medical school and AI Research Institute of Zhejiang University have (6)_____ in developing an intelligent recognition and auxiliary diagnosis system for keratitis, which has greatly improved diagnostic (7)_____ for the disease.

Besides these interdisciplinary (8)_____ adopted in the university, there is also a growing (9)_____ for universities to strengthen links with industry in AI technology. Nanjing University has cooperated with e-commerce giant JD.com in creating an AI training base for students. Students will conduct (10)_____ learning for real AI applications under the guidance of high-level instructors.

Text B

The Education Cloud: Delivering Education as a Service

1. Introduction

The massive proliferation of affordable computers, internet broadband connectivity and rich education content has created a global phenomenon in which Information and Communication Technology (ICT) is being used to transform education. Cloud computing is beginning to play a key role in this transformation.

The U.S. National Institute of Standards and Technology gives the following definition of cloud computing:

"Cloud computing is a model for enabling ubiquitous, convenient, on-demand network access to a shared pool of configurable computing resources (e.g., networks, servers, storage, applications and services) that can be rapidly provisioned and released with minimal management effort or service provider interaction."

Simply speaking, cloud computing is a set of hardware and network resources that combine the power of multiple servers to deliver different kinds of services via the web. When discussing cloud computing technology in education, it is important to mention its three most important categories:

● Software-as-a-Service (SaaS). It refers to any type of application software that is managed remotely and delivered via the web.

● Platform-as-a-Service (PaaS). The service provider delivers the platform or OS, which frees users from installing and maintaining the hardware and software.

● Infrastructure-as-a-Service (IaaS). IaaS is a service model that delivers computer infrastructure on an outsourced basis to support users' operations.

That is, the service provider hosts the hardware and software on its own infrastructure. The users simply access it via the Internet, freeing selves from complex software and hardware installation and management. Figure 11-1 illustrates these three layers of services.

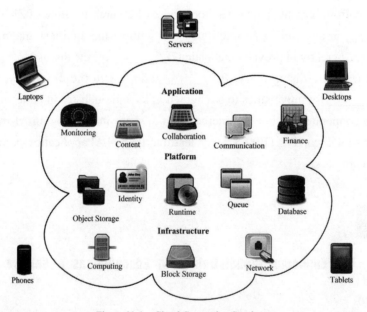

Figure 11-1　Cloud Computing Services

In education, each of these three models plays an important role in general education transformation. By storing complex IT infrastructure on remote servers, cloud vendors make advanced computing tools available to institutions at low price, which contributes to a rapid adoption of these services. Additionally, new provisioning models have triggered proliferation of various cost-efficient software programs, collaborative platforms and web applications. Their adoption is often seen as a major form of education innovation. By making ICT more affordable to implement and easier to integrate into classrooms worldwide, education can be transformed—students across the globe can develop the critical skills they need to compete and prosper in today's information society.

2. Cloud Computing Simplified

There has been much hype about cloud computing, and cloud computing has the potential to play a vital role in education transformation. However, there remains a need to distill it into a practical, consistent, accessible framework for education. To understand cloud computing in the context of education, it helps to begin by understanding the notion of "service". A service is a type of software function or capability that is accessible anytime and anywhere via a computing device such as a laptop, desktop, handheld PDA or cell phone. Some of the more common examples of cloud services are Google Apps, Amazon EC2 and SalesForce.com. Other more generic services include wikis, blogs and email.

From a user's perspective, a cloud can make all of these (and more) services available in such a way that the user does not have to be concerned with where the services originate or even where the services are running. The services are just "out there" somewhere, in the cloud, and the user can access them at any time, from any device (see Figure 11-1). In reality, cloud services might originate in one place but actually run on a standalone laptop or cell phone, or on a server somewhere in cyberspace. It is also possible for a single service to be running on some combination of devices. Google Earth, for example, can run standalone on an individual laptop, but when the Earth image on the laptop has to be updated, those updates come from one or a combination of Google's data centers around the world.

3. The Education Cloud

To support education transformation, cloud computing can help government leaders, educators and IT decision makers answer key strategic questions such as:

- What is the quickest, most efficient and affordable way to deliver education?
- How do I develop students' 21st-century skills and prepare students for the new job market?
- How do I encourage local innovation within a country or region?
- How do I share resources across districts, regions or the entire country?

With the flexibility and affordability of cloud computing, it is possible to answer these questions and develop education programs and strategies that also:

- Simplify, speed and reduce the cost of development, integration procurement, and operation and maintenance of ICT infrastructure;
- Capitalize on worldwide innovation of developers;
- Focus on the user experience and expected outcomes, not on infrastructure;
- Simplify management of vendors;
- Provide better visibility of results and impacts, using cause-and-effect analyses for continuous improvement.

For example, the ePortfolio is a cloud service that can be delivered to the members of an education community. A student portfolio is a valuable record of a student's academic life. The record may include items such as assessments, evaluations, assignments, homework, and classroom projects. These portfolios are critical for managing each student's academic progress, and—when student portfolios are collectively reviewed by the Ministry of Education (MoE)—they can also play an important role in managing the performance and progress of an entire education system.

Moreover, ePortfolios present significant advantages over paper-based alternatives. One reason is their accessibility. End users—that may include students, teachers, parents, administrators and government officials—can access the ePortfolios at any time, from computers, cell phones or other devices. The ePortfolios can be accessed by teachers to issue assignments, and by students to access assignments. A school principal can use students' ePortfolios to monitor the performance of the school, and parents can access their own child's portfolio in order to become more involved in their child's education.

Using cloud computing, the ePortfolio service can be designed in several ways. For instance, the service can run as a standalone service on a laptop, without connectivity. The service can also run from local school servers, from a MoE data center or from a third-party services provider that is accessed via the Internet.

4. A Model of Education Cloud

The real power of education clouds becomes evident when viewed from a user's perspective. As depicted in Figure 11-2, a set of users (including students, teachers, parents and others) can access a variety of education cloud services, using whatever device or devices they have access to (laptops, desktops, PDAs, etc.). A common cloud infrastructure like the one illustrated in Figure 11-2 can scale services across dozens or even thousands of schools. If an ICT infrastructure is

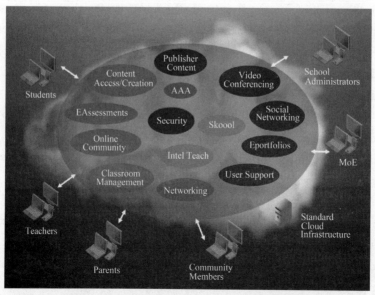

Figure 11-2　K-12 Education Cloud Example—User's Perspective

already in place, an education cloud facilitates the integration of this existing infrastructure with new technology and solutions. The cloud also "wraps around" the existing infrastructure so that it can be accessed as services. In instances in which there is little or no existing infrastructure, an education cloud helps to make cloud-based services available more quickly to schools, as well as to teachers and students.

In the connected age, it does not matter where the information is, where the student is, or where the faculty member is. What matters is the value that comes from the connection. In the connected age, data, collaboration tools, and communities can come together in ways never possible before.

5. Concluding Remarks

Every coin has two sides. Cloud education is becoming a trend and benefiting an increasing number of learners. Its application is not without limitations. This table summarizes both the benefits and limitations of cloud education.

Benefits	Limitations
Access to applications from anywhere	Not all applications run in cloud
Support for teaching and learning	Risks related to data protection and security and accounts management
Software free or pay per use	Organizational support
24-hours access to infrastructure and content	Dissemination politics, intellectual property
Opening to business environment and advanced research	Security and protection of sensitive data
Protection of the environment by using green technologies	Maturity of solutions
Increased openness of students to new technologies	Lack of confidence
Increasing functional capabilities	Standards adherence
Offline usage with further synchronization opportunities	Speed/lack of Internet can affect work methods

Although still quite a vague term for some, cloud computing is definitely one of the major innovations that enter worldwide classrooms in recent years. With the ability to cut IT costs and at the same time to create a modern collaborative environment, educational institutions can see some important benefits from moving to the cloud. Modernizing learning processes and introducing the latest technologies in classrooms encourage students to develop skills and knowledge necessary for achieving their academic and professional goals. From this perspective, it is obvious what a valuable resource the cloud is in the education sector. Together with other forms of technology implementation, the cloud can substantially increase learning opportunities for students all over the world, and eventually contribute to equipping future generations with skills and competences necessary for international career advancements.

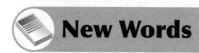 **New Words**

proliferation [prə,lɪfə'reɪʃən] *n.* 扩散，增殖

broadband ['brɔːdbænd] *n.* 宽带；宽频

configurable [kən'fɪɡərəbl] *adj.* 可配置的；结构的

provision [prə'vɪʒən] *v.* 供给，供应

remotely [rɪ'məʊtli] *adv.* 遥远地；远程地

infrastructure ['ɪnfrəstrʌktʃə] *n.* 基础设施

outsource ['aʊtsɔːs] *v.* 外包，委外

prosper ['prɒspə] *v.* 繁荣，昌盛；成功

simplify ['sɪmplɪfaɪ] *v.* 简化；使单纯；使简易

hype [haɪp] *n.* 大肆宣传；炒作

distill [dɪs'tɪl] *v.* 提取，提炼

wikis [wɪkɪs] *n.* 维基百科

standalone ['stændə,ləʊn] *adj.* 单独的，独立的

cyberspace ['saɪbəspeɪs] *n.* 赛博空间，网络空间

affordability [ə,fɔːdə'bɪləti] *n.* 支付能力；负担能力

procurement [prə'kjʊəmənt] *n.* 采购；获得

maintenance ['meɪntənəns] *n.* 维护，维修

visibility [,vɪzə'bɪləti] *n.* 能见度，可见性

portfolio [pɔːt'fəʊliəʊ] *n.* 公文包；作品集；系列产品

principal ['prɪnsəpəl] *n.* 首长；校长

account [ə'kaʊnt] *n.* 账户；账号

dissemination [dɪsemɪ'neɪʃən] *n.* 宣传；传播

maturity [mə'tʃʊərəti] *n.* 成熟；完备

adherence [əd'hɪərəns] *n.* 坚持；依附；忠诚

synchronization [,sɪŋkrənaɪ'zeɪʃən] *n.* 同步，同时发生

substantially [səb'stænʃəli] *adv.* 实质上；大体上；充分地

advancement [əd'vɑːnsmənt] *n.* 前进，进步；提升

 **Phrases**

cloud computing 云计算

wrap around 环绕

intellectual property 知识产权；著作权

 Abbreviation

Personal Digital Assistant (PDA) 掌上电脑；个人数字助理

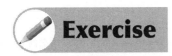

Exercise

Answer the following questions according to Text B.

(1) Could you define cloud computing?

(2) What is SaaS?

(3) What is PaaS?

(4) What is IaaS?

(5) What are the advantages of storing complex IT infrastructure on remote servers?

(6) Could you define "service" in terms of cloud computing?

(7) How could cloud computing help with stakeholders in terms of education transformation?

(8) What is a student portfolio?

Supplementary Reading

Text	Notes
How Teachers See the Classroom Redefined by the Cloud	
1. Everyplace Becomes a Learning Space with Cloud Technology	
Teachers are incorporating[1] cloud tools and content into instruction in ways that change how they interact with students both in and outside the classroom. They are no longer limited to face-to-face instruction or constricted[2] by class schedules. Instead, teachers are using both tools that are imposed by administrators and more ad-hoc[3] resources. For example, algebra teachers can spend more time troubleshooting individual students' problems by using content like Khan Academy to cover the core material. In other cases, Khan Academy can be used as additional support material.	[1] incorporate v. 包含；吸收；把……合并 [2] constrict v. 限制；限定 [3] ad-hoc adj. 特别的；专门的
Mark Miazga, an English and language arts teacher at Baltimore City College High School, is an example of a teacher who is taking the more ad-hoc approach. Miazga, who also mentors new teachers and writes curriculum for Baltimore City Public Schools, was featured[4] with his English class in the documentary *Experiencing Shakespeare*, produced by the Folger Shakespeare Library. Miazga regularly uses Folger's	[4] feature v. 以……为特色

resources, including *Hamlet*[5], Folger's online catalog plays by Shakespeare and other eminent[6] playwrights[7], and an image repository[8] called Luna.

However, Miazga said the largest role that the cloud has played in his teaching has been in shaping his students' writing process. "Most essays in our classes are turned in electronically via Google Docs[9]," he explained. "Students share their essays with a peer or their teacher, and we offer live comments. The student can then resolve the comment and make the changes."

"That collaboration between student and teacher can happen from anywhere", Miazga said, "on their tablet[10], laptop, or phone. This is a continuous conversation done in the cloud that vastly improves the student's writing ability." He has worked with this process for just the past two years, and he noted, "The difference it makes is amazing."

2. Blended Learning[11]

Jennifer Schmitt is a secondary world language educator at Lawrence High School in Lawrence, Kansas. She said her school's route to the cloud began with a "blended learning" process seven years ago and has continued to evolve as technology has changed. "We're changing the way we teach not for change's sake, but to bring 21st-century technology into the mix because it's not to be avoided."

Schmitt uses GoogleDocs for students and Office 365 OneNote for professional use, like generating reports to administrators and curriculum development. Like Miazga, she also uses content from the cloud to enhance instruction, including KU Acceso, a free cloud application provided by the University of Kansas, which works well for her students taking Spanish Level 4.

At home, Schmitt said, she also uses Khan Academy with her own kids—primarily for math during the summer to serve as a refresher. She noted that if she were to use it in the classroom, Khan Academy would function as a tutorial for students who needed extra help and not as a primary source. Regardless of what cloud tools are used, Schmitt emphasizes that teachers at her school use them to accentuate[12] the core material. Teachers, she insists, will always remain the primary source of material.

[5] *Hamlet n.* 《哈姆雷特》

[6] eminent *adj.* 杰出的；有名的

[7] playwright *n.* 剧作家

[8] image repository 虚拟镜像库

[9] Google Docs 谷歌在线办公软件

[10] tablet *n.* 平板电脑

[11] blended learning 混合式学习

[12] accentuate *v.* 强调，突出

Cloud tools enable Schmitt to do her job more efficiently, effectively, and creatively. They give her inspiration[13] for teaching activities, and she can access units of study and notes for the classroom from her phone while she is taking a walk. Schmitt grades papers and gives students feedback in real time from her house if necessary. She points out that the cloud has changed the way she educates in many of the same ways it has changed how businesses do business: by expanding the workspace.

Schmitt admits that she went through a learning curve when jumping into the new environment. At first, she spent more time planning things, familiarizing herself with the technologies, investigating which ones best suited her needs, and making contributions to the core shells. She carefully researched which tools were worth her time because she was not interested in using something just because it was fun and cool. A tool had to be functional and educational, too. "It took some time on the front end, but it's paid off in the long haul[14]."

Miazga illustrates how the use of cloud technology helps him be more fluid[15] in his curriculum design on the fly[16]. "I might see a great example from first period, snap a picture of it with my phone, then upload it into my presentation so the second period can benefit from it and I can share it with my colleagues." Another useful cloud environment, according to Miazga, is Google Classroom. He explains the power of its video upload and reveals that his students' next unit will be about social media. "They'll be creating their own TED Talk and uploading it to the app for other teachers to score after studying various aspects of the subject."

3. Benefiting from the Cloud

Students benefit from the cloud because the technology helps them make more efficient use of their time in the classroom. Miazga says that using Google Slides in the classroom has taken hold[17]. "Students will create slides, share them around, make changes, and, at the end of class, they review the class period's work." Kids get more done in their 45-50 minute class each day and have richer homework and research capabilities delivered anywhere they choose to study, be

[13] inspiration n. 灵感；启发

[14] in the long haul 长期，长时间

[15] fluid adj. 优雅流畅的

[16] on the fly 在运行中，在工作中

[17] take hold 生根；固定下来

it at home, the library, or Starbucks. This practice also benefits students who were sick or unable to attend class because they have immediate access to what was done that day. The cloud keeps them up to speed with their classmates.

Ken Roberts, head of marketing at Pathmatics, is father to two children who use different cloud applications in school. The youngest uses the School Loop[18] program. Roberts definitely sees an improvement in communication between teachers and parents, noting a higher degree of responsiveness from the teachers, which helps them work more as a cohesive[19] team. Parents can see grades, check to ensure that all assigned homework has been completed, and nudge[20] their children along if a piece is missing. "I like that everything is recorded within the app and nothing goes outside of the system, so there is a consistent thread." His oldest is a sophomore in high school and uses Windows-based tablets and OneNote to input and route all assignments.

As with all experiments, some cloud tools work better than others. Roberts points out that, in the case of his youngest, cloud technology is producing a better indirect, secondary role with the improved communications. However, Roberts also feels that the cloud is not as successful in the way it is being used with his oldest child. "With the older one, the way they've integrated a PC into it, the results are mixed. Just like in our corporate life, the kids spend a lot of time recuperating[21] from system and app crashes."

From a scholastic standpoint, the cloud offers educators outside of urban and private school environments equal access to world-class, global educational sites and teaching environments. As a result, their methodologies and their students' learning opportunities have a chance to flourish along with the best schools in the world, equalizing the playing field.

[18] School Loop 一个允许学生在网上查看自己成绩，并与老师沟通的在线应用程序

[19] cohesive *adj.* 有凝聚力的；紧密结合的

[20] nudge *v.* 推动；用肘轻推

[21] recuperate *v.* 恢复；挽回损失

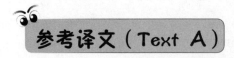

参考译文（Text A）

教育中的人工智能

几十年来，科幻小说作家、未来学家和电影制作人一直在预测，人工智能的普及将会带来惊人的（有时是灾难性的）变化。到目前为止，人工智能（AI）还没有掀起任何疯狂的风浪，以各种不同的方式，它已经悄悄地在我们日常生活的许多方面变得无处不在。从

帮助我们拍摄完美照片的智能传感器，到汽车的自动泊车功能，再到智能手机中有时会令人沮丧的个人助理，各种各样的人工智能每时每刻都在我们身边。

尽管我们还没有造出像《2001太空漫游》和《星球大战》等热门电影中那样具有自我意识的机器人，但我们已经在广泛的应用领域巧妙地使用了人工智能技术，这通常意义重大。这些应用虽然没有机器人那么令人振奋，但仍在改变我们的日常生活。人工智能即将做出重大改变（在某些情况下已经如此）的一个领域就是教育。

虽然我们可能不会在未来十年看到类人机器人担任教师，但已经有许多项目在进行中，这些项目利用计算机智能帮助学生和教师从教育体验中收获更多。以下的这些方法和工具将塑造和定义未来的教育体验。

1. 人工智能可以使教育中的基本活动自动化，比如评分。

在大学里，批改大型课程的作业和试卷可能是一项乏味的工作，即使有助教们来分担这部分工作。甚至在低年级，评分也占用了教师大量的时间，这些时间本来可以用于与学生互动、备课或职业发展。

虽然人工智能可能无法真正取代人类评分，但它已经非常接近了。现在，几乎所有的多项选择题都可以进行自动评分，填空题和学生写作作业的自动评分可能也不会落后太多。如今，文章批阅软件还处于初级阶段，尚未达到标准，但它可以（而且会）在未来几年得到改进，这将使得教师可以更多地注重课堂活动和学生互动，而不是评分。

2. 教育软件可以适应学生的需求。

从幼儿园到研究生院，人工智能影响教育的一个关键途径是应用更高层次的个性化学习，其中一些已经通过越来越多的自适应学习程序、游戏和软件实现了。这些系统会对学生的需求做出反应，重点强调某些主题，温习学生没有掌握的知识，而且不管怎样都会帮助学生按照自己的节奏学习。

这种量身定制的教育可以成为一种机器辅助教学方案，帮助同一个教室里不同层次的学生一起学习，老师会在需要的时候提供帮助和支持来促进学生学习。适应性学习已经在全国范围内对教育产生了巨大的影响（特别是通过可汗学院这样的项目），随着人工智能在未来几十年的发展，像这样的适应性项目很可能会得到改进和扩展。

3. 它可以指出课程在哪些地方需要改进。

教师不一定总能意识到他们的讲座和教学材料中的不足，这些不足可能会让学生对某些概念感到困惑。人工智能提供了一种解决这个问题的方法。大型在线公开课程提供商Coursera已经在实施这一计划。当发现大量学生提交了错误的作业答案时，系统会向老师发出警告，并向学生提供一条定制的信息，给出正确答案的提示。

这种系统有助于填补课程中可能出现的没有解释清楚的地方，并能确保所有学生都打下了相同的概念基础。学生不必再等待教师的答复，便可以得到即时的反馈，帮助他们理解某个概念，并记住下次如何正确地解答。

4. 学生可以从人工智能导师那里得到额外的支持。

很明显，尽管教师可以提供一些机器无法提供的东西，至少目前是这样，但未来可能会有更多的学生接受机器导师的指导。一些基于人工智能的辅导项目已经存在，可以在基础数学、写作和其他科目方面帮助学生。

这些项目可以教授学生基础知识，但到目前为止还不适合帮助学生学习高阶思维和创造能力，这些方面仍需要现实世界的教师指导。然而，这不排除人工智能导师在未来能够做这些事情的可能性。随着过去几十年技术的快速进步，先进的辅导系统可能不再是白日梦。

5. 人工智能驱动项目可以给学生和教育者提供有用的反馈。

人工智能不仅可以帮助教师和学生根据自己的需求定制课程，还可以在总体上为了课程的成功向教师和学生提供反馈。一些学校，尤其是那些提供在线课程的学校，正在使用人工智能系统来监控学生的学习进度，并在学生学习可能出现问题时提醒教授。

这些类型的人工智能系统可以让学生得到他们需要的支持，让教师找到可以改进教学的地方，为那些在学科方面可能遇到困难的学生提供帮助。然而，这些学校的人工智能项目不只是针对个别课程提供建议。一些人正在努力开发一套系统，帮助学生根据自己擅长和困难的领域来选择专业。虽然学生们不一定要采纳这些建议，但这可能标志着未来学生选择大学专业的一个崭新世界。

6. 它正在改变我们获取信息并与信息互动的方式。

我们日常很少注意影响我们看到和发现信息的人工智能系统。例如，谷歌根据用户的方位调整结果；亚马逊会根据之前的购买情况做推荐；Siri 语音助手能适应你的需求和命令；几乎所有的网络广告都会适应你的兴趣和购物偏好。

这类智能系统在我们的个人生活和职业生涯中与信息互动方面发挥着重要作用，也可能改变我们在学校和学术界发现和使用信息的方式。在过去的几十年里，基于人工智能的系统已经从根本上改变了我们与信息的交互方式。随着更新、更集成的技术发展，未来的学生在做研究和寻找事实方面的体验可能与现在的学生有很大的不同。

7. 它可以改变教师的角色。

教育中总会有教师的角色，但由于智能计算系统这一新技术的出现，教师的角色以及它所包含的内涵可能会发生变化。正如我们之前讨论过的，人工智能可以代替诸如评分这样的任务，帮助学生提高学习，甚至可以代替现实世界中的辅导。不过，人工智能也可以应用于教学的许多其他方面。人工智能系统可以通过编程来提供专业知识，作为学生提问和查找信息，甚至可能取代教师来教一些基础课程内容。然而，在大多数情况下，人工智能将把教师转变到引导者的角色。

教师将补充人工智能课程，帮助有困难的学生，并为学生提供人际互动和实践经验。在很多方面，技术已经在推动课堂上的这些变化，尤其是那些网校或提倡翻转课堂的学校。

8. 人工智能让试错法学习不再令人生畏。

试错是学习的重要部分，但对许多学生来说，一想到失败，或仅仅是想不出答案，就会令人却步。有些人就是不喜欢在他们的同学或老师这样的权威面前难堪。有了一个旨在帮助学生学习的智能计算机系统，试错学习就不会那么令人生畏。人工智能可以为学生提供一个相对而言没有评判的环境来进行实验和学习，尤其是当人工智能导师能够提供改进的解决方案时。事实上，人工智能是支持这种学习的完美形式，因为人工智能系统本身经常通过试错法来学习。

9. 人工智能提供的数据可以改变学校招生、教学和支持学生的方式。

由智能计算机系统驱动的智能数据收集，已经在改变大学与未来学生和在校学生之间的互动方式。从招生到帮助学生选择最好的课程，智能计算机系统可以使大学生活的方方面面更适应学生的需求和目标。

数据挖掘系统已经在当今的高等教育领域发挥着不可或缺的作用，但人工智能可能会进一步改变高等教育。一些学校已经开始采取行动，为学生提供人工智能指导的培训，以缓解大学和高中之间的过渡。大学的选报可能会像亚马逊或网飞那样，有一个系统会根据学生的兴趣推荐最好的学校和节目，谁知道呢？

10. 人工智能可能会改变学生的学习地点、授课主体以及学生获得基本技能的方式。

尽管可能仍需几十年才能发生重大变化，但现实是，人工智能有可能彻底改变我们对教育理所当然的理解。

通过使用人工智能系统、软件和支持，学生可以在任何时间在世界任何地方学习。随着这些程序取代了某些类型的课堂教学，人工智能可能会在某些情况下取代教师（可能更好，也可能更坏）。由人工智能驱动的教育项目一直在帮助学生学习基本技能，但随着这些项目的发展和开发者的进一步学习，它们可能会为学生提供更广泛的服务。

Unit 12

Bringing the Maker Movement to the Classroom

1. Defining Maker Movement

Maker Movement, a technological and creative learning revolution underway around the globe, has exciting and vast implications for the world of education. New tools and technology, such as 3D printing, robotics, microprocessors, wearable computing, e-textiles, "smart" materials, and programming languages are being invented at an unprecedented pace. Maker Movement creates affordable or even free versions of these inventions, while sharing tools and ideas online to create a vibrant, collaborative community of global problem-solvers.

Fortunately for teachers, Maker Movement overlaps with the natural inclinations of children and the power of learning by doing. By embracing the lessons of Maker Movement, educators can revamp the student-centered teaching practices to engage learners of all ages.

Maker education refers to using a wide variety of hands-on activities (such as building, computer programming, and sewing) to support academic learning and the development of a mindset that values playfulness and experimentation, growth and iteration, and collaboration and community. Typically, "Making" involves attempting to solve a particular problem, creating a physical or digital artifact, and sharing that product with a larger audience. Often, such work is guided by the notion that process is more important than results.

2. Three Big Game-changers

- Computer-controlled fabrication devices

Over the past few years, devices that fabricate 3D objects have become an affordable reality. These 3D printers can take a design file and output a physical object. Plastic filament is melted and deposited in intricate patterns that build layer by layer, much like a 2D printer printing lines of dots line by line to create a printed page. With 3D design and printing, students can design and create their own objects.

- Physical computing

New open-source microcontrollers, sensors, and interfaces connect the physical and digital worlds in ways never before possible. Many schools are familiar with robotics, one aspect of physical computing, but a whole new world is opening up. Wearable computing—in which circuits are made with conductive thread—makes textiles smart, flexible, and mobile. Plug-and-play devices that connect small microprocessors to the Internet, to each other, or to any number of sensors mean that low-cost, easy-to-make computational devices can test, monitor, and control your world.

- Programming

From the *Next Generation Science Standards* to the White House, there is a new call for schools to teach computer programming. Programming is the key to controlling a new world of computational devices and the range of programming languages has never been greater. Today's modern languages are designed for every purpose and learners of all ages.

3. "Hard Fun" and the Process of Design

The tools and ethos of the maker revolution offer insight and hope for schools. The breadth of options and the "can-do" attitude espoused by the movement is exactly what students need, especially girls who tend to opt out of science and math in middle and high school.

However, hands-on making is not just a good idea for young women. All students need challenge and "hard fun" that inspire them to dig deeper and construct big ideas. Making science hands-on and interesting is not pandering to young sensibilities; it honors the learning drive and spirit that are all too often crushed by endless worksheets and vocabulary drills. Making is a way of bringing engineering to young learners. Such concrete experiences provide a meaningful context for understanding the abstract science and math concepts traditionally taught by schools while expanding the world of knowledge now accessible to students for the first time.

Tinkering is a powerful form of "learning by doing", an ethos shared by the rapidly expanding Maker Movement community and many educators. Real science and engineering is done through tinkering. We owe it to our children to give them the tools and experiences that actual scientists and engineers use, and now it is time to bring these tools and learning opportunities into classrooms. There are multiple pathways to learning what we have always taught, and things to do that were unimaginable just a few years ago.

4. Lessons from the Maker Movement

- "Doing" is what matters

Makers learn to make stuff by making stuff. Schools often forget this as they continuously prepare students for something that is going to happen next week, next year, or in some future career. The affordable and accessible technology of Maker Movement makes learning by doing a realistic approach for schools today.

- Openness

Maker Movement is a child of the Internet but does not fetishize it. Makers share designs, code, and ideas globally but making occurs locally. Makers share their expertise with a worldwide audience. "We" are smarter than "me" is the lesson for educators. Collaboration on projects of intense personal interest drive the need to share ideas and lessons learned more than external incentives like grades.

- Give it a Go

Back in the 1980s, *MacGyver*[1] could defuse a bomb with chewing gum and paper clips. Modern MacGyvers are driven to invent the solution to any problem by making things, and then making those things better. Perhaps grit or determination can be taught, but there is no substitute for experience. The best way for students to become deeply invested in their work is for their projects to be personally meaningful, afforded sufficient development time, given access to constructive materials, and the students themselves encouraged to overcome challenges.

- Learning is intensely personal

The current buzz about "personalized learning" is more often than not a scheme to deliver content by computerized algorithm. Not only is it magical to believe that computers can teach, it confuses learning with delivering content. Learning happens inside the individual. It cannot be designed or delivered. Learning is personal—always. No one can do it for you. Giving kids the opportunity to master what they love means they will love what they learn.

- It is about the technology

Some educators like to say that technology is "just a tool" that should fit seamlessly into classrooms. In contrast, Maker Movement sees tools and technology as essential elements for solving unsolvable problems. To makers, a 3D printer is not for learning to make 3D objects. Instead, it is the raw material for solving problems, such as how to create inexpensive but custom-fit prosthetics for people anywhere in the world, or how to print a pizza for hungry astronauts. The Maker philosophy prepares kids to solve problems in the way their teachers never anticipated before.

- Ownership

One motto of Maker Movement is "if you can't open it, you don't own it". Educators often talk about how learners should own their own learning, but if the learner doesn't have control, they can't own it. Teachers should consider that prepackaged experiences for students, even in the name of efficiency, are depriving students of owning their own learning. Learning depends on learners with maximum agency over their intellectual processes.

5. Getting Started with Classroom Making

Luckily, getting started with making in the classroom is not just about shopping for new toys. Making is a position on learning that puts the learner in charge. Giving students time to

---

1　*MacGyver*：《百战天龙》，一部美剧。剧中的主人公从不带工具，而专门创造性地利用身边的物品来解决问题。

brainstorm, invent, design, and build—and then time to fix mistakes, improve, test, and improve again is crucial. The most important element of classroom making is allowing the students to have agency over their own creations.

This does not mean that the teacher does nothing! Far from it. Being a guide, studio manager, and motivator is the important work of the teacher. Resist the urge to lecture students about invention and just get busy.

Whether you are getting started in your classroom or building a Makerspace, the most important thing to remember is that making is about making sense of the world, not about the "stuff". Making connections and making meaning are the true results of classroom making, not the plastic or cardboard artifacts. However, you will be even more beneficial to your students if you develop fluency with the materials, tools, and processes available in your learning environment.

The Common Core and the *new Next Generation Science Standards* emphasize critical thinking, creativity, and 21th-century skills. To achieve these goals requires taking a hard look at both what we teach and how we teach it. Maker Movement offers lessons, tools, and technology to steer students toward more relevant, engaging learning experiences.

New Words

maker ['meɪkə] *n.* 制造者；创客

robotics [rəʊ'bɒtɪks] *n.* 机器人学

microprocessor [ˌmaɪkrəʊ'prəʊsesə] *n.* 微处理器

e-textile [i:'tekstaɪl] *n.* 电子织物

vibrant ['vaɪbrənt] *adj.* 充满生气的；振动的

revamp [ˌri:'væmp] *v.* 修补；改进

iteration [ˌɪtə'reɪʃən] *n.* 迭代；反复，重复

fabricate ['fæbrɪkeɪt] *v.* 制造；伪造；装配

filament ['fɪləmənt] *n.* 纤维

deposit [dɪ'pɒzɪt] *v.* 放置；存放

intricate ['ɪntrɪkɪt] *adj.* 复杂的；错综的

interface ['ɪntəfeɪs] *n.* 界面；接口

circuit ['sɜ:kɪt] *n.* 电路

conductive [kən'dʌktɪv] *adj.* 传导的；传导性的

programming ['prəʊɡræmɪŋ] *n.* 编制程序

ethos ['i:θɒs] *n.* 民族精神；社会思潮

espouse [ɪ'spaʊz] *v.* 支持；赞成

sensibility [ˌsensə'bɪləti] *n.* 情感；敏感性；感觉

tinkering ['tɪŋkərɪŋ] *n.* 修补；东敲西打；动手能力

fetishize ['fetɪʃaɪz] *v.* 盲目迷恋；以……为偶像

defuse [ˌdi:'fju:z] *v.* 去掉……的雷管，排雷

grit [ɡrɪt] *n.* 勇气；决心

prosthetics [prɒs'θetɪks] *n.* 修复学，修补学；假肢

motto ['mɒtəʊ] *n.* 座右铭，格言

prepackaged [pri:'pækɪdʒd] *adj.* 预先包装好的

brainstorm ['breɪnstɔ:m] *n.* 集思广益；头脑风暴；灵机一动

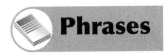

Phrases

wearable computing 可穿戴计算机	hard fun 寓学于乐
layer by layer 逐层	opt out of 决定不参加；决定退出
plug-and-play 即插即用	pander to 迎合；取悦
Next Generation Science Standards《新一代科学教育标准》（美国）	paper clip 回形针
	deprive of 剥夺，使失去

Exercises

Ex. 1 Give the English equivalents of the following Chinese expressions.

(1) 创客 _____

(2) 电子织物 _____

(3) 倾向，爱好 _____

(4) 编制程序 _____

(5) 社会思潮 _____

(6) 修补；动手能力 _____

(7) 集思广益；头脑风暴；灵机一动 _____

(8) 即插即用 _____

(9) 决定不参加；决定退出 _____

(10) 通常；多半 _____

Ex. 2 Decide whether the following statements are true (T) or false (F) according to Text A. Give your reasons for the false ones.

(　　) (1) The 3D printers can take a design file and output a physical object.

(　　) (2) Wearable computing in which circuits are made with conductive thread makes textiles smart, flexible, and mobile.

(　　) (3) The American government does not encourage schools to teach computer programming.

(　　) (4) "Hard fun" inspires students to dig deeper and construct big ideas.

(　　) (5) The major purpose of making science hands-on and interesting is to pander to the sensibilities of young students.

(　　) (6) Making is a way of bringing engineering to young learners.

(   ) (7) Tinkering does not promote "learning by doing".

(   ) (8) It is still not realistic to practice learning by doing for schools today.

(   ) (9) The maker education proposes that "we" are smarter than "me".

(   ) (10) Both grit and experience can be taught.

Ex. 3 **Answer the following questions according to Text A.**

(1) Could you define "maker education"?

(2) What does "tinkering" mean in terms of education?

(3) What does the term "openness" mean in terms of Maker Movement?

(4) What is the best way for students to become deeply invested in their work?

(5) How do you understand "learning is personal"?

(6) What does Maker Movement see tools and technology as?

(7) What is the most important element of classroom making?

(8) What is the role of a teacher in the classroom making?

Ex. 4 **Fill in the blanks with the words given below.**

project	communal	tools	part	improve
hands-on	idea	activities	share	goal

Makerspace is a buzzword that has been floating around for a few years now. However, what, exactly, is it? A makerspace is a room that contains (1)_____ and components, allowing people to enter with an (2)_____ and leave with a complete (3)_____. The best part is that makerspaces are (4)_____. The (5)_____ is to work together to learn, collaborate, and (6)_____. Most importantly, makerspaces allow us to explore, create new things, or (7)_____ things that already exist.

Makerspace is (8)_____ of what we call Maker Movement, which started in the early 2000s. Of course, scrapbooking, tinkering, and other arts and crafts (9)_____ have been around for quite some time, but Maker Movement emphasizes (10)_____ discovery in a world that has become increasingly automated.

Text B

NuVu Studio as a Makerspace

1. A Space to Invent and Create

Down an alley off Massachusetts Ave. in Cambridge, there's a "makerspace" called NuVu Studio, where local high school students leave their classrooms behind to design robots, websites, board games, medical devices, and clothing, among other things. However, they're not playing hooky— in fact, it's part of their education.

As the brainchild of MIT alumnus Saeed Arida PhD'10, NuVu (pronounced "new view") enrolls students from local schools—both during the academic year and the summer—to focus on real-world projects. In so doing, they're exposed to the collaborative, experimental, and demanding design process typical of architectural design studios.

"We walk students through a rigorous process to get to this real, final product," says Arida, who modeled NuVu after designing studios in MIT's School of Architecture and Planning, where he studied design and computation and taught several studios.

Over the course of 11 weeks, students choose to attend a selection of two-week studios under themes such as "science fiction" "health" "home of the future", or this summer's theme, "fantasy". Sometimes, studios even bring students to international destinations—such as India and Brazil—for research.

During studios, NuVu coaches present students with real-world problems to solve. The coaches include full-time employees and local experts such as doctors, engineers, and graduate students from MIT and Harvard University.

A brief research period gives way to the bulk of the two-week studio—the rigorous design process— that includes prototyping, critiques from the coach, and constant documentation of progress. Students have full use of NuVu's equipment, including 3D printers, designing software, art and photography equipment, and other machines.

At the end of each studio, students present finished projects to guest experts—including professors, practitioners, entrepreneurs, and designers—for evaluation. The rapid design process is "intense", but beneficial, Arida says.

"Students come in at the beginning of two weeks, and it's all sketches and scraps of paper. They come out at the end of two weeks and you see results," Arida explains. "We have this culture here, where you can have an idea, but if you don't go through this rigorous process, you have nothing."

Students hail from partner schools around the Boston area, including Beaver Country Day School in Brookline, Phoenix Charter Academy in Chelsea, and Inly School in Scituate.

Co-founded with Saba Ghole MS'07 and David Wang, a PhD student in MIT's Computer Science and Artificial Intelligence Lab, NuVu brought in about 150 students last year. Around 400 students have participated in the studio, creating more than 130 projects including robotic arms, modular shelters, sustainable and futuristic clothing, and strategy games.

Such programs are difficult to implement broadly, Arida admits, and private institutions tend to favor them, rather than public schools. However, this fall, NuVu is entering its first public-school partnership, with Cambridge Rindge and Latin School, which will send 10 students for the entire semester—and those 10 students will earn credit. It is a step in the right direction, Arida says.

"Within a year, we hope to have three to five centers opening in different places in the United States and internationally," he adds. "There's been a lot of interest from people in this educational model."

2. A New Model of Education

NuVu arose from Arida's 2010 PhD dissertation, which suggested that architectural design studios train youth in "learning by doing" at an accelerated pace. The idea is that in design studios, students spend the bulk of the semester focused on building one project over multiple iterations, receiving constant feedback from professors and other students.

For a case study, Arida approached Beaver Country Day School, which allowed 20 students to participate in a pilot program on its campus, with two-week studios that centered on alternative energy, balloon mapping, interactive music, and filmmaking.

Among other things, Arida's dissertation suggested that NuVu's model could help students, in a two-month timespan, understand complex systems and recognize the importance of rapid prototyping. It also helped inform NuVu's current model of combining instructors with mixed backgrounds—such as pairing a filmmaker with an engineer, or a doctor with an architect—for more effective teaching.

For students like Liam Brady, a recent Beaver graduate, going from a classroom setting to NuVu was like "night and day".

"With studio-based learning, we can see the application," says Brady, who in a 2011 studio designed an interactive floor projection for playing games such as soccer. "As a result, I tend to remember things I learned in a studio environment rather than a classroom environment."

Brady is one of the 10 NuVu alumni returning as interns this summer; another is Cambridge School of Weston junior Harper Mills. As part of a NuVu studio, Mills traveled to Rio de Janeiro for 10 days to research urban inclusivity, and designed an interactive website that laid out prominent challenges facing the city.

For Mills, who enrolled in many studios over the course of an entire year, one benefit of the studio was the time pressure. "You're constantly asking yourself if you're being as productive and efficient as possible, and you're also forced to be self-driven," she says. "There is no bell or strict schedule moving you through your day, just you and your determination to create the best product you possibly can."

Another perk, she says, is the iterative design process, where "failure is an integral part of success".

"In school you get one shot and if you blow it, then that's the end," Mills says. "At NuVu, when you show the first iteration of your project, it's to say, 'I know this isn't great; how can I make it better?'"

3. Rich Portfolios

At NuVu, students are not graded. "But they end up with a really rich portfolio," Arida says. "This is important, as portfolios are increasingly becoming integral to the college application process."

Some projects have found life outside the studio. An interactive music installation that one group of students helped design with an MIT architecture student is now on display at the MIT

Museum. Other students produced animations explaining social-media phenomena including "selfies" and the "deep Web" that were presented at a conference on youth and media at Harvard.

Last winter, two students created a medical device that expanded and improved upon research to reduce tremors caused by Parkinson's disease. The device measures, in real-time, the frequency and amplitude of a patient's tremors, creating and sending a feedback signal to the brain that helps suppress the tremors. Being developed further by Wang, the device will begin clinical trials at Beth Israel Hospital this summer.

Moreover, in a recent "do-it-yourself prosthetics" studio, two students developed a 3D printed "artistic" prosthetic hand for children under age 12. Using an online open-source design called "Robo Hand", they built a hand with interchangeable cylinders to fit a brush, pencils, and other artistic utensils.

Now the student inventors are organizing prosthetic design events next fall at NuVu, where students creating prostheses can display their inventions at the studio and share their knowledge.

"You can really see the impact on these kids," Arida says. "It's phenomenal."

 **New Words**

alley ['æli] *n.* 小巷，胡同

hooky ['hʊki] *n.* 逃学；逃学者

brainchild ['breɪntʃaɪld] *n.* 某人的发明或主意；脑力劳动的产物

alumnus [ə'lʌmnəs] *n.* 男校友；男毕业生

rigorous ['rɪɡərəs] *adj.* 严格的；严密的

fantasy ['fæntəsi] *n.* 幻想；想象产物；幻想作品

bulk [bʌlk] *n.* 体积，容量；大多数，大部分

prototyping [prəʊtə'taɪpɪŋ] *n.* 样机研究；原型设计

entrepreneur [ˌɒntrəprə'nɜ:] *n.* 企业家；承包商

sketch [sketʃ] *n.* 素描；草图

scrap [skræp] *n.* 碎片；小块（纸、织物等）

modular ['mɒdjulə] *adj.* 模块化的，组装式的

dissertation [ˌdɪsə'teɪʃən] *n.* 论文

accelerated [ək'seləreɪtɪd] *adj.* 加速的，加快的

iteration [ˌɪtə'reɪʃən] *n.* 迭代；反复

pilot ['paɪlət] *adj.* 试点的；试验性的

mapping ['mæpɪŋ] *n.* 绘图；测绘

intern [ɪn'tɜ:n] *n.* 实习生

inclusivity [ˌɪnklu:'sɪvəti] *n.* 包容性

perk [pɜ:k] *n.* 额外收入；外快

iterative ['ɪtərətɪv] *adj.* 迭代的；重复的

animation [ˌænɪ'meɪʃən] *n.* 卡通片绘制，动画

selfie [selfi] *n.* 自拍；自拍照

tremor ['tremə] *n.* 震颤；颤动

amplitude ['æmplɪtju:d] *n.* 振幅；丰富，充足

cylinder ['sɪlɪndə] *n.* 圆筒；圆柱状物

utensil [ju:'tensəl] *n.* 用具，器皿

phenomenal [fɪ'nɒmɪnəl] *adj.* 惊人的，非凡的

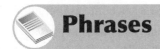 **Phrases**

board game 棋盘游戏，棋类游戏
model after 模仿；仿造
the bulk of 大多数，大部分
hail from 来自；出生于

deep web 暗网
Parkinson's disease 帕金森氏病；震颤性麻痹

 **Abbreviation**

Massachusetts Institute of Technology (MIT) 麻省理工学院

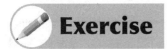 **Exercise**

Decide whether the following statements are true (T) or false (F) according to Text B. Give your reasons for the false ones.

(　　) (1) The so-called NuVu Studio is not part of education.

(　　) (2) Saeed Arida came up with the idea of NuVu Studio under the inspiration of design studios in MIT's School of Architecture and Planning.

(　　) (3) During studios, NuVu coaches present students with real-world problems to solve.

(　　) (4) The finished projects of students do not have to be evaluated in the NuVu Studio.

(　　) (5) Both private institutions and public schools tend to favor this kind of studio like NuVu.

(　　) (6) Each pair of instructors usually have the same professional background in the NuVu.

(　　) (7) For students like Liam Brady, studio is a better learning environment than classroom.

(　　) (8) The learning in the studio usually has no pressure.

(　　) (9) The learning in a makerspace does not allow failure.

(　　) (10) The projects finished in the makerspace have no real-world value.

Supplementary Reading

Text	Notes
How Technology Is Shaping the Future of Education	
Technology in the classroom can be so much more and so much better than the stereotypical[1] cell phone going off in the middle of class. Technology can actually be a major tool, both in terms of pedagogical resources and in terms of connecting with the younger generations. New technologies like AI, machine learning, and educational software aren't just changing the field for students; they're shaking up the role of educators, creating philosophical[2] shifts in approaches to teaching, and remodeling[3] the classroom. With an influx[4] of new learning models available, traditional educational methods are bound to evolve in the next decade.	[1] stereotypical *adj.* 老一套的; 一成不变的
	[2] philosophical *adj.* 哲学的; 哲学上的
1. Technology Is Providing a Way for Learning Models to Become Increasingly Personalized.	[3] remodel *v.* 改变; 重塑
	[4] influx *n.* 流入; 汇集
Every student learns differently, and technology allows educators to accommodate[5] unique learning styles on a case-by-case basis.	[5] accommodate *v.* 使适应; 供应; 调解
"We're currently challenging the paradigm that all seven-year-olds are exactly the same and should be exposed to the same content," said Brian Greenberg, CEO of Silicon Schools Fund, in an interview with Business Insider. "We're starting to question what's right for this seven-year-old versus what's right for that seven-year-old."	
Technologies like DreamBox, a math education software that's used in a number of classrooms across the U.S., adapt to each student's skill level and let students learn at a pace best suited to their needs.	
Adaptive learning software is quickly replacing the role of textbooks in the classrooms and students are tackling[6] subjects with the aid of tailor-made computer programs that assist their needs.	[6] tackle *v.* 处理; 与……交涉

2. Technology Is Going to Present Some Philosophical Shifts in Education.

With technology making it easier than ever before to query Google or effortlessly calculate a math problem, educators are determining the types of knowledge students need in order to thrive[7] in a technology-saturated[8] workforce.

While educational models of the past focused on providing students with the requisite[9] skills to turn them into skilled workers, the educators of today are more concerned with teaching students how to learn on their own.

"The real purpose of education is for the brain to be empowered with information," said Greenberg. "We're teaching students to learn to think, to learn to learn, and to critically assess a situation."

3. Teachers Will Be as Important as Ever.

CEO of Silicon Schools Brian Greenberg says that evolving technology doesn't undermine a teacher's role in the classroom; instead, it augments[10] it.

"Technology is important, but it's really just the means to an end," Greenberg said. "The real magic is in giving great educators freedom and license into how school works."

With more data available to track each classroom's progress, educators are provided with increasing insight into how their students are struggling.

Math education software DreamBox provides educators with recordings and data into how students are learning and progressing so that educators can focus on the areas where their classrooms need the most help.

In order for technology to function successfully in the classroom, DreamBox's SVP[11] of Learning, Tim Hudson, says that it needs to be in touch with educators and their needs. "It's important that we listen to teachers and administrators to determine the ways technology can assist them in the classroom," Hudson told *Business Insider*.

4. Artificial Intelligence Is Poised[12] to Play an Integral Role.

AI makes one-to-one tutoring increasingly possible at enormous scale. The U.S. Navy has introduced an AI-based

[7] thrive v. 繁荣，兴旺；从容应对

[8] saturated adj. 饱和的；渗透的

[9] requisite adj. 必备的，必不可少的

[10] augment v. 增加，增大

[11] SVP 高级副总裁

[12] poised adj. 做好准备的；蓄势待发的

tutoring system called Education Dominance into an entry-level IT school in Pensacola. The platform works similarly to a human tutor, monitoring each student's progress and providing personalized assessments and tests.

The Navy reported that the students who had worked with the digital tutor made enormous strides[13] in their education, and that they consistently tested higher than students who had studied without the program's benefit.

The platform provides a glimpse into how educational models might work in the next 15 years: computers acting as individual tutors in classrooms filled with diverse learning styles.

5. Students Can Assume More Responsibility in the Classroom.

With educators better equipped at understanding a student's learning process, classrooms are being formed around small groups, with students who match each other's skill level working together. Greenberg says that this shift in tailor-made learning groups provides students with independence in the classroom.

"There's an increasing push for students to take more ownership and have more involvement into how they learn," said Greenberg. "Creating agency in the classroom improves student's motivations."

With adaptive technology assisting individuals at every skill level, students are better equipped to learn on their own.

6. Despite the Inundation[14] of Technology, its Role Still Remains to be Determined.

"Technology is not silver bullet[15] solution," said Greenberg. "We have to be honest that we don't have definitive proof one way or the other yet that technology is improving education. We are cautiously optimistic that technology is having a very bold impact."

Technology's benefit in the classroom is all in the way it is used. When paired with interpersonal relationships, thoughtful educators, and deliberate programs, technology can be an incredible asset, but Greenberg warns that it is not the end-all[16] solution to education.

[13] stride *n.* 大步；进步；进展

[14] inundation *n.* 洪水；泛滥

[15] silver bullet 银子弹；良方，高招

[16] end-all *n.* 终结；最终目标

"It's not about having a kid stare at a screen for six hours a day," Greenberg said. "The real story for the future of education will center on how educators structure and run their classrooms."

Teaching is all about introducing students to a whole world of concepts that they do not know about yet. Technology in the classroom is like a foray[17] into modern invention—and you get to be the expedition leader. Rather than viewing digital devices and Internet spaces as a threat to your duties, view them as unexplored areas of growth for both you and the young minds trusting you to show them what is out there.

[17] **foray** *n.* 涉足，初次尝试

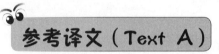

将创客运动带入课堂

1. 定义创客运动

创客运动是一场正在全球范围内进行的技术和创新学习革命，它对教育界有着令人振奋和广泛的影响。3D 打印、机器人技术、微处理器、便携计算机、电子织物、"智能"材料和编程语言等新工具和新技术正以前所未有的速度被发明出来。创客运动为这些发明提供了价格低廉甚至免费的机会，同时通过在线分享工具和想法，创建了一个充满活力、相互协作的全球问题解决者社区。

对教师来说，幸运的是，创客运动与孩子们的自然天性和"在做中学"的能力相吻合。通过引进创客运动课程，教育者可以改进以学生为中心的教学实践，让所有年龄段的学习者都参与其中。

创客教育是指利用各种各样的实践活动（如建筑、计算机编程和缝纫）来支持学术学习，并培养一种重视玩和实验、成长和迭代、协作和社区的心态。具体而言，"创"试图解决一个特定的问题，创建一个物理的或数字的制品，并与更多的受众共享该产品。通常，这种学习的指导思想是过程比结果更重要。

2. 三大"搅局者"

● 计算机控制的制造设备

在过去的几年里，制造三维物体的设备已经变得不再昂贵。这些 3D 打印机可以输入一个设计文件并输出一个物理对象。塑料纤维被融化并一层一层地以复杂的图案堆积，很像 2D 打印机逐行打印墨点来形成页面。通过 3D 设计和打印，学生可以设计和创建自己的作品。

- 物理计算

新的开源微控制器、传感器和接口以前所未有的方式将物理世界和数字世界连接起来。许多学校都熟悉机器人技术，这是物理计算的一个方面，但一个全新的世界正在打开。便携计算机——电路由导电线构成——使纺织品变得智能、灵活、可移动。即插即用设备将小型微处理器连接到互联网，或彼此相连或连接到任意数量的传感器，这意味着低成本、易于制作的计算设备可以测试、监控和控制您的世界。

- 编程

从《新一代科学教育标准》到白宫，都有一种新的呼声要求学校教授计算机编程。编程是控制计算设备这一新领域的关键，编程语言的范围从未如此之大。现代的编程语言是为各种目的和各个年龄段的学习者设计的。

3. 寓学于乐和设计过程

创客革命的工具和思潮为学校提供了洞见和希望。这场运动所倡导的选择的广度和"能做"的态度正是学生所需要的，尤其是那些在初中和高中往往选择放弃科学和数学的女孩。

然而，动手制作不仅仅对年轻女性来说是一个好主意，所有的学生都需要挑战和"寓学于乐"来激励他们更深入地挖掘和构建宏大的创意。让科学实践变得有趣并不是为了迎合年轻人的情感，这是对学习动力和精神的一种尊重，而这种学习动力和精神常常被无休止的练习题和词汇练习所摧毁。创客之创是将工程学带给年轻学习者的一种方式。这些具体的经验为理解学校传统教授的抽象科学和数学概念提供了一个有意义的背景，并首次让学生接触到了这个知识世界。

反复尝试是一种"在做中学"的强大形式，也是迅速壮大的创客运动团体和许多教育者共有的一种思潮。真正的科学和工程是通过反复尝试来完成的。我们有责任给孩子们真正的科学家和工程师所使用的工具和体验，现在是时候把这些工具和学习机会带到课堂上了。学习传统传授的知识有多种途径，而这些事情在几年前是无法想象的。

4. 从创客运动中学到的经验

- "做"才是最重要的

创客通过制造东西来学习制造东西。学校经常忘记这一点，因为他们不断地让学生为下周、明年或未来的职业生涯做准备。创客运动技术的廉价性和易进入性，为当今的学校提供了一种现实的"在做中学"的学习方式。

- 开放

创客运动是互联网的产物，但并不依恋它。创客们在全球范围内共享设计、代码和想法，但在本地进行制造。创客与全球受众分享他们的专业知识。对教育工作者来说，团队比个人更有智慧。在本人感兴趣的项目上进行合作，比分数等外部激励更能促进想法和所学的分享。

- 尝试

早在 20 世纪 80 年代，马盖先就能用口香糖和回形针拆除炸弹。现代的"马盖先"通过制造东西来发现解决问题的方法，然后让这些东西变得更好。勇气或决心也许是可以传授的，但没有什么能取代经验。让学生对自己的工作更投入的最好方法是让项目对他们自己有意义，有足够的研发时间，有机会接触到建造材料，并鼓励他们勇于接受挑战。

- 学习是非常个性化的

当前流行的"个性化学习"往往是一种通过计算机算法来传递内容的方案。相信计算机可以教学不仅是神奇的，它还混淆了学习和内容传递。学习发生在个体内部，它不能被设计或传递。学习永远是个人的事情，没有人能为你做这件事。给孩子们机会去学习他们喜欢的东西意味着他们会喜欢他们学到的东西。

- 这与技术有关

一些教育工作者喜欢说：技术"只是一个工具"，应该无缝地融入课堂。而创客运动将工具和技术视为解决尚待解决的问题的基本要素。对创客来说，3D 打印机不是用来学习制作 3D 物体的，相反，它是解决问题的原材料，比如如何为世界上某个地方的人们制造廉价但量身定制的假肢，或者如何为饥饿的宇航员"打印"一份披萨。创客哲学让孩子们以老师们从未预料到的方式解决问题。

- 所有权

创客运动的座右铭之一是"如果你不曾打开它，你就无法拥有它"。教育工作者经常谈到学习者应该如何拥有自己的学习，但如果学习者没有控制权，他们就不能拥有它。教师应该考虑到，即便是以效率的名义，为学生提前打包好的体验也正在剥夺学生拥有自己学习的权利。学习取决于学习者对他们的心智发展拥有的最大能动性。

5. 在教室开始制作

在教室里开始制作不仅仅是购买新玩具。制作是一种让学习者对自己负责的学习态度。给学生一些时间来进行头脑风暴、发明、设计和建造，然后再花时间来修正错误、改进、测试和再改进，这是至关重要的。课堂制作最重要的元素是让学生对自己的创作拥有自主权。

这并不意味着老师什么都不用做！绝非如此。教师的重要职责是做一位指导者、工作室的管理者和激励者。不要急着给学生讲授如何发明创造，而是要做好上述准备。

无论你是在教室里开始制作，还是要建立一个创客空间，最重要的是要记住，制作最终是为了理解这个世界，而不是为了某个"东西"。课堂制作的真谛是建立关联和做有意义的事，而非塑料或纸板制品。然而，如果教师能熟练掌握学习环境中的材料、工具和过程，你将会对你的学生更有帮助。

《共同核心课程标准》和新的《新一代科学教育标准》强调批判性思维、创造力和 21 世纪的技能。为了实现这些目标，我们需要认真考虑我们教什么和如何教。为引导学生获得更相关、更吸引人的学习体验，创客运动提供了课程、工具和技术。